Eter

Our Courtship

Mary Ann Marasco
2015

Copyright © 2014 Mary Ann Marasco
All rights reserved. This book or any portion thereof may not be reproduced in any manner whatsoever without the express written permission of the publisher except for the use of brief quotations in a book review or scholarly journal.

ISBN 978-0-9960262-0-8

Cover: Painting by Joe Marasco

Mary Ann Marasco
Fairport, NY 14450

Acknowledgements

I have to thank my daughters-in-law for starting me on this journey. Joe's sudden death took my family and me by surprise, and I was looking for ways to heal. When I found Joe's love letters (300) to me during our courtship, I put them in binders and read them repeatedly, especially the ones from Korea after our wedding. My daughters-in-law asked me if they could read them, and I consented. They asked me if I was sure, there was nothing in them I didn't want them to know. I told them there was nothing in the letters I didn't want them to know or would be embarrassed by. When they finished reading the letters, they told me I should publish them because boys did not write that way anymore.

I would like to thank my family and many friends who encouraged me to complete this book through their patient listening. I couldn't have done it without them. My editor and close friend, Jennifer Litt, for helping me retrieve memories I thought were long forgotten. We worked well together and shared many laughs, tears and epiphanies during the three years we spent editing the book. Tom Mc Elroy, my English professor at Empire State, read portions of the manuscript and offered me some helpful suggestions.

Dedication:

To Joe Marasco (1933-2006)

My first love that became a lifetime commitment.

Introduction

The world I was born into over seventy-eight years ago was not as complex as that of today. Computers, television, microwave ovens, cell phones, e-mail, credit and debit cards and other progressive electronic devices were unheard of.

We walked everywhere. Few families owned their own cars. We grew up walking to school, temple, church, the local movie theater, ice cream shops, shoe repair and neighborhood grocery stores.

Respect for elders, family, teachers, the military and other positions of authority were taught at home and in school. Discipline was administered immediately if you misbehaved at home, school or in public. A verbal reprimand or spanking of a child was not called child abuse.

On occasion, I was upset and angry at the discipline handed me by my mother or the double standard in our house between my brothers and me, but talking back or trying to get my point across were ignored. I rebelled silently, not verbally.

Mom stayed at home as did the majority of woman at the time. Few women worked outside the home. Those who did were teachers, nurses, office workers or caregivers.

My mother passed down her moral values to me. Most girls with the exception of a few, remained virgins until marriage. Boys of the same persuasion didn't admit it to their peers for fear of being ridiculed. My mother began my instruction at an early age that you had sex and a baby after you were married, not before. One of the consequences of making the wrong choice and getting pregnant out of wedlock not only would my reputation but the family would have to endure the whispers and rumors of my mistake.

Falling in love and getting married was the objective of

most girls and some of the boys too. When we saw someone we were attracted to we took the time to learn and know the qualities he or she possessed not only outward appearance. True, good looks were an advantage, but as my mother reminded me often, "Good looks don't last forever; it's what and who you are that matters." Sometimes our attraction for the opposite sex was acquired at a young age. Limits and rules given by our parents were followed regarding those friendships. Girls may have admired and flirted with boys from a distance, but they knew the proper time to respond to their advances. If a friendship resulted, nothing was rushed. It took its due course over time and matured as fruit on the vine.

I was almost nineteen in 1954 when I married my high school sweetheart. We dated for five years. The friendship ring he gave me when I was fourteen was my commitment to him to be faithful. If I wanted to go out with other boys, I had to return it. He was not permitted to be in the house with me unless my parents were there. Under no circumstances were we allowed to be in my bedroom for any reason. I had curfews. If I broke them, and I did a few times, punishment was quickly administered by my mother. I learned early in my teens I was responsible for my actions, choices and responsibilities.

Letter writing was the common way of communication. A three-cent stamp was less expensive than the dollar or more, a long distance phone call cost. Pen and paper were the instruments to pour out your heart to someone you loved and missed. Reading the letters from a loved one drew images in the mind of them speaking the words. They could be read many times over to bring the loved one closer in the heart.

Flirting, or having a crush on someone you met or wanted to meet occurred but you adhered to and followed the rules of etiquette prevalent at that time. Boys were supposed to be gentlemen and respect you. In those days, we kissed with a closed mouth, and the only form of public affection tolerated was holding hands or a boy's arm. I thought about what was forbidden and had to fantasize about the reality until marriage.

I dreamed and thought about my wedding day and the

gown I would wear. Traditionally, the color of the bride's gown and veil was white or ivory and stated she was a virgin. It modestly covered the upper chest. A strapless wedding gown may have been appropriate in Hollywood, but not in church. The gown was never seen by anyone but the mother and perhaps grandmother and maid of honor. It was kept a secret until the day of the wedding. In my day, it was the bride's decision on a choice of her gown.

In New York State before a couple could apply for their marriage license they had to have a blood test. It was a countrywide test for venereal disease. It was later abolished. Then and now venereal diseases are treatable but abortion was unthinkable and illegal. Abortions were available if you knew the right people and could afford it. The dark sides were the horror stories of back street amateurs who performed them illegally and the deaths that occurred. I was Catholic and the only acceptable birth control to this day is abstinence or the rhythm system proposed by the Catholic Church.

The business world was dominated by men who were not about to relinquish or share their stately positions and private boardrooms. With the outbreak of World War II, women took off their aprons and worked in factories, businesses, banking and other fields previously controlled by men. They tasted the promise of independence and in its wake; their former cultural role was on the threshold of change. That change would affect the atmosphere and upbringing of their children.

Most of the moral values I was taught have been trodden under foot. Legalized abortion, contraceptives handed out in high school, teen age pregnancies, single parents, highest divorce rates in our history, children before marriage (no shame involved) and multiple sex partners have become normal behavior. The sexual revolution that began in the sixties has leveled the playing field for a girl to be as promiscuous as a boy.

Every generation has its cultural standards of behavior and morality. However, what was acceptable in one may be rejected or eliminated in the next. I believe that the values I grew up with have radically changed. Responsibility, integrity, morality and respect seem to have silently slipped between the cracks. I can't accept all the changes that have occurred in my life time, but I must accept what I have no control over and hope corrections will be part of the next generation.

The End of the Beginning

April 2006

    I woke up before the alarm went off, went to the kitchen and made a pot of coffee. Making coffee was a task Joe assumed on the first day of our honeymoon. I prepared our breakfast of orange juice, scrambled eggs, bacon, toast and coffee. He drank the juice ate the eggs, bacon and toast, but, when he sipped my coffee he set his cup on the table smiled at me and said,

    "Honey, you make breakfast; I'll make the coffee."

    "You don't like my coffee?" I asked.

    "It's okay, but I'll make it from now on."

    I followed his proportions of one rounded scoop of coffee to two cups of cold water but his always tasted better, and he made a pot every morning before I got out of bed.

    I filled my cup, opened the door to the sun porch and sat at the table. The room, warmed by the sun, was in sharp contrast to the cool house. Joe had remodeled the porch into a sunroom by replacing the screens with sliding glass doors on three walls. "This will be a great place for me to recuperate after my knee surgery," he said, installing the last door latch.

    Chipmunks, daily visitors, scurried across the patio when the door opened. I glanced around the back yard. Tulips, daffodils, and crocuses were pushing up through the warmed soil, and faint signs of color appeared on winter bare tree branches. I glanced at the mature magnolia tree, heavy laden with buds ready to burst into bloom. I couldn't recall the last time it did so. Sunday was Easter, the perfect day for them to blossom.

I wanted to be at the hospital by ten or eleven to see Joe. Today was his last day there. His long overdue knee replacement surgery on Wednesday went well. He had postponed it for years until the pain forced him to have it done. I had hoped he would wait until after Easter, but he was anxious to have the surgery as soon as possible. Tomorrow he would transfer to Aaron Manor in Fairport, a rehab center closer to home for the remainder of his therapy. I wouldn't be preparing Easter Sunday dinner for the family because I'd be spending most of the weekend there with him.

The phone rang.
"Hi, Honey, did I wake you?" Joe asked.
"No. I'm on the porch drinking my coffee."
"What time do you plan on getting here?"
"Around eleven. Why?"
"I need my grey sweats."
"How was your night?"
"OK. Had some pain but I can handle it."
"Do you need anything else?"
"No."
"Love you. See you soon."

Park Ridge Hospital was located on the west side of the city and was a half hour drive from home. I reached the hospital at 11:30. Joe was in bed. Shortly after lunch, the nurse reminded him of his 2:00pm therapy session.

"Honey, will you help me get into my sweats?" Joe asked pushing aside his bed tray. "I can't do it alone." He sat on the edge of the bed for a moment and stood up slowly. I helped him gain his balance and knelt down in front of him. He put his left hand on my shoulder and leaned against the bed.

Gently, I lifted one foot at a time into the legs of the sweats, got up, pulled the band to his waist and adjusted it. He lowered his hand from my shoulder, put his arm around my waist and pulled me close to his side.

"I love you. I've loved you all my life," he whispered in my ear. Bewildered, I looked at him. The tenderness of his voice and the love in his eyes caught me off guard. Why tell me now? Here? I kissed him gently and looked into his eyes.

"What made you say that?" I asked.
"I just want you to know. That's all."

It was completely out of character. He never displayed any affection toward me in public other than holding my hand. A few minutes later the therapist arrived, helped Joe into the wheel chair, and said he'd be back in about an hour. I visited with his sister Marigrace and her husband Mario who arrived shortly after they left. We were still talking when Joe returned. His face was pale and he looked tired. He climbed into bed.

"I think I pushed myself too far this time," he said.
He joined the conversation and at 3:45, he interrupted his sister and looked at me.
"Mary Ann, I think it's time for you to leave."
"I will, but not yet."
"I want you to leave now. It's Good Friday; the expressway will be heavy with traffic because of Easter weekend."

I wanted to stay, but he insisted. I kissed him, said goodbye and told him I'd be at Aaron Manor in the morning.
Arriving home, I called my son Jeff and asked him if he wanted to go out for supper. He said yes.
Joe's sister called at 5:30 to let me know Joe was fine when she and Mario left the hospital.

3

Jeff and I were about to leave when the phone rang. I answered it.

"Hello is this Mrs. Marasco?" asked the women's voice on the other end. I said it was.
"This is the hospital. How long will it take you to get here?"
"Why?" I asked.
"Your husband is not responding. He may need to go to ICU."
My blood pressure plummeted.

"How long will it take you to get to the hospital?" she repeated.
"It's going to take a half hour or more depending on the traffic."
Jeff must have seen the panic in my face and heard it in my voice.
"Let's go," he said.

I called Joe's sister and Jim and Bob, my two other sons on my cell phone as we rushed down the expressway to the hospital. Marigrace said she'd meet us there. Neither of my sons answered their phones. Suddenly, the foreboding I had prior to Joe's surgery two days earlier returned, and it overwhelmed me.

The nurse had told me I could see him in the pre-op cubicle before he went into surgery. When I got there, he was talking to the anesthesiologist. I stood by the side of the bed and noticed he'd removed his wedding band and was holding it in his hand. A chill went through me. It was the first time he'd taken it off since the day we were married.

"Why have you taken your ring off?"
"I can't wear it during surgery," he said and handed it to me.

"Why can't they tape it like they did for your other surgeries?"

"I asked them. They said it was hospital policy."

The anesthesiologist continued to question Joe about the report from his cardiologist.

"Do you have a heart issue?" Joe said, "No." I butted in. "What about your failed stress test in December?" Joe looked at me. I knew that look. I'd seen it over the years. I didn't say anymore. I sat in the chair next to the bed holding his ring in my hand. A few minutes later, he was taken to surgery. I slipped his ring onto my thumb and went to the family waiting area for patients in surgery. As soon as he returned, still groggy from the recovery room, I put the ring back on his finger.

. . . .

At 6:30pm, Jeff and I reached the fourth floor of Park Ridge Hospital. A nurse saw us rushing to Joe's room and asked us to follow her to a small waiting room at the end of the corridor. I looked down the hall in the direction of his room and saw a nurse closing the door. We made brief eye contact. I wondered why she closed the door so gently. What had happened to the normal hustle and bustle of the floor? My heart pounded through my blouse like a jackhammer-breaking pavement as we entered the room.

"Please sit down," the nurse said. "Would you like something to drink?"

"No! I want to see my husband."

"Someone will be in shortly to speak with you."

I tried again to reach my sons. No answer. I don't know how long we sat there before Dr. Little and two nurses came in. He got down on one knee in front of me, his eyes filled with compassion, and he took my hands.

"I'm so sorry," he said. "I don't know why Joe died."

"He asked me for a glass of ginger ale," said one of the nurses. "When I returned, he was unresponsive."

I was numb to their remarks. I tried to absorb the fact my husband was dead. I thought I was going to the ICU to see him, not to a waiting room to hear, "I don't know why your husband died." Tears, disbelief and confusion clouded all reason. I didn't want to believe that this separation was permanent. I went on autopilot. Every minute seemed like an hour.

"I'll take you to his room now," the nurse said. When she opened the door, a faint odor of antiseptic was in the air. I glanced quickly around the room. Everything had been removed except the bed, the cabinet next to it and the tray table against the wall. Even the wastebasket had been emptied. I held on to Jeff for support.

Joe looked asleep. A hospital gown replaced the grey sweats he had on when I left. I stood by the side of the bed, leaned over his body and kissed him as I often did when he fell asleep on the couch.

"I love you, honey. My life will never be the same without you. I need to look into your eyes one last time." I opened them gently. I remembered when they'd looked at me with such tenderness and love only a few hours earlier. I'd never again see his eyes smile, show anger, or silently say I love you. I touched his hands and remembered how soft they felt on my face when he kissed or held me. How they looked when he painted a canvas with an artist's brush or cut a miter on exotic woods for a piece of furniture or picture frame.

I removed his wedding band and remembered what my mother said when I informed her I was going steady with Joe. "Your wedding ring you will wear until death parts you," she'd told me. I slipped the ring onto my right index finger, a symbol of fifty-two years of love, marriage and commitment. As I turned to leave, I noticed on the cabinet next to the bed was an empty syringe, forgotten or overlooked when the room was cleaned. Was it a silent witness to the struggle for life?

I returned to the waiting room. Joe was an organ donor and release forms had to be signed for his organs to be harvested as soon as possible. I finally reached my sons.

The weekend was spent making arrangements for Joe's funeral. Terri Ross and her husband Herb were close friends for over thirty years. Herb and Joe met while serving in the reserves with the 98th Division Reserve Center in Rochester. Herb called me Saturday morning and said he would make the necessary phone calls and arrangements for Joe's military funeral.

"Put my uniform away for the day of my funeral," Joe had said jokingly when he retired from twenty-eight years of service in the Army and Reserves. He removed the belt buckle, brass, ribbons and shoulder boards from the jacket, and handed them to me. "I remember the day you were drafted," I said, "the day you were commissioned from OCS, and now I'm holding the shoulder boards of a Bird Colonel. You've come a long way, honey." I put them in a box in the bottom drawer of his dresser.
He smiled at me and left the room.

I took the garment bag with Joe's dress blue uniform from the closet and removed the box in the bottom drawer of the dresser.
I slipped the shoulder boards in place and polished the buckle and brass. As a young lieutenant's wife, I'd received his instructions on their proper placement on a collar or lapel. Our oldest son Jim, who would retire from the Reserves as a Lt. Colonel, pinned the polished brass and ribbons on his father's jacket. Watching him, I remembered his graduation from ROTC at Ft. Bragg, NC and the pride Joe felt pinning on his son's bars.

At the cemetery, rifles fired their final salute and the haunting sound of Taps filled the silent sunny morning. The Honor Guards lifted the Flag from the casket, held it taut and with meticulous precision began to fold it. They snapped and tucked each fold tightly against the other. I never knew that each fold of the flag had a significant meaning.

The first fold of our Flag is the symbol of life.

The second fold is a symbol of our belief in eternal life.

The third fold is in honor and remembrance of those veterans departing who gave a portion of life for the defense of our country and to attain peace throughout the world.

The fourth fold represents our weaker nature; for as trusting American citizens, it is to Him we turn to in times of peace as well as war for His Divine guidance.

The fifth fold is a tribute to our country, for in the words of Stephen Decatur, "Our country in dealing with other countries; may she always be right; but, it is still our country, right or wrong."

The sixth fold is where our hearts lie. It is with our heart that we pledge allegiance to the Flag, of the United States of America, and to the Republic for which it stands, one Nation under God, indivisible, with liberty and justice for all.

The seventh fold is the tribute to our Armed Forces, for it is through the Armed Forces that we protect our country against all her enemies, whether they are found within or without the boundaries of the Republic.

The eighth fold is a tribute to the one who entered into the valley of the shadow of death that we may see the light of day, and honor mother, for whom it flies on Mother's Day.

The ninth fold is a tribute to womanhood, for it has been through their faith, love, loyalty and devotion that the characters of the men and women who have made this country great have been molded.

The tenth fold is a tribute to father, for he, too has given his sons and daughters for the defense of our country since he or she was first born.

The eleventh fold, in the eyes of a Hebrew citizen represents the lower portion of the seal of King David and King Solomon and glorifies, in their eyes, the God of Abraham, Isaac and Jacob.

The twelfth fold, in the eyes of a Christian citizen, represents an emblem of eternity and glorifies, in their eyes, God the Father, the Son, and the Holy Ghost.

The thirteenth fold. When the Flag is completely folded, the stars are uppermost reminding us of our Nation's Motto, "In God we trust."

As the flag was folded, a spent shell was tucked into each corner of the flag. The first shell was for Duty, the second Honor, and the third Courage.

Pride welled up within me when an Honor Guard handed me Joe's flag, conveyed condolences, stepped back and saluted.

I invited family and friends to return home with me for a light brunch. Gone was the solace of their company when they said good bye. I faced the reality that I would be living alone. Everyone had gone back to the business of their own lives and the stillness of the house was disquieting. I turned on the TV to drown out the silence. Financial obligations and household responsibilities awaited me, but I wasn't ready. Later, not now. There was no rush, no schedule to adhere to. It would all be accomplished in due time. Who else but me cared or would know?

Looking Back

Months later, it was time to remove Joe's clothes from the closet. A familiar box on the top shelf caught my attention. I removed the contents and found it difficult to hold back tears from eyes that should have been dry from endless days and nights of crying. Our memories were scattered on the bed. Pictures and mementos from our junior and senior proms, and places we visited. Bundles of letters neatly tied with faded, blue satin ribbon, written by the boy of fifteen who flirted with me in eighth grade and married the year after I graduated from high school. I stared at the familiar handwriting on the envelopes, the smiling young faces in the pictures, so young, so in love, so committed to each other and their future, in such a hurry to grow up, get married and raise a family.

Untying the ribbons on the bundles, I found the letters weren't in any particular order. As I looked through them, I noticed pages with the ink smeared and illegible words. I dusted cobwebs from past memories and recalled the unpleasant evening I had last read them. We had been married for eight years and we had two sons ages five and six.

. . . . .

Joe and I were in the kitchen quarrelling. I don't remember exactly what we were arguing about, but I had unresolved issues of concern. Three nights a week for the past six years Joe had been attending the Rochester Institute of Technology to complete his degree in Mechanical Engineering, and one night a week, he served in the Army Reserves to fulfill his military obligation. Weekends he devoted to studying. Friday was his only free night, and I'd ask him if we could go out to dinner or a movie. Most of the time his answer was no. His excuse: "I work all day and go to school and reserves four nights. I'm tired, and I want to stay home and relax."

I resented not being able to enjoy an occasional evening out alone with him. I felt lonely, neglected. I worked every day and night, too; raising our children, washing clothes, cleaning the house, paying bills, grocery shopping and dressmaking. During the summer, Joe had the advantage of being away from his family and his job for two weeks while he trained with the Reserves.

Our two sons came into the room to kiss us goodnight before going to bed. I didn't want to continue quarreling in front of them so I started to walk away. Joe grabbed my arm and held it tightly. I jerked it away. "Don't you ever do that to me again," I told him. I put the boys to bed and went down to the rec room to be alone.

I mixed a shaker of Manhattans, poured the first glass and sat on the couch to mull over the past eight years of our marriage.

We had been married a short three months, living in Ft Leonard Wood, Missouri, when Joe reccived orders to report to Patrick Air Force Base in California for a new assignment. It would be for a year, and Joe hoped it wouldn't be Korea, a hardship tour where I wouldn't be allowed to join him. We packed the car and left for home.

I wanted my own apartment, but Dad said I could live at home rent-free while Joe was gone. The money I saved and Joe's allotment check would probably be enough to make a down payment on a house when he returned. Joe thought it was a good idea also. It was only for a year; I'd get a job to help time pass. I was used to being independent and wondered if Mom expected me to continue following the same rules she had imposed on me when I was single. I hoped not. Was living at home their way of keeping an eye on me while Joe was gone?

One evening, after Joe left, Mom and Dad returned from a visit with friends who knew Joe's parents. Dad had some interesting information regarding comments from Joe's father.

"According to your father-in-law, your marriage won't last six months."

"Why would they say that?" I asked.

"They think you and Joe are too young, and won't be able to handle the pressures you will face."

"Really? They said that. How do they know what we are capable of? Yes, we are young and have a lot to learn, but we'll do it together. They did their best to separate us and prevent our marriage. How am I supposed to feel about them now?"

"You will respect them," Mom said. "They are his parents."

I never shared with Joe what Dad told me. He didn't have to know what his parents said about us. Perhaps he already knew.

I filled my glass a second time . . .

I thought about our two boys and how anxious we had been to start a family. Jim was born in May 1956, and I'm almost positive I conceived him the first night Joe made love to me after he returned from Korea. Ten weeks after Jim was born, I went for my postnatal checkup. During my examination, I felt the draped sheet pulled to one side like the Wizard of Oz revealed. "Mrs. Marasco, you're pregnant again," Dr. Sax said. I couldn't believe my ears.

On the way home, I stopped to see Mom to tell her I was going to have another baby. She was holding Jim.

"I remember the letters Joe wrote after he left asking if you were pregnant," Mom said, and how disappointed he was when you weren't. He's always wanted a daughter who would look like you."

"It doesn't matter if it's a boy or girl, Mom."

"You weren't pregnant when he left, but now the Lord has blessed you with another to make up for the one you didn't have while he was gone."

"I know. I wonder what Joe's going to say."

I drove to my Brother Sonny's house to visit my sister-in-law. We were invited to Joe's parents' house for supper, so I didn't have to go right home. I unbuckled the strap and was lifting Jim out of his car seat when I heard a familiar voice.

"Hello, how are you?" I turned around and saw Tony, the man I met four months before my wedding, the man who almost stole my heart and postponed my wedding. The last time I'd spoken to him was when he called me the morning of my wedding.

"I'm fine, Tony. How are you?" He looked at Jim.

"You have a son?" he asked.

"Yes. We saw the doctor this morning, and I'm pregnant again."

"It will be another boy." Tony said to me.

"I hope it will be a girl this time" I said, balancing Jimmy in one arm while I shut the car door with the other.

"It will be another boy," he said again confidant with his prediction.

"It was nice to see you." I smiled and walked into the house.

Angie was more of an older sister to me than a sister-in-law. She was an only child and I had brothers. I looked up to her as someone other than my mother to confide in

The smell of fresh perked coffee filled the kitchen. She set the cups and saucers, creamer and sugar bowl on the table and stood by the counter until the pot stopped perking.

"Having another baby so soon is going to be very hard on you," she said and poured the coffee.

"I didn't know I could get pregnant again so quickly."

"You'd better think about birth control or you'll be having a baby every 9 months."

"The only birth control allowed by the church is the rhythm method or abstinence."

"The church doesn't have to raise them. Let your conscience guide you."

I finished my coffee, went home and waited for Joe.

When he came home from work, I told him he was going to be a father again. He kissed me and said he hoped it would be a girl.

Joe's mother stood peeling potatoes at the kitchen counter when we arrived. Joe took Jimmy into the living room and I asked my mother-in-law what I could do to help. She said I could set the table.

"Mom, I saw the doctor today for my post-natal checkup," I said as I placed the dishes on the table. "Guess what she told me?"

"What?"

"I'm pregnant again."

She stopped peeling the potatoes, set the knife down, turned slowly and looked at me.

"Oh no. Please don't say anything to your father-in-law before supper, Mary Ann. It will upset him."

It was not the response I expected. The only reason I knew they were against our marriage was because they thought we were too young. Why should they get upset because I was going to have another baby? After supper, I told my father-in-law he was going to be a grandfather again. He didn't say anything. I knew by his silence that he wasn't pleased.

In April 1957, Bobby was born. Jim wasn't even out of diapers.

I filled my glass a third time . . .

The stress of being alone most of the time depressed me. I was just going through the motions. I remembered the day I decided to leave. Fed up with paying bills, cleaning the house, taking care of the children dressmaking and feeling lonely, I packed a suitcase one Friday afternoon and went to my parents' house with the boys.

"What's going on?" Dad asked when I walked in the door.

"I can't take it anymore. I'm unhappy."

"Take the boys into the kitchen with your mother and come on the porch."

I sat next to him on the glider.

"Does Joe know what you're doing?" he asked.

"No, I haven't told him."

"Is he abusive to you or the boys?"

"No, of course not."

"Does he bring his paycheck home every week?"

"Yes, but he's hardly ever home."

"Is he going to college to benefit your future or mine?"

I knew what he was leading up to; his defense of Joe.

"Mine, but I need his attention, too. He works all day, comes home and has supper, and leaves for school or the Reserve Center. I'm practically raising the boys alone. I feel like a single parent."

Dad lit a cigarette and didn't say anything.

While we sat and rocked in silence, I thought about the night I had the notion that he was going to leave my mother. I was eleven or twelve when I woke up to the sound of her crying. I got out of bed and noticed they weren't in their bedroom. They were downstairs. I quietly snuck down the steps. By the side of the front door was a suitcase. Who was going away? Looking through the balusters, I saw my mother on her knees in front of my father.

"Mike, please, I need some rest from the kids and this house. I can't keep doing everything alone. I can't take it anymore."

Dad didn't say anything. He stood there expressionless.

"Can't we go away for a weekend alone?" she pleaded.

I got up and walked into the room.

"Mom, get up off your knees," I said. "You kneel only to God."

I looked at my father. His face reflected the shock of what I had said. I loved my father, but at that moment, I didn't like what he was doing to my mother. Dad was a trucker and spent many days on the road. Mom had the responsibility of raising the five of us almost entirely alone. All she wanted was to spend some time alone with him.

My mother told me to go back to bed. When I got up the next morning, the door to my parents' bedroom was slightly ajar. I was relieved to see both of them sleeping.

Dad stopped the glider. He looked at me.

"You don't belong here. If you told me Joe were abusive and not providing for you and the boys, you could stay. You belong home with him. I know it must be difficult, but he is working and going to school to earn a degree to provide a secure future for you and the boys."

"I'm lonely, Dad. We're always saying goodbye. It began in high school, continued when he went to college, the military, and the year he spent in Korea after we were married. It has been going on forever. Nothing has changed. We are still apart most of the time and I miss him."

"How's your love life?"

"There isn't much of that lately. We make love, but it is not the same as it used to be. Romance is just a word. The only time we can be away and alone is when I join him the middle weekend he is at summer camp with the Reserves. It's tight financially right now."

Dad reached into his pocket and handed me a twenty-dollar bill.

"Mom and I will watch the boys this weekend. Buy a couple of steaks and set the table with flowers and candles. Before Joe gets home, take a bubble bath, have soft music playing on the stereo and greet him at the door wearing your sheerest nightgown. Pretend you are waiting for your lover. You seduce him."

I took his advice.

. . . . .

"You should do that more often honey," Joe said.

"I would, but I can't walk around in a sheer nightgown in front of the boys."

"That's not what I mean."

"What do you mean?"

"You know what I mean. Your being aggressive."

I turned toward him, my hand on his chest.

"You want me to initiate making love to you?" I whispered in his ear.

"Yes, I do," he said half smiling.

"I will if that's what you want, but you have to promise to be my lover more often."

Dad had talked to me the night before the wedding regarding the responsibilities of a wife. Not a written list, just a discussion. The last item on the list was "Be his mistress in the bedroom." Is this what he meant?

I poured the fourth glass . . .

I looked around the room; the box with Joe's letters was in the bookcase. I decided to read them again. I turned on the stereo and stacked the record holder with romantic music we listened to when we went steady and fell in love. "You Belong to Me," "Little Things Mean a Lot," "Beloved Be Faithful," "Because of You," Tenderly," "Harbor Lights" and others.

I pulled the ribbon on each bundle and untied them. They were sorted by the day, month and year he wrote them. Randomly, I pulled a few from each bundle. Every letter professed his love, passion and longing for me. What happened to the passion? When did I last hear him speak of his love for me the way he did in his letters? I longed to hear him say those loving thoughts to me. My heart hurt when the next record to play was "Tenderly," our song. I couldn't hold back the tears. They fell onto the letters. The wet ink spread like wildfire across the page I was reading and the pages on my lap, leaving behind smudged watermarks that were once the passionate loving thoughts Joe had written.

The shaker was empty.

With tearless eyes, I gathered the letters into the box and decided it was time to go upstairs. I wasn't used to drinking and was clumsy trying to hold the box in one hand, the handrail with the other. I looked up and saw Joe coming down.

"What do you have in your arms?" he asked.
"Your letters." My voice was slurred.
"What are you going to do with them?"
"Burn 'em."
"Why?"
"Because the person who wrote them is not the same person standing next to me."
"You can't burn my letters."

Taking the box from my hand, he put his arm around me.

"I'm sorry, Honey. Come to bed."

I bundled and tied the letters the next morning. I had no reason to read them until now, more than sixty years later. I sorted them by the day, month and year Joe wrote them. Reading them again, I remembered the first time I saw Joe, fell in love with him, and the trials of our young love.

The Beginning

September 1948

My first semester at Benjamin Franklin High School. I was assigned to room 212, Mrs. Peterson's homeroom on the second floor. I expected to see my class from grammar school when I walked into the room, but only three or four of them were there. The final bell rang.

Mrs. Peterson introduced herself and said she would be our homeroom teacher for the next five years. After she passed out an attendance sheet for us to sign, she read our names and handed each of us an envelope containing a five-day schedule of subjects, study halls, classroom numbers and first or second lunch period.

The bell rang at 8:55. Five minutes was the allotted time between periods. Running up and down unfamiliar stairways and corridors from one part of the building to another to get to class before the final bell was hectic. Once I was lost and asked for help. A smart aleck upperclassman gave me the wrong directions. By the end of the week, I knew my schedule, where I was going and how to get there.

One afternoon after lunch period, my girlfriends and I were walking down the hall to Mr. Hennessy's algebra class. As we turned the corner I heard, "Hi, Red." I looked in the direction of the voice and saw a group of boys standing near a classroom door. "Hi, Beautiful." Only one of them was staring at me.

He was leaning against the wall with his hand in his pocket. His straight dark brown hair matched deep-set eyes that spoke a language all their own. His face was tanned and when he smiled at me I felt my heart jump. Creases down the center of his chestnut- brown gabardine slacks were neatly pressed, the shirt cuffs on his cream-colored sport shirt were evenly rolled up twice, and his loafers were polished. He reminded me of the illustrations I'd seen in *Seventeen* magazine of the well dressed student. I returned his smile and walked past him.

Every day as I walked by that corner on my way to class, I glanced in that direction. If he was there, he smiled and said, "Hello, Rusty," "Hi, Beautiful" or "I love your red hair." Sometimes he just smiled and said, "Hi." Whatever he said, I kept walking.

My girlfriends thought I was rude not to respond. "He's so good looking!" they kept saying. "Why don't you go over and talk to him?" I was flattered and attracted, especially to his smile, but I didn't want to be the one to open the conversation. I looked forward to his flirting, but he never attempted an introduction. We enjoyed our game of cat and mouse. In class, I thought of him standing there with his hand on his waist or in his pocket as he stood against the classroom wall. He was very handsome, but it was his smile that captured my heart. On other occasions, I'd heard references to my red hair from boys with voices loud and boisterous. When this nameless boy spoke, his voice was calm, quiet and sincere, pleasant to my ears. His eyes invoked Svengali when he looked at me, but I refused to fall under his spell. The fall semester ended without any change in our routine. Etiquette dictated he was to approach me first. Girls didn't chase after boys.

During the two weeks of Christmas recess, I thought about him occasionally. I wondered when I saw him again if he would make the effort to come and talk to me or if I would break the rule and talk to him. The answers to these questions had to wait until the New Year.

January 1949

I barely made it through lunch. I walked down the hall, the conversations of my girlfriends fading from my ears as we approached the end of the corridor. All I could think about was the winning smile, dark brown eyes and voice of the handsome boy who flirted with me. Would he be there?

I turned my head to the left as we reached the corner. He was there, looking my way. When he saw me, he said, "Hello, Beautiful." This time I paused, returned his smile and said, "Hello." He smiled but didn't come toward me, so I continued on to my algebra class. A few months of "hellos" later, our yearbooks arrived. I vacillated. Should I break my own rules and ask him to sign mine? At lunch, I made my decision. I walked toward him on my way to class with my yearbook in hand. He looked surprised, moved away from the wall, and took his hand out of his pocket. I had to look up to talk to him. He looked down into my face and smiled. I was so nervous I could feel my heart pound and the blood rush to my cheeks.

"Will you sign my yearbook?" I asked.
"Yes, if you'll sign mine. It's in my locker, but I'll have it later for you to sign."

I looked into his brown eyes and handed him my book. He wrote quickly and closed the cover. His hand touched my fingertips when he smiled and handed it back to me. I felt the blood rush to my face again when our eyes met. When I was out of his view, I stopped in the middle of the hallway and flipped to the back cover. *To a swell girl I wouldn't mind getting really acquainted with, Joe Marasco.* Now I knew the name behind that wonderful smile. The next afternoon after lunch when Joe saw me, he walked toward me with his yearbook. He handed it to me. I signed his; *To a handsome guy*

I wouldn't mind getting better acquainted with, Mary Ann Mastro. When I handed it back to him, he smiled and said thank you. That was our first written communication. The semester ended, summer vacation began and the handsome boy who flirted with me became a fond memory.

I spent the summer riding my bike, going to the movies, eating strawberry sundaes at the United Dairy Ice Cream Store, or just sitting on the front porch with my girlfriends. Most of our conversation was about plans to go somewhere and the boys we thought were good looking or not. Sandwiched between our girl talk were my chores. I dusted my room, dried the dishes, and folded the flat pieces of laundry Mom removed from the clothesline. I didn't mind folding them, but Mom said my job was to iron them, a chore I felt cut into playtime with my friends.

On a hot, sunny afternoon in July following my 14th birthday, my friends and I decided to take a bicycle ride to Irondequoit Bay to go swimming. "Let's wear our bathing suits under our clothes, so our parents won't know we're going swimming," someone suggested. We all agreed. After lunch my brother Jim, my girlfriend Mary Navarra, her brother Joe, and my other neighborhood friends Lillian Di Bernardi, Frances (Babe) Sortino and Al Battaglia headed down Goodman Street and turned right onto Norton and headed for Bay Road. We got off our bikes and anxiously looked down the curving road, uncertain if we wanted to go through with our plans. Al finally broke the silence.

"I think we better go down in single file. The guys first. You girls follow, but not too close in case we have to stop suddenly."

Cautiously, we began our descent. Our fingers tightly gripped the handlebars as we shoved off, our feet positioned to press down hard on the pedals to brake as we coasted down the hill. With the wind in our faces, and our hearts pounding, we followed each other down and around the curves in the road. Exhilarated, we reached the bottom and breathed a sigh of relief from the exciting three-minute ride.

We took pictures on a sailboat (fortunately the owner was nowhere to be seen.), swam, and sat on the dock all afternoon until our swimsuits dried. We enjoyed the three-minute thrill of coasting down the hill, but none of us enjoyed the twenty-minute ordeal of pushing our bikes back up to the top. I never told Mom that we swam in the bay. She would have gone into orbit. I can't imagine what our punishment would have been had she known.

Our front porch was the gathering place for my friends and my brother's friends. One day in late August, I sat on the porch with Stella Russo, Nancy Azzanno and Cecilia Perrone. We were laughing, talking, and just hanging out.

"Mary Ann, Mary Ann, look who's riding his bike toward your house," Cecilia said. She poked me repeatedly. I looked up and saw that certain someone who flirted with me all during the school year. I walked to the end of the porch to meet him. He got off his bike and stood at the bottom of the porch steps.

"What are you doing here?" I asked, shifting my weight from one foot to the other. I felt the blood rush to my face as I leaned against the porch post; nervous as the day he signed my yearbook.

"I want to ask you to go out with me," he said, coming up the steps onto the porch.

"You'll have to ask my Dad first." I opened the screen

door. "Dad, there's someone here I want you to meet. He wants to ask your permission to take me on a date."

Dad came out the door and I introduced them.
"Where do you live?" Dad asked.
"Irondequoit," Joe answered.
"Where are you going? How will you get there?"
"To a movie downtown. We'll take the bus."
"What day and time?"
"Next Friday at 6:30."
"She has a 10:00 curfew."
"I'll have her home before 10:00."

Dad hesitated, looked at Joe, at me, smiled and said, "She can go." I was surprised. Dad knew all my friends, boys and girls from the neighborhood, but this was the first time he'd met Joe. Perhaps he knew the distance Joe had traveled from his house to ours. I didn't. Did he see something in this boy and respect his asking permission to take out his daughter? I didn't know why, but I was happy and appreciated he said yes. Joe said goodbye, said he would see me Friday and rode off. When he was out of sight, my friends asked me questions all at once. They were as excited as I was about my first date with Joe.

I asked my mother if I could get a new dress. She said yes. We went shopping at Nathan's and she noticed a dress in my size in a soft shade of turquoise. "This would be a lovely dress for you; it's in your size and the perfect color for a redhead." I tried it on. She was right about the size and color. When we arrived home, I held it in front of me and asked Dad if he liked it. "It's pretty," he said with a smile. I ran up to my bedroom to try it on again. I didn't have a full-length mirror in my bedroom. The dresser had a mirror above it and the reflection was from the waist up. I decided to stand on the bed to get a full view. Taking off my shoes, I stood in the middle of the bed trying to keep my balance on the soft mattress while I turned to the back and front. I wondered what Joe would think when he saw me in it.

Finally, it was Friday. I could hardly wait for 6:30 to arrive. I took the new dress out of the closet and put it on the bed next to my full slip, stockings, garter belt and underwear. I washed my hair and set it with large pin curls so it wouldn't be so frizzy. My thick curly hair was unruly after I washed it. I tied a kerchief over the pin curls and went on the porch to polish my nails. Mom reminded me I had to dust my room. "You might smear the polish if it isn't dry." I went to my bedroom, dusted the furniture and the floor and ran down to the porch to do my nails. My nails were always a problem. They never grew long. The afternoon dragged towards supper where I barely touched my food. Mom asked Dad to raise the flame on the hot water tank so I could bathe and she could do the dishes at the same time.

A little before 6:30 I went on the porch to wait for Joe. The angle of the setting sun cast shadows of the houses across the street. As they elongated through the canopy of elm trees toward our house, my anticipation grew. I didn't want to get too excited because it would cause me to blush and I didn't want my freckled face to look like a strawberry when Joe arrived.

When I finally saw him, he smiled and raised his hand to say hello. My heart beat faster as each step brought him closer to our front porch. I was impressed with the way he looked and the way he walked. I had only seen him wearing slacks, sport shirts or sweaters in school, jeans and a "T" shirt when he rode his bike to my house. Today he wore a grey suit, white shirt and a maroon tie. He strode forward with a determined pace, shoulders squared, not slouched. As he got closer, I saw his neatly combed hair and polished loafers. His tanned face looking straight ahead at me. How handsome he looked as he walked up the steps, smiled and winked at me.

"Hello, Beautiful, is your dad here? I want to tell him we're going to the Regent Theater." Joe told Dad where we were going. We said goodbye and walked to the bus stop.

On the bus, Joe deposited both our fares into the coin box and we sat down. I asked him how he knew where I lived.

"After you signed my yearbook, I looked up your name In the phonebook."

"I'm glad I used the shorter version of Mastrolonardo, but there is more than one entry with my last name."

"I know, but yours was in the school district we attended. How long have you lived there?"

"We moved there in 1941. Why do you want to know?"

Joe did not say anything for a moment or two. He looked at me with a Cheshire cat smile. "There's something else I have to tell you later on," he said.

We were downtown in twenty minutes and in the theater for the start of the movie. I don't remember the movie, but I do remember him holding my hand and telling me he had been thinking about asking me for a date all summer. After the movie, we went to the Goodie Shop ice cream parlor next to the theater. A waitress came to our table with water and asked if we needed a menu. We said no, we knew what we wanted. I ordered a strawberry sundae and Joe ordered a hot fudge sundae with peanuts. He looked at me for a moment or two. He folded his arms, rested them on the table and leaned toward me.

"Why did you ignore me for so long?" he asked.

"You kept flirting, but you didn't come toward me. I would have stopped and talked to you."

"Why didn't you stop?"

I smiled and slowly leaned toward him.

"I did, but you didn't move from where you were standing. Boys are supposed to make the first move in an introduction," I whispered. "Would we be sitting here if I hadn't broken the rule and asked you to sign my yearbook?" He smiled at me.

The waitress brought our sundaes. We started to eat and Joe spilled ice cream on his jacket sleeve. I dipped the edge of my napkin into my glass of water, squeezed out the excess and patted the area so the stain wouldn't set. When I finished, he thanked me.

"That saves a trip to the dry cleaners," he said.

I continued where I left off.

"I was flattered that you were flirting with me. I liked your smile, but I didn't know you, and you weren't in the circle of friends I had known all my life."

"That's silly. You need to make new friends as you go through life; that's part of growing up and maturing. Remember on the bus I said I had something else to tell you?"

"Yes, I remember."

"When you told me how long you lived at that address, I knew you had to be the girl I admired in grammar school."

"Grammar school? I went to School 39".

"So did I. You were the only redhead in the whole school. You had long curly red hair. I thought you were the prettiest girl I'd ever seen."

"What street did you live on?"

"Randolph."

"That's only a few blocks from my house." I folded my napkin and set it on the table. The waitress asked if we wanted anything else. We said no and she gave Joe the check.

"I was in sixth grade when we moved to the suburbs; you must have been in fourth grade when I first noticed you."

"Who were some of your friends?" I asked.

"Joe Scibona, Dick Tambe. Nick Mastromatteo, Bill Ruoff, to name a few."

"Nick's sister Angie and her twin brother Steve were in my class and I know Joe. I don't remember you."

Our conversation ended abruptly when he looked at his watch and said we had to hurry to catch the bus so I would be home by ten-o'clock. On the way home, he mentioned the frightening experience he had when he lived on Randolph Street.

"I played baseball in a KPAA (Kodak Park Athletic Association) league at the age of eleven or twelve and had to ride the bus to the city where the teams played. One day I got on the wrong bus and panicked when I had no idea where I was. I couldn't locate familiar landmarks and knew I was lost. I became more frightened the further the bus traveled."

"What did you do?" I asked.

"I had money for the ride back, but if I used it to change buses, I wouldn't have enough to get home. I had no choice. I had to ask the bus driver for help. When I told him my problem, he gave me a transfer, didn't charge me and told me which bus to take to reach the ballpark. I was concerned because we were going to have our team picture taken that day and I didn't want to miss being in it."

"What did your parents say when you told them?"

"I never told them. I was afraid they wouldn't let me play ball anymore."

Mom and Dad were sitting on the porch glider waiting for us to get off the bus. Dad asked Joe how long it would take him to get home. Joe said about forty-five minutes. The buses ran every 20 minutes and he knew he'd make it home before his midnight curfew. Dad offered to drive him home. He winked at me and said, "Why don't you and your mother come along, too." We got in the car. Dad backed into the street; Joe reached over and took my hand.

"You can take Goodman to Ridge Road and turn right," Joe said as he squeezed my hand. No one spoke until we approached Culver Road.

"Turn left at Culver," Joe said as he caressed the top of my fingers with his other hand. I looked in the rear view mirror to see if Dad was watching us.

"After Titus Avenue the first left is my street." Dad drove past the street and had to turn around.

"You can let me off on the corner."

Joe poked his head in my open window after closing the door and asked if he could call me. I agreed without asking permission I didn't think my parents would mind. They let me go on a bus to a movie with him and drove him home, so I didn't think there would be a problem.

On our way home, Mom asked if I had a nice time.

"Yes, I did, and he knew me from grammar school."

"How did he know it was you after such a long time?

"My hair. He remembered me because of my red hair,"

Mom smiled. "You were the only redhead in the neighborhood and in school."

"He's soft spoken and polite. I love his smile, but he seems very quiet."

"Still waters run deep," she said.

I didn't hear from Joe after our date. I spent the last couple of weeks before school started with my girlfriends going to the movies, eating strawberry sundaes at the United Dairy Ice Cream Store, or sitting on the front porch with them or my family.

Right before Labor Day Joe called and asked me to meet him in front of the school by the flagpole. He had a camera in his hand. "How about my taking your picture leaning against the flag pole?" he asked with a smile. I smoothed my brown corduroy skirt, brushed the dust from my penny loafers, and straightened my bobby socks. I leaned against the flagpole, and he snapped the picture

"Would you like to have a locker next to mine?" he asked as we walked to the school entrance. I said yes. We looked for two near the exit and found them on the second floor across from the tailor shop classroom. We'd meet there every morning before class and after school to walk home.

The only time we saw each other was in school. Joe's part time job at Greenberg's Pharmacy kept him busy after school and on weekends. He was busy working and hanging out with friends in his neighborhood, at the Hub Theater, indoor roller skating rink, miniature golf course and bowling alley near Sea Breeze Amusement Park. I was busy with chores at home and friends from my neighborhood.

After Joe died, I went to lunch in Irondequoit with Sue Rudman, a friend of Joe's from his neighborhood where I also met Mary Lu, a classmate of Joe's at Durand. When I told her I was Joe's widow and writing about our courtship, she told me she was so infatuated with him she asked her mother daily if she needed anything from Hart's Grocery Store, so she could see him. Joe's first job when he moved to Irondequoit was working after school at Hart's Grocery Store.

Sue gave me a picture taken in March 1949 of Joe and his friend Camille, who are standing behind her and Vic Kane, one of Joe's best friends.
Joe was quite popular with the girls. He captured many

hearts with his smile and handsome face when he transferred from School 39 to Durand. Dick Saxe, one of his friends from Durand told me the day Joe started school and walked into the classroom, all the girls stared at him.

. . .

When we walked home from school, Joe always positioned himself on the street side of the sidewalk. He said it was the "proper" thing to do. The first time he put his arm across my back and his hand on my shoulder, I put my arm around his waist. He gently removed it, and took my hand.

"You're a lady, and ladies don't put their arms around boys in public. I'll put my arm on your shoulder or you can put your arm in mine."

He slipped my hand into his arm.

"This is what I want; your arm in mine, or my arm on your shoulder when we're in school or when I walk with you."

His concern for my reputation if seen in public with my arm around his waist was something a *good girl* didn't do.

We'd walk together to Portland Avenue and Norton Street where he would wait for the bus to take him home or to work. Ritz's, a hangout for the after school crowd, was on the same corner. If Joe didn't have to work, we'd stop in and order burgers, Cokes and French fries. Dick Saxe and Ken Latimer, two of his best friends, often walked with us. Joe and Ken played the pinball machine waiting for our order. When it was time to leave, Joe got on the bus if he had to go to work, if not he'd walk me home.

Our friendship continued throughout the fall semester. We talked, laughed, and enjoyed the same music and the joy of being good friends. We spent the holidays at home with our families and saw each other again after Christmas recess.

Going Steady

March 1950

    Joe asked me to his junior prom. I asked Mom if I could get a new dress or gown and she said yes. We went downtown to Thompson's, a shop off East Avenue. I liked the first gown I was shown. The fabric was a soft sheer in sea foam green. The bottom edge of the fitted bodice where the gathered skirt was attached rested just above my hip and accentuated the waist. Other than the length, it fit perfectly. I decided to shorten it myself to save the added expense of an alteration. Mom said with the savings I could purchase an evening bag. I chose a small gold mesh bag that I could use for future proms or other special occasions. Arriving home, I opened the box, and showed the gown to Dad. He gave his usual "It's pretty" response.

    The night of the prom Joe handed me a white box with a cellophane top. I looked inside and saw a corsage of roses. "They're Talisman roses. I chose them because their color reminds me of the color of your hair," he said. It was the first time I'd ever seen roses with petals of burnt sienna and tips of yellow. I pinned it on the left side of my waist because I knew if it were on my shoulder it might be crushed when we danced. The prom started at 7:00. Dad said I had to be home before midnight.

The decorating committee had transformed the gym into a ballroom with crepe paper streamers of pink, lavender, pale green and yellow suspended from the second floor hall balcony, over raised bleachers and basketball hoops. Flowers and tablecloths covered the cafeteria tables where bowls of fruit punch, trays of cookies and other snacks awaited the happy crowd. In one corner of the gym, a photographer took keepsake pictures of the happy couples.

We danced, talked with friends and had our picture taken. We were dancing to "Tenderly" when Joe asked me to go steady. I looked up into his eyes. "Yes," I said, and he held me a little tighter. We were oblivious to anyone else around us. The song became "our song" from then on.

We went home after the prom and sat on the porch glider. Dad bought it in the summer of 1945, and it remained in the same spot in front of the window by the front door from the day it was delivered. Anyone sitting on it was visible from the front hallway. Uncovered during many seasons of rain, snow, and damp weather, the glider squeaked from rusty rails. Dad never found time to paint the glides. Occasionally, he oiled them but we still heard the squeaks when we sat and glided. It was the place we were told to sit as punishment with a stern, "Until your father comes home." Reading a book, doing homework, talking with friends, or eating bologna sandwiches with homemade lemonade on a summer day was routine. Joe left at midnight to be home before his 12:30 curfew.

After lunch, Joe and I would wait in the hall on the second floor overlooking the gym for the bell to ring for afternoon classes. Ken often joined us. The week after the prom Joe handed me a small braided ring he made in metal shop. "Now we are officially going steady," he said. "I'll replace it with my senior ring next year."

When I walked in the house that day, I went into the kitchen, said hi to Mom, and opened the refrigerator to have a snack. She noticed the ring on my hand.

"Where did you get that ring?" Mom asked.
"Joe. He made it for me."
"Are you and Joe going steady?"
"Yes."
"You're fourteen, too young to be going steady."
"You and Dad were childhood sweethearts and married at nineteen."
"That's true, but times were different then."
I sat at the table to drink my glass of milk. She sat across from me folding the dishtowel in her hand.
"This ring may be one of three Joe will give you if you continue to go steady with him."
"What do you mean?"
"You and Joe are very young, and he is the first boy you feel strongly about. If you accept his ring, it means you'll be faithful to him."
"I know."
"When you're older, the second ring may be an engagement ring, your promise to marry and your fidelity to him. Third and last is your wedding ring if you marry Joe. That ring is your commitment to God and Joe of your faithfulness in marriage forever."

I finished my glass of milk and put the glass in the sink.

"If you're faithful to the first ring, you'll be faithful with the last."
"I know that. We want to get married some day in the future."
"I want you to know, the first two you can return if you change your mind, but your wedding ring you will wear until death parts you. There is commitment and responsibility in accepting each one of them."

I understood her sincerity and instructions, unaware that one day in the future, they would be tested. I was young, and didn't intend to change my mind. I loved Joe and hoped to marry him some day.

Going steady with Joe wasn't as easy as I thought it was going to be. He didn't appreciate my talking to other boys or walking to class with them for any reason. If he saw me with them, he would question what we were talking about. I assured him he was the only one I loved, but his jealousy and suspicions troubled me. He said he trusted me but not the other guys who might try to change my mind about him. I noticed other girls looking at him with adoring eyes and smiles, and I felt a pull on my heartstrings. I knew I was not the only girl who was attracted to him, but as far as I knew, I was the only one he gave a ring to and asked to go steady. I asked my mother about his attitude.

"He doesn't want to share you with anyone."

"Why is he so possessive and jealous?"

"I don't know why, but as long as you are going steady and wearing his ring, you have to accept how he feels."

"I'm not doing anything wrong, just talking to boys."

"Maybe he's afraid you'll find someone else and break up with him."

"That's not true. It won't happen."

"If you disagree, return his ring and you can do what you want to do."

I didn't want to return his ring so I ignored her last remark.

Our relationship continued to grow and Joe's confidence about my feelings toward him seemed more secure. I knew how he felt about me so it never occurred to me to question him about Sally Ashmore and Barbara Williams, two girls from his neighborhood he talked to or took home the few times he drove the family car to school.

We spent a lot of time talking about college and marriage. We knew that it was a long way off, but we enjoyed dreaming of that day wondering what is was going to be like.

"Honey, I wish I could put you in a test tube and keep you there until the day I marry you," Joe said one day walking home.
"Why?" I asked.
"So I can keep you only for me and not have to worry about someone else changing your mind about me."
"Don't worry, honey; no one will."

The semester ended and a week later Joe said his family was going to Archibald, Pennsylvania to visit his favorite aunts, uncles and cousins. His mother was born there. He said he'd be gone about 10 days. I wasn't sure when I would receive his letter. This was the first of many that he wrote to me during the years of our courtship and marriage.

June 30, 1950

Hi Honey,

I suppose you're mad at me for not writing sooner, but you know how I am. My cousin's vacation was changed so I decided to stay. I hope you're still thinking about me because I have been thinking of you. It probably hasn't seemed that way because I didn't write sooner but they say better late than never.

I'll keep writing so you can write back to me. Soon please.

Love always,
Joe

P.S. Keep thinking of me no matter what may go through your mind. Remember that.

I thought it odd his postscript told me to keep thinking

of him no matter what. Was it a tinge of guilt that perhaps he was doing something he shouldn't? Unknowingly he had planted a tiny seed of doubt where none had existed.

Returning from his trip Joe continued to work through the summer and we'd see each other on Friday night or the weekend when he didn't have to work.

One Saturday afternoon he came over to my house with his cousins Mary and Ralph from Archibald, Pennsylvania. Mary was petite with dark brown hair and Ralph was about Joe's height with brown eyes and hair. They were warm and friendly. We were friends almost instantly.

"How long have you been going with Buddy?" Mary asked.
"Who?"
"Buddy is what the family calls Joe."
"Oh. I didn't know that. Two years."
"Have you been to his house?"
"No."
"Why not?"
"Joe never asked me."
"We'll be going home in a few days. Why don't you stop by?" she asked.
"I don't think I should."
"You're coming to see me."
"No. It's not right unless Joe asks me."

It wasn't until that moment I realized Joe had never asked me to his house. I wavered about going. I rationalized Mary invited me, but Joe didn't. I knew I'd be breaking a rule of etiquette if I went, but I was curious about where he lived.

The following day after lunch, I told my mother I was going for a bike ride, not where I was really going.

I learned how to ride on a bike that belonged to Mike (Sonny), my older brother. I was too short to reach the seat so I pedaled standing up. Many times while I was trying to brake, my foot slid off one of the pedals and I'd fall onto the cross bar. That hurt.

I went to the garage to get my bike. I was so proud of it. The morning of my twelfth birthday, Mom and Dad woke me up and told me they had a surprise for me. I went downstairs; in the front hall by the window was a blue and cream girl's Schwinn bicycle. The tires were rubber, white walled with inner tubes. Not until the end of the war was rubber available for civilian use. The chrome handlebar had a basket, cream handle grips with blue and white streamers attached at the end, a horn built into the frame and a carrier on the back fender. Mom and Dad said they cashed my war bonds to purchase it.

I had no idea how long it would take to get to Joe's house. I took the same route Dad drove the night we took Joe home after our first date. I rode down Goodman Street and turned onto Ridge Road. I kept asking myself, "Should I have told Joe I was coming? Will he be angry? Should I turn around and go home?" I reached Culver Road and had to stop for the signal light to change. Waiting, I felt the hot afternoon sun on my back. I didn't feel its heat until I stopped. I signaled left when the light changed and continued down Culver Road. It's not too late to turn around I thought.

Passing Titus Avenue, I turned onto Joe's street. I was hot and thirsty when I got off my bike and stood in the driveway. Joe and his cousins were in the back yard. Joe wasn't smiling when he saw me and began to walk toward me. The look in his eyes told me I'd made a mistake going there.

"What are you doing here?" he asked.
"Your cousin Mary asked me to stop over." Mary came up to me.
"Hi, would you like to meet Aunt Lena?" she asked. Before I could answer her, Joe took my hand.
"Your face is red; I think you need a glass of water," he said.

We walked to the side door of the house and went into the kitchen. The first thing I noticed was the black and white ceramic tiled kitchen counter and the matching linoleum floor tile. A built in china cabinet in the corner held a variety of teacups, china and glassware. I compared the difference between our house and Joe's, the quiet street, manicured lawn and the tastefully decorated formal dining room and living room. His mother was in the kitchen standing by the table. I felt awkward and stood at the doorway.

"Mom, this is Mary Ann." We both said hello at the same time. Joe reached into the cupboard and took out a glass filled it with water and handed it to me. I drank it hurriedly and handed the glass back to him. He put it in the sink. I told his mother I was glad to have met her and we went outside. Embarrassed, I said goodbye and told Mary I had made a mistake in coming. I got on my bike and left. The long ride home gave me time to think about what happened and ask myself questions regarding Joe's attitude.

Was he angry with Mary for asking me to come or did I put him in a position where he had no choice but to introduce me to his mother? Was he afraid to tell his mother I was his girlfriend? Did she know he had a girlfriend? I may have made the wrong decision going there, but that was no excuse for him to be rude and make me feel uncomfortable. He was never treated that way when he came to my house.

The next time we were together he commented on my going to his house.

"Mary shouldn't have asked you to visit her."
"Why not?"
"I wanted to wait until the proper time for you to meet my family."
"When is the proper time, Joe?"
"After we've dated for a little longer."
I knew then his parents would not accept the fact that he had a girlfriend and that they probably thought that he was too young to be serious about any girl. If first impressions mattered to him or his mother, I probably failed.

Joe was nominated to run for senior class president. "No way," he said. Ken and his friends convinced him.
He asked me if I would write a campaign slogan. I did. It wasn't long, just a few lines
.
Get on your mark,
Get set, let's go.
Get in the swing and vote for Joe.
It was catchy and Joe liked it. The slogan, printed in dark green ink on yellow cards was given to classmates. He was up against some stiff opposition; the most popular guys in school.
Campaign banners had to be painted for the rally, so Ken, Joe, Mary, Babe, and I agreed to help make them. Joe said he and Ken would pick up the supplies and we'd meet after school on Thursday, the day before the rally at Connie Massero's house on Norton Street. Walking home after we finished, I remembered that I didn't tell my mother I'd be late. I knew the consequences for not doing so. I walked in the house at 5:00 and braced myself for the inevitable confrontation.

"You're late. Where were you?" Mom asked.
"At Connie's house making banners for Joe's rally."
"Were her parents' home?"

"No."

"You and your friends were in the house alone?" Her expression changed from upset to fury.

"Yes. All we were doing was painting banners for the rally." I tried to reason with her and defend my position. My disobedience just fanned the fire of her anger.

"You're not going to school tomorrow," she said.

"What? You can't do that," I yelled.

"Oh yes, I can."

"Why are you being so mean?"

I didn't understand her reasoning. For the first time in my life, I didn't like my mother. Hate may be a better word to describe how I felt. I was too old to have my hair pulled, but her taking something away from me as important as being at Joe's rally pushed me to the limit. Her punishment didn't fit my crime.

I was sitting on the stairway crying when my father came home from work.

"What's going on?" he asked.

"She said I can't go to school tomorrow to help at Joe's rally because I got home late. I have to Dad. It's important."

"Your mother is not 'she'. She has a name."

He looked at me and walked into the kitchen. He came in a few minutes later and told me I was going to school the next day. Once again, he came to my rescue. I didn't speak to my mother during or after supper. I cleared the table, washed the dishes and went to my room to do my homework.

I have not forgotten the lesson I learned that afternoon. You don't have to punish someone physically to hurt them. Take away something that is precious or important, and the pain lasts longer. Joe didn't win, but a large number of students voted for him.

My Wounded Heart

Joe was a senior and this was our last year in high school together. As promised, he gave me his senior ring which I banded with tape. I put away the friendship ring.

As a senior, he drove the family car to school occasionally. After school, he drove Ken, Sally Ashmore, Barb Williams, and me home. Ken sat in back with the girls and I sat in front with Joe. After school on the days he didn't have to work, we stopped at Ritz's. When we left, Joe took me home first; Ken hopped in the front seat with him and was taken home next and then Joe drove home with Sally and Barb.

A few weeks into the semester, I noticed a change in Joe's attitude and affections towards me. He made excuses not to meet me for lunch, or if we did meet at our spot overlooking the gym, he was quiet. He talked with Ken and left me out of the conversation. He didn't put his arm on my shoulder walking to class or home after school. When I attempted to slip my hand into his arm, he took his hand out of his pocket so I had nowhere to rest mine. Was something going on I should know about?

This change continued for a time, but the reasons for it were not evident until the week he and Ken received their white cardigan class sweaters with their class letters and names embroidered on the pocket. I asked him if I could wear it.

"No, I just got it. I want to wear it for a while," he said abruptly. Again, that little voice inside of me warned me something was wrong because he had never spoken to me that way.

"OK, someday."

Maybe he was having difficulty at home or at work. He never mentioned problems at either place, and I wouldn't allow myself to think otherwise. He wore his sweater every day that week, except Friday. When I met him at our locker, he didn't have it on. I was about to ask him where it was, but the bell rang and we had to leave for homeroom. I told him I'd meet him after assembly.

I walked to my seat in the auditorium and was about to sit down when I noticed Sally, six rows ahead of me wearing a familiar white sweater. I put my books on the seat and walked to where she was sitting.

"Is that Ken's sweater you're wearing?" I asked.

"No, it's Joe's," she said with a smirk. She turned to Barb sitting next to her and whispered something. They giggled. Barb also had a white sweater on. It was Ken's.

A hot arrow pierced my heart as I walked back to my seat. Now the pieces of the puzzle were falling into place. Joe's coolness toward me, not putting his arm on my shoulder while we walked to class, his unresponsiveness toward me at our place after lunch and dropping his arm so I couldn't hold it. Driving me home, instead of Ken getting in the front seat of the car, Sally did. I stupidly thought it was because Ken had a crush on Barb, so I didn't think anything of it. How naive I was.

I thought of nothing but Joe's unfaithfulness during the entire assembly. Was giving Sally his sweater a way of telling me he wanted to break up with me? My knees felt like rubber and my heart ached as I left the auditorium. I waited for Joe in the foyer.

"Why is Sally wearing your sweater?" I asked when he was close enough to hear me.

"She wanted to wear it."

"I asked you if I could wear it and you told me later. When did you give it to her? How long have you been seeing her?"

He didn't answer my questions. The look on his face told me that he didn't want to answer. I pulled his ring off my finger.

"Take this, she has your sweater. You might as well give her your ring too". I turned and walked away as fast as I could, tears filling my eyes and my heart breaking. I kept asking myself "Why?" I had no answer to that painful question.

Second period was gym. I walked into the locker room and saw Sally wearing Joe's sweater and something new added. Around her neck was Joe's ring with my tape still on it. He didn't waste any time giving it to her.

"I see you have Joe's ring."
"Yes," she said.
I felt emptiness in the pit of my stomach and the ache in my heart worsened. "He's a great guy."
"Yes, I know," she said.

I changed into my gym suit. I don't know how I made it through the period. I was a mess. I still loved him. What should I do? How could someone I love and trust hurt me? Everything he planned for our future, the promises he made, flooded every thought. I fought back tears during the next period. I knew if I were to get through the day, I had to do something or I'd fall apart. I also knew I had decisions to make. Did I or didn't I want him back in my life? Would he come back? If he did, could I forgive and trust him again? Questions without answers. I knew I had to do something, but what.

I didn't go to the lunchroom that day. I went to our lockers and removed my picture from inside his locker door and everything else that belonged to me and put them in my locker. Then, I took of all his things from my locker and put them into his. I walked across the hall to my tailoring class and went to the back of the empty room. It was too early for class to start, and I wanted to be alone. I sat there for a few minutes when all of a sudden the silence was shattered by the sound of locker doors slamming shut. Startled, I heard my name. Joe stood in the doorway, his hands resting on his hips. I got up from the chair and walked toward him.

"What is that all about?" he asked.

"What?"

"Why have you removed everything of yours from my locker?"

"Why not? We're not going steady anymore. You broke your promise. I didn't. You wasted no time giving Sally your ring. Now, I'm free to do whatever I want, go wherever I want, see whomever I choose and talk to whomever I please without worrying if it will hurt your feelings, anger you or make you jealous."

The bell rang and he didn't have a chance to respond. I asked Mr. Mohr for a pass to go to the office where I called home and asked my mother to pick me up after school. She knew something was wrong when I got in the car. I told her what happened.

"Is there anything I can do?" she asked.

"No, there's nothing anyone can do."

"Loving someone will always have trials, and some of them are painful."

"I was faithful. Why couldn't he be the same?"

"I don't have the answer. When love opens your heart, you become vulnerable to disappointment, rejection, jealousy, anger and unfaithfulness."

"I'm not ready to forgive him for what he did to me."

"Perhaps, but forgiveness and understanding will mend the wound. True love endures all trials. You're young. He may have been your first love, but there's someone else for you in the future."

"I know I'm young, Mom, but I trusted him. I'm not ready to forgive. I need time to get over the ache in my heart."

Neither one of us spoke the rest of the way home. I remembered what Mom said two years earlier about returning his ring if I wanted to go out with someone else. I gave it back to him because he wanted to.

I spent the weekend with girlfriends, and most of the time the conversation was about my breakup with Joe. They wanted to know what happened. I didn't have an answer. How could I? I told them he'd been a little distant, but I thought it was because he had so much on his mind taking the extra courses he needed to get into college in night school. I never thought he would be unfaithful to me. Maybe he preferred blonde, blue-eyed girls to those with red hair and brown eyes.

On Monday morning, I went directly to homeroom. I didn't want to take the chance of seeing Joe at my locker or running into him in the hall. If I saw him, I knew the tears would start and I wouldn't give him the satisfaction of knowing I still cared or the heartbreak I was experiencing.

The annual Sadie Hawkins Day dance was Saturday, and the rules stated girls were supposed to ask the boys for a date. What better way for me to get even than by asking Ken, Joe's best friend, to be my date. That afternoon after lunch, I saw Ken near his classroom talking to Joe. When Joe saw me walking toward them, he thought I wanted to talk to him. I ignored him.

"Hi Ken, do you have a date for Saturday's Sadie Hawkins Day dance?"
"No."
"Will you be my date?"
"Aren't you going with Joe?"
"Didn't Joe tell you? We're not going steady anymore; I broke up with him."
Ken looked surprised, glanced at Joe and said, "Sure, I'll go with you." I touched his arm, said thank you and walked

away. The rest of the day flew by, and after my last class, I saw Ken, his eye swollen, waiting for me at my locker.

"What happened to your eye?"

"After you left, Joe was mad because I said I would go to the dance with you."

"Why was he mad?"

"He didn't say, but I told him if the two of you weren't going steady, I could take you. That's when he punched me."

"I'm sorry, Ken. I was thinking of myself. Let's forget about it."

The next Monday morning Joe was waiting at the school entrance for me to arrive. I walked past him and up the stairway to my locker. He followed me down the hall and stood next to me as I put away my lunch, took out my books and attempted to leave. He blocked my leaving with his arm against his locker. I leaned back against my locker, not looking up.

"I have to talk to you," he said in a soft-spoken voice.

"About what?"

"About us."

"We have nothing to talk about."

"I need to talk to you."

I started walking without answering him.

"Please, Mary Ann, meet me at our place by the gym after lunch," he said when I reached my homeroom.

I wanted to say yes. My heart racing, I looked up at him. and walked into homeroom without giving him an answer. I wasn't sure what I wanted to do. I felt stupid trusting him so completely.

I didn't meet him after lunch; I walked to classes with boys and talked to them free of guilt, stress or concern. I didn't have the pressure of making excuses to Joe, but it was a bittersweet victory. Thoughts of him and Sally remained fresh in my mind.

The following week dragged by. I did homework, helped around the house and sat on the porch glider most of Saturday morning. I sat there nervously curling a strand of my hair around my fingers as I rocked and the glider squeaked. I didn't want to cry, but the vision of Joe kissing and holding Sally, filled my eyes with tears. I continued to twist my hair around my finger in the attempt to forget. Doing so, I recalled the time in third or fourth grade that my mother grabbed my hair during an argument.

After a severe snowstorm, the sides of driveways were piled high with shoveled snow that resembled small mountains. Walking home from school my friends and I climbed up one side and slid down the other in every driveway along the way. I was having so much fun I lost track of time, and it was late when I got home. I knew I was in trouble when I closed the door and saw Mom standing in the kitchen doorway with her hands on her hips. I barely had time to remove my boots and walk up the steps when I felt one of her hands on the seat of my snow-laden leggings and the other grabbing my hair.
"Why are you so late?" she shouted. I wiggled loose and ran up to my bedroom with her in close pursuit. I slid under the bed to avoid her getting hold of my hair again, but she took the dust mop from outside the bedroom door and began to poke under the bed in an attempt to reach me. She tried a few times and then gave up. "Stay in your room until your father comes home."

I took off my leggings and jacket, put them in the bathtub so the melting snow wouldn't drip on the hard wood floor, and laid my gloves on the floor register to dry. My second floor bedroom was the only room with a register in the floor. I liked to feel the warm air when I stood on it on cold fall or winter mornings and I enjoyed the touch of warmed clothes laid on it for a minute or two before dressing.

I looked out the window when I heard Dad's truck in the driveway. A few minutes later, I heard him coming up the steps to my bedroom.

"I'm supposed to spank you for worrying your mother," he said.

"Spank me? Daddy, you've never spanked me," I cried.

"I know, but your mother is angry because you came home late. What happened?"

I explained why.

"This is what we'll do, he said. "When I clap my hands, you say 'Ouch'."

He clapped his hands twice, I said "Ouch," and we went downstairs. I put my leggings and jacket in the hall closet and apologized for being late. Mom said she was sorry she pulled my hair. I promised myself that some day in the future to have it cut short, so she would never again have the advantage of grabbing it so easily.

I stopped rocking the glider.

Joe liked it long, too. What did I want? Did I want it long or short? I got up from the glider and marched into the kitchen.

"Mom, I want to cut my hair!"
"What will your father say if I let you cut it?" she asked.
"It's time I decide how long I want it."
"How short?"
"I'm not sure, maybe to the collar of my dress."

She called her friend Ann Luciano, a hairdresser who lived two doors away, and asked her to cut my hair.

Ann covered me with a cape and spritzed my hair with water. Because my hair was so thick and curly, she thinned and layered it with a razor cut. My red curls, and with them my childhood, fell silently to the floor with each stroke of the razor. When she finished cutting, I looked in the mirror. My hair length was just above the collar on my blouse; it looked softer, framed my face and didn't stick out on the sides or back. I liked the reflection I saw in the mirror. I was not a little girl anymore.

"I hope your father won't be angry I cut your hair." Ann said. "He loved your long hair."

I walked in the kitchen and asked Mom what she thought about the haircut.

"It makes you look older."

I knew she was wondering what Dad was going to say to us when he came home from work. I went out on the porch and sat on the glider to wait for him.

Dad waved to me as he pulled into the driveway. Normally, he went into the house by the side door. This time he came around to the front door.

"What did you do to your hair?" he asked, walking on the porch.

"I had it cut."

"I can see that. It makes you look older. What does your mother think?"

"She and Ann were more concerned about your feelings."

He opened the screen door looked at me again and smiled.

"It will grow back." He went in the house.

Monday morning, I wondered what Joe was going to think. I wasn't sure when he would be at his locker, so I waited by mine until I saw him. I had purposely avoided him until then. I wore my brown fitted skirt and the gold sweater he liked. When he came down the hall, I said, "Hi." He looked first at me, and then at my hair. He tilted his head to one side and smiled. I closed my locker door and started to walk down the hall when I felt the familiar touch of his hand on my shoulder. I looked up at him. He looked in my eyes.

"I want you back," he said. "What do I have to do to get you back?"

I paused a moment before I answered. I looked up at him.

"For starters, a ring and sweater."

"I can't hurt her feelings."

That did it! All the stored up anger and hurt within me surfaced. I pushed his hand off my shoulder.

"You can't hurt HER feelings? What about MY feelings?" I said in a tone of voice that I had never used talking to him.

I didn't want anyone else nearby to hear what I had to say, so I lowered my voice to a whisper, moved closer, looked up and stared in his face.

"I don't care what you do anymore, Joe Marasco. I don't want or need you in my life. You're not the only boy in this world." I left him standing there. This time, there were no tears.

The next morning, he was waiting at my locker with his sweater in one hand and his ring in the other. He handed me his sweater.

"I'm sorry I hurt you. I love you and don't want to lose you." He took my hand. "Will you wear my ring and forgive me for being so stupid?" I wanted him back, and he did have the sweater and the ring.

"Yes," I said. He slipped his ring on my finger and I put on his sweater.

Walking down the hall with his arm on my shoulder, I thought about my mother's words. *Forgiveness, time, and*

understanding will mend the wound. It would take time, but I'd work it out. Ken joined us as we walked to my homeroom.

"You're back together?" he asked.
"Yes," we said
He looked at Joe. "Great, I don't want another punch in the eye."

We met Ken and Dick for lunch on the school lawn. We were busy eating and talking, but Joe kept looking at me.

"Why did you cut your hair?" he asked.
"I thought it was time for a change. I'm not a little girl anymore. I wondered what your reaction would be when you saw it short.
"It makes you look older; my young sweetheart is growing up."
"I like the change in how I look."
"Please don't change too fast, Pumpkin."

I worked through my nagging emotions of broken trust and forgiveness for the next few weeks. Every now and then moments of doubt entered my mind, but I loved him and love won over my uncertainty. I saw Sally after Joe and I made up. She didn't say anything to me, and I said nothing to her. If Joe drove the family car to school, she and Barb did not join us.

One Friday night a few weeks later, we double dated with Ken and Mimi to the amusement park at Sea Breeze. I told my parents where we were going and left. We walked to the bus stop on Portland and Norton and got on the same bus Joe took after school to go home or to work. We went on the roller coaster a few times and rode the merry go round, where Joe stood on the edge of the platform trying to grab the brass ring for a free ride. We played ski ball, shot duck decoys, tossed hoops onto bottles, and ate hot dogs and French fries. After taking the boat ride, I asked the time. It was 11:30. I was past my curfew, and there was no phone available for me to call my parents and tell them I was going to be late. We waited fifteen minutes for the bus. It was the last bus of the day.

Would it be all right if Ken and Mimi took you home?" Joe asked. "It is 12:15 and I have to be home by 12:30."

I hesitated to answer. I knew it was wrong for him not to take me home, but I said, "Yes." Joe got off at his stop. I was worried about what my mother was going to say and didn't talk much the rest of the ride. By the time we got to Portland and Norton and walked to my house, it was after 1:00. No one was on the porch. We walked to the side door. It was locked; I didn't have a key.

I knocked.

Dad opened the door. Before I had a chance to explain what happened, he slapped me on the cheek. *Why in the heck did he do that? Why didn't he give me chance to explain why I was late?* It was the first time in my life he'd raised his hand to me. I said nothing, turned toward Ken and Mimi and saw the blank expressions on their faces. I said good night and went into the house.

"I was worried because you're so late, but what really upsets me is your boyfriend didn't respect you enough to bring you home," Dad said. "You tell Joe I want to talk to him. You're grounded for a month."

Another first; this was the only time he ever punished me. Feeling the sting on my cheek, I climbed the stairs to my bedroom. I was mad at Joe for not bringing me home, and mad at myself for not saying something in my defense. I should have said no when asked if it was okay for Ken and Mimi to take me home. Joe was worried about the consequences he would face if he got home late and didn't think about the trouble I'd be in getting home almost two hours past my curfew.

I called him the next morning.

"My father wants to talk to you about not bringing me home last night."

"Is he angry?"
"Angry enough to slap me when he opened the door."
"I'll be over when I get out of work."

When Joe arrived, we went into the living room and sat on the couch. Waiting, he held my hand. I knew he was nervous. Joe stood up when Dad came into the room. Dad motioned for him to sit down as he sat across from us.

"Joe, if you pick up my daughter, I expect you, not your friends, to bring her home. I know you have a 12:30 curfew, but if you called me when you got home, we wouldn't be having this conversation now. The proper thing would have been to bring her home and call your parents as to why you were late. I would have driven you home.
"I'm sorry. It won't happen again," Joe said.
"Apology accepted, but she's grounded for a month."

This was the first time he imposed punishment. Dad got up to leave; Joe stood up. Dad gave him a half smile and left the room. Joe's expression changed to one of relief.

During the month of my punishment, Joe came over as often as he could. We watched TV or sat on the couch with his head in my lap running my fingers through his hair.

"Would you still love me if I became bald?" he asked."
"Don't be silly. It's not only your hair I care about. I would have your wonderful smile and eyes to look into and your arms to hold me. It won't matter if your hair thins or gets grey. I love all of you, even your body," I whispered in his ear.

Shortly after Mom said she wanted to discuss something with me. The look on her face and the tone of her voice told me it was important. We went out to the porch and sat on the glider. She rested her elbow on the arm of the glider.

"You and Joe have been dating for a long time. You're in love and you want to be with him as much as you can. That's all right, it's normal, but because you're always together, you may want to do more than just hug and kiss each other.

"I know what you're going to tell me. We're not doing anything."

"No, not yet, but there will come a time when Joe will want to do more than just kiss you. If he fondles and caresses you, it can lead to sex. It's your responsibility to say no before it happens."

"Why is it my responsibility to say no?"

"Because you decide where and how he touches you."

"He hasn't tried to do anything!"

"I'm trying to tell you that when you're in love or think you're in love, things happen."

"I don't think I'm in love. I know I love Joe."

"Some boys will go as far as a girl will let them, but when they get married, they want their bride to be a Virgin. They want to be the first and last she will be intimate with."

"I know that. You've preached often enough that making love for the first time should be with my husband."

"You love Joe now, but suppose that changes and you don't get married? If you get pregnant before marriage, it could ruin your reputation and future. Your virginity belongs to you and is proof of your fidelity on your wedding night.

I thought about her words and was troubled. Joe hadn't asked or tried to have sex, but I wondered about the future. Would I heed my mother's advice or would I allow my emotions to rule?

I think God endowed all mothers with a sixth sense. After a movie at the Dixie, Joe parked a couple of blocks from my house. We kissed, embraced and Joe put his hand on my chest. I moved it away. He did it again. I opened the car door and started to walk home. He followed me down the street and asked me to get back in the car. I told him no and continued to walk home. When I reached the house, I saw Dad on the porch.

"Where's Joe? What happened?" he asked as I walked up the steps.

"Ask him," I said, pointing back to Joe, and walked in the house.

Dad came in a few minutes later.

"Your boyfriend wants to apologize to you," he said.

"I don't want to talk to him."

"He wants to apologize."

I went out to the porch and we sat on the glider.

"I'm sorry. It isn't easy being in love with you, wanting to be closer, and having to keep my hands off of you," Joe said.

I knew then our relationship had changed. It was up to me to decide where and how he would touch me. Mom was right again.

Joe left. I went inside and looked at my father. He didn't say anything to me, and I didn't question him about his conversation with Joe. It was between the two of them.

. . . . .

Majorette uniforms, flag corps and cheerleaders' skirts, and graduation gowns in school colors of ivory with red trim were made by the tailoring classes.

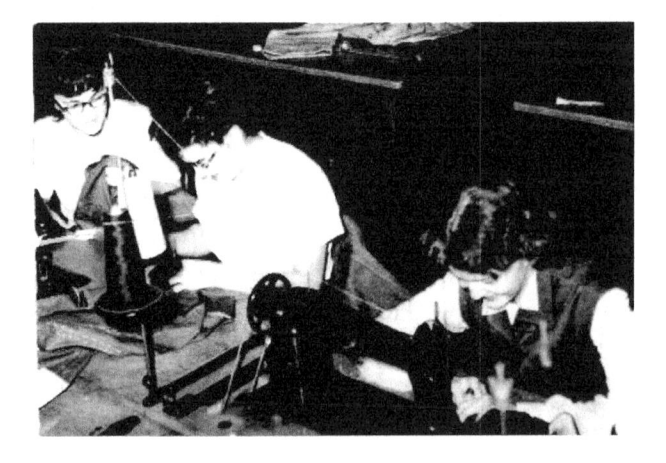

If Joe needed a pair of slacks shortened, I altered them in class. One day, he brought in a pair for me to shorten. Ken came up to me.

"Mary Ann, sew the legs so he can't get into them," he said. I laughed, but I did it anyway. I shortened them and then I hand basted across each leg between the crotch and knee, folded and handed them to Joe after class. The next morning, he was wearing the slacks I had shortened. He wasn't smiling when I got to the locker.

"Why in the heck did you do that? Why did you sew the legs up?" I smiled. "Because Ken asked me to," I said. He had to laugh.

Joe and I spent the rest of the semester meeting at our lockers in the morning before class, eating lunch on the grass or in the cafeteria, going to football games, walking home, and stopping at Ritz's for a coke, burger and fries. On Friday or Saturday night, he'd drive us to the movies in his Dad's Ford pickup truck. Dad drove tractor and trailers and kidded Joe about my being a trucker's daughter, used to being around trucks. His first tractor was either an International or Fruehauf; my name was on the front bumper. When he wasn't working, Dad parked the tractor next-door on the vacant lot, not used as a play area any longer.

Thanksgiving and the Christmas holidays came and went in the usual manner. Before we knew it, the New Year was upon us. In June of 1951, Joe would be graduating and going to college if he wasn't drafted into the Army. Also another year that brought challenges in our relationship and more confrontations with my mother. I was growing up and wanted more freedom to make choices. I wasn't rebellious. I just wanted to be and feel more independent to make decisions on my own without fear or repercussions.

January 1951

Short Lived Independence

The night of Joe's senior banquet, he planned to pick me up after the dinner about 9:30 and take me back to the restaurant to spend the balance of the evening with mutual friends. While I walked out the door, Mom told me to be back by 11:00. I turned around.

"Why so early? Can't it be 12:00 or 12:30?" I asked.
"No, I said 11:00."
"You're not being fair, Mom. The restaurant is on the other side of the city. We'll just get there and have to turn around and come home.
"I said 11:00."

I knew when I got in the car I wasn't going to be home at 11:00. This time I was going to be late on purpose. This was the first time I chose to assert myself and openly disobey her, regardless of the consequences. I knew I'd be grounded, but I didn't care.
Mom greeted us at the door at midnight.

"I told you I wanted her home at 11:00, Joe. Why didn't you do what I asked?"
"It's not his fault," I said. "I made the decision to stay."
"This is my last year to be with friends we both know and I wanted her to be a part of it," Joe said, ignoring my remark.
"She's past her curfew and grounded again."

"Why did you allow her to stay out until 12:30 for my junior prom and change your mind about the banquet?"

"I told her what time I wanted her home."

I interrupted the conversation again.

"It was my decision, not his, to stay beyond 11:00."

"It doesn't matter whose decision it was. You're late and grounded."

Joe tried to reason with her.

"You're not acting fairly. Why is there a difference between my junior prom and the banquet curfew?"

She looked at him.

"I make the rules and she has to follow them."

Nothing we said would change her mind. He kissed me good night and left. I turned to her.

"I've always done what you asked, and yes, I've broken curfew a few of times since dating Joe. Why is there a double standard in this house?"

"What do you mean?"

"Sonny would come home late and wasn't punished. You and Dad would argue and ask where he was, but when you heard his car in the driveway, you said nothing to him except, 'Why are you late, or where have you been?' I never heard you say to him, 'You're grounded for a month'. If Jimmy came home late, he was never punished. Why was it okay for them but not me to break the rules? Why are my rules harsher?"

"They are boys."

I stomped my foot.

"It's not fair just because they're boys!"

"It may not be fair as far as you're concerned, but that is the rule in this house, one you have to follow."

I went to bed wondering, if there would ever be a time I'd make my own decisions. Following the rules at home choked the fun and freedom out of doing something I wanted to do. I was fearful of the consequences if I didn't follow them.

Maybe someday.

We continued to go the movies on Friday night or the weekend if Joe didn't have to work. If there were a scheduled football game, we'd attend it with Ken and his date and go to Ritz's after for something to eat. Most of the time we would stay at home and watch TV with my family.

Joe had his senior picture taken and shortly after completed the night school courses he needed to get into college.

His senior prom was May 26. Mom took me to Friedman's, a formal dress shop. I tried on a few gowns, but none of them had the sophisticated look I wanted. They were too frilly with bows, ruffles, or the wrong color.

"Would you be interest interested in a strapless gown?" the salesperson asked. Strapless? I looked at Mom, pleading with my eyes for her to say it would be all right.

"Yes, you can try one on." The gown was pale aqua chiffon and taffeta with a matching stole. When I modeled it for my mother, she smiled at me. "You're not my little girl anymore," she said.

It was too long, but I could shorten it. We purchased the gown and shopped for shoes to match. The gold evening bag I carried for Joe's junior prom would be perfect with this gown also.

I showed the gown to Dad.

"Strapless?" he said.

His "little girl" was not little anymore either. His glance toward my mother said it all. I kissed him. Over the course of the next week, I ordered a red carnation from the florist for Joe's lapel and shortened the gown. We made plans to double date with Ken and my girlfriend Ursula Losardo. The weeks passed quickly and Saturday, May 26, had arrived. I stepped into my gown and tried to zip up the zipper on the side but it wouldn't come up past the waist. I kept pulling, but the seam fabric beneath it caught in the slide, and the more I pulled, the more it jammed. Frustrated, I called for help.

"Mom, will you come up? I need help with the zipper on my gown."
"What's the matter with it?" she asked when she came into the room.
"It's stuck. I can only get it up half way."
"Hold the gown at the top so the zipper is straight."

She closed it with one upward stroke and handed me the shoes from the box. I put my lipstick and handkerchief in the evening bag, picked up my gloves, and took a last look in the mirror and went downstairs.

I took the carnation out of the refrigerator and set it on the hall table so I wouldn't forget to pin it on Joe. He arrived about 5:45. When I opened the door, my heart skipped a beat. His tuxedo, a white double-breasted jacket with black pants, looked tailor made. The shoulders, sleeves, and pants length were a perfect fit. Joe smiled, kissed me on the cheek and said, "You look beautiful." I told him how handsome he looked, and he put his arm around me. "We make a perfect couple," he said, squeezing me. He slipped the corsage of pink sweetheart roses on my wrist; I pinned the carnation on his lapel.

"Be careful, and drive safely," Mom and Dad said as we left. For dinner, Joe had made reservations at Rupert Gray's restaurant in Pittsford. Following the waiter to our table, I noticed everyone glancing our way and smiling. I felt like Rita Hayworth in *Gilda,* a movie where everyone wore formal clothes to dinner.

The first thing we did after arriving at the prom was to have our picture taken. While we danced, Joe talked about it being his last year in high school and his plans for college.

"I don't like the idea of you being alone in school for the next two years without me."
"Why?"
"I don't want to lose you to some other guy."
"You won't. We will be writing to each other and you will be home for the holidays. You're not that far away. Maybe you can come home for the weekend."
"I promise I'll write to you at least twice a week."
"So will I."

We danced or sat on the bleachers and talked with friends. The Korean War was always a topic of conversation.
Joe mentioned the possibility of being drafted while in college. Ken spoke up quickly.

"I'm joining the Coast Guard or Navy," he said. "I want no part of the Army."
"You, not the government, will make the decision about which branch of the service you will be assigned to if you're drafted," Joe said. "It's your choice."

Mr. Mohr taught tailoring, but he was also a senior class advisor and a chaperone at the dance. Joe stood up as he walked toward us.

"Still going steady?" he asked with a smile.
"Yes," Joe answered.

We left our friends to dance when the band played "Tenderly."
"Do you remember the first time we danced to this?" he asked.
"It was last year at your junior prom when you asked me to go steady."

Once more, he held me tighter. We left the prom around 11:00 p.m. and drove to Durand Eastman Park overlooking Lake Ontario, Rochester's version of Blueberry Hill. Between kisses, we talked about the prom, graduation, college, and his plans for our future.

Joe glanced at the clock on the dashboard.

"Honey, you have to be home by 12:00. We better leave now."
He drove Ken and Ursula home, and he pulled into my driveway a few minutes after midnight.
"Did you have a nice time?" Mom asked when we walked in the house.
"Yes, we did. We're going on the porch for a little bit."
"Take a sweater with you. It's cool outside."

I grabbed a sweater from the closet. Joe put it on my shoulders and we sat on the glider. The air was brisk and the cloudless sky sparkled with diamond bright stars. The houses across the street and the one next door were dark. We sat in the glow of the corner streetlight and watched the moths and gnats perform their crazy dance around the light bulb.

Joe put his arm around me. Stretching his legs set the glider in motion. During the day, traffic muffled the sound of its squeaking rails, but in the still of the night, they sounded like shrieking cats with their tails being stepped on. He stopped the glider in fear of waking up the entire neighborhood. We kissed and embraced. I rested my head on his shoulder.

"I'm really concerned about going away to college and leaving you home alone."

"Will you please stop worrying about me?"

"It's not you I'm worried about. I know you love me; I'm worried some wise guy will think you're available and make a pass at you."

"I can take care of myself," I said.

Mom came to the door. "Mary Ann it's late. It's time to come in."

Final exams and Joe's graduation were just a few weeks away. We tried to spend as much time as we could together because Joe was planning a trip to California after graduation, and he'd be away for a month. I knew I'd be lonely, but I didn't want him to know how I felt, so we talked about his trip with an upbeat attitude.

Joe's graduation ceremony held in the school auditorium allowed only four tickets per graduate. The ticket that I thought would be mine I believe was given to his sister's girlfriend or his cousin. I was disappointed that they had taken precedence over me.

Joe picked me up after the ceremony. The proper time that Joe had referred to on the day of my bicycle ride to his house finally arrived. Joseph Senior was reserved, and his sister Marigrace, cordial. I said hello a second time to his mother and then I was introduced to his cousins from Italy — Ralph and Adeline and their daughter Mary, John and Maria Antonia, her mother Mary, Uncle Fred, Joe Senior's brother, his wife Lisa, and their son Armando. They were warm, friendly and gracious to me. Joe's cousin Lee and her husband Paul Anspach were an interesting couple. They both had worked for the Federal Government. When Paul retired from the Cavalry, he became an investigator for the Alcohol, Tax and Tobacco division. His stories about being shot at while destroying stills during Prohibition were fascinating.

For the past year, Joe had saved silver dollars toward the trip to California in a glass block bank made by his father. He accumulated $150.00 (minimum wage was seventy-five cents an hour in those days), enough to pay for the train fare and spending money. He planned to leave July 10 for Sherman Oaks and stay with his aunt, uncle and cousins.

The week prior to leaving, he went with his family on a vacation to Wasaga Beach in Ontario, Canada. Unfortunately, the day before they left, he contracted a serious case of poison oak. He called me the day before he was leaving for California and asked me to go to the train station with him and his parents. His face was all broken out with a pimply rash in various stages of healing. Calamine lotion covered the blemishes, and he wore his aviator sunglasses.

He was upset and self-conscious. "No one will want to sit next to me the way I look," he said. Nothing I said would cheer him up. While boarding, he told me the trip to Los Angeles would take three days, and he would write as soon as he arrived. His first letter arrived almost two weeks later.

July 16, 1951

Hi Beautiful,
Well I guess you know by now what happened to me. We left Chicago on schedule but never arrived in LA on time. We were marooned by a flood outside of Newton, Kansas for about three days. Boy was it lousy. The first day wasn't so bad but the second day we ran out of water. Some farmer flew in some food (Spam and canned milk). We couldn't wash or go to

the bathroom because of no water. Finally, a farmer brought some well water, about 50 gal. That didn't last long among 342 passengers. It was only used for drinking but still it went fast. One night I was so hot and thirsty I went up to the dining car and asked the porter for a glass of water. He said there wasn't any, I tossed him a half dollar on the counter and he gave me two glasses of iced cold water, boy was that good.

Friday morning about 7:30, the National Guard came and took us out by Army trucks. Was that ever rugged, but I didn't care it was the first time I moved in three days. They brought us to a town called Newton, Kansas. There they had a train waiting for us and gave us breakfast. From the time we were marooned to the time we arrived in LA, the meals were free. They were good too. On the new train, they stuck us anywhere there was room. I was stuck with two old women. I couldn't sleep there because it didn't look right. So two sailors and I grabbed pillows and went into the men's washroom. We arrived in LA about 10:30 p.m. Saturday night. I met everyone at the station, and went home where I slept on a bed. The first time in about 5 days, boy did that feel good.

Well that's all for now, write soon.

I wrote him I was thankful he was all right and he would have quite a story to tell someday about being stranded in a flood on a train in Kansas.

My birthday was approaching, and I was waiting for a card or letter from him. I was disappointed that the letter I received from him the day before on July 23 didn't mention it at all. Thinking he didn't remember, I was hurt. When I answered his letter, I started by writing *Dear Joe* instead of *Hi honey* and signed it *Love always* instead of *All my love always*. It was short. I wrote in part, *if you are so busy having fun that you can't remember my birthday, you can stay there as long as you want.*

I knew it was sarcastic, but I wanted him to know how I felt. A few days later, a special delivery letter arrived.

July 31, 1951

Dear Darling Mary Ann,

What a terrible surprise I got when I opened your letter. I never expected you to act that way. Boy, you sure can change from night to day. Maybe there's no use explaining because you've already made up your mind, but there is more to the story than you think.

First, there are 10 kids running around this house ranging from 1-10 and I usually am with them in the daytime, and it's quite a job for me. The wedding plans have everyone running around like chickens with their heads cut off. Then my cousin works in the daytime and the only time we can go out is at night and by the time they finish feeding 30 people it's about 9:00. Now if you think I've forgotten about your birthday you're crazy and don't take that seriously about being crazy. I never forgot about it. I changed my intentions from good to what I thought better but by then it was too late.

I was going to send a card, and then I was going to call you until I learned the cost of a person-to-person call from California and I said for that amount of money I could buy you a beautiful gift you would appreciate more.

I thought I was doing something good, but I guess I wasn't. No matter what you think I could never forget about you. After receiving that letter, I can't understand what has gotten into you. That letter wasn't at all like you starting out, "Dear Joe," and signing it "Love always." I thought we always signed it "All my love always." Did you do it purposely? Don't forget we've been going steady a long time and you've only hurt me once before like this. Do you have some other reason? Is there something I know nothing about? I know it's difficult loving me 3000 miles away, but I thought we made promises to one another.

The other day before your letter arrived, I was sitting alone and my mind started to wander. I suppose I was feeling kind of lonesome, but just then, I realized how much I loved you and how much I missed you being so far away. Maybe it sounds silly but you know I don't usually talk like this unless I really mean it. So please darling, forgive me, but I had good intentions, and if this doesn't explain it, I don't know what to do. Say hello to everyone and please write soon and tell me things that I like to hear from you. So long, and I am sorry.

His rationalization that *I had hurt him once before* confused me. If he was talking about my breaking up with him because of Sally, there was no comparison. I wasn't unfaithful; he was. To compare forgetting my birthday to being unfaithful was out in left field as far as I was concerned.

Shortly after, I received a package. His gift was a pearl necklace.

"Do you know pearls represent tears?" my mother asked when I showed it to her.
"I didn't expect a gift. All I wanted was a card or mention of my birthday in his letter."
"Perhaps you should apologize."
"Why?"
"Because you jumped to conclusions."

I wrote and apologized. There were only a couple of weeks before he came home and I would tell him in person.

As the time drew closer for him to come home, he wrote that his sister had joined him and he was going to extend his stay until the end of August. I was disappointed. The summer would be over, and I'd be returning to school the week after his return. I wondered how he could afford to stay the extra month and why all of a sudden had his sister decided to join him.

August 20, 1951
Hi Beautiful,
Well here I am in the same place, anxious to get home. Boy do I miss everyone, especially you. I was wondering when

you were going to answer my letter and yesterday it came, what a relief. Yesterday I called the Santa Fe Station to see about reservations on the El Capitan. Well they didn't have any for the 28th. She said it wouldn't be until the 3rd of Sept. Well I can't wait that long so I am going to take the Grand Canyon instead. No seats reserved so I will go down to the station early and hope to get a seat. I am going to get there early enough so that I'll be sure. So don't worry. I will be home next week. The Grand Canyon takes 10 hours longer but after what I went through on the E-Cap it will probably be better on the Grand Canyon.

I'll bet you are all excited about school. It's going to seem funny me not going too, but don't worry I'll be there enough. I haven't received any news from Wanakena. Oh well, maybe I'll just go to work with my dad. My sister got her license I hear. I pity our car. Well sweetheart this is all for now, keep writing and stay in my dreams like you have been.

Joe arrived home the week before Labor Day. We missed spending the entire summer together.

After I had returned to school, he received notification of his acceptance to the New York State College of Forestry in Wanakena, a program of Syracuse University. The semester didn't begin until January of 1952, so he worked full time as a clerk in Greenberg's Pharmacy.

School wasn't the same without him. I missed his arm on my shoulder, meeting him for lunch, and walking to class or home. I felt lonely when I walked past our spot near the gym remembering the day he gave me the ring he'd hammered for me in metal shop and his talks and plans for our future. However, I enjoyed the new freedom of walking and talking with male classmates without having to look over my shoulder to see if Joe was watching me.

Majorette practice and marching at football and basketball games filled most of my time after school. I joined the bowling team, Craft Guild and was a member of the Junior and Executive Councils. I had three study halls every week and changed them for three classes in tailoring. I had plans to apply to Trapagen School of Dress Design in New York after graduation and thought knowledge of tailoring would be an asset if accepted.

Joe picked me up from school on the afternoons he wasn't working or we spent the weekend together as often as his work schedule allowed. If I marched at football games, he attended them with me.

Later on in the semester, he often called to break a date with excuses about a change in his work schedule or use of the family car. Maybe I shouldn't have been so naive. Maybe I should have been concerned with what Joe was doing. I had a gut feeling something was going on, but I couldn't put my finger on it. He was always attentive when we were together, but I couldn't get rid of that nagging familiar little voice inside feeding my suspicions.

Thanksgiving came and went, and it was December. Joe picked me up after school one afternoon and we stopped in Ritz's. I sipped my coke and I looked at him.

"Is there something you want to tell me?" I asked.

"What do you mean?"

"I'm not sure what it is, Joe. I just feel something's wrong."

"Nothing is wrong."

"Lately, I have the impression that there is something bothering you."

"Honey, I love you. Nothing is going on."

"I hope not."

Joe came over late Christmas Eve for the midnight buffet, and I didn't see him again until the middle of the following week. He told me he had to work extra hours because of the holidays. We made plans to spend New Year's at home.

We were sitting on the couch when he handed me a special delivery letter he'd received two days earlier.

"I think you should read this," he said.

December 29, 1951

Dear Joe,
    Well, it is now past 10:30 pm. I have waited all day for the phone to ring and to hear your voice again. I guess I knew all along that you wouldn't call, but like the fool I am I kept my hopes up. If you're certain about everything-your feelings towards myself and Mary Ann and as of now, they still remain in her defense, I think I'll call everything, absolutely everything quits. I had hoped that there may have still been an ember burning in you, but I guess I was wrong. I am sorry that I have made such a fool of myself Joe and I promise that you will never hear from me again.
    My feelings remain as I told them to you last night, but I suppose that means nothing.
    This whole thing will undoubtedly remain in your mind as something very funny. I hope you get a real good laugh out of it someday-sorry I can't laugh with you.
    You can tell Mary Ann all about this if you already haven't, maybe she too will get a big laugh. I don't care anymore who knows or who laughs even her.
    Please don't ever think that you should have pity on me. I detest pity.
    As you desire it, we will forget about even talking or maybe caressing, there's no sense to it when you have no real desire to.
    I'm sorry if I have bored you,
        Sheila

p. s. *Just like that.*

I didn't laugh when I read it. She still cared for him and it must have hurt her to know that he loved me. ` I added her letter to my other saved mementos. After Joe died, Sheila told me the reason she broke up with Joe was because he lost the school ring she gave him. It was after their breakup he started to see me. I'm not sure of the circumstances surrounding their relationship, how they got in touch with each other, or who contacted whom, but she wanted to renew her association with him. I knew there was something going on; my intuition knew what it was telling me.

January 1952

Wounded a Second Time

In early January, Joe asked me to help him pack for college. I was apprehensive because his parents had taken a trip to South America to see his dad's brother and I would be in the house with him alone. My parents' rule was that Joe and I couldn't be in the house alone when they were out. I agreed to go, but I was uneasy, knowing I shouldn't be there.

The large steamer trunk was in the living room. We packed it with the folded clothes that were on the dining room table, couch and chairs. When the trunk was full, he set the removable tray on the supports and asked me to get his handkerchiefs and socks from the small right hand drawer in his bedroom dresser. He told me the blue room at the top of the stairs was his. When I walked in, I got a warm feeling in my heart, noticing where he slept and how the room was furnished. His bed was on the front wall right between two windows and the dresser was on the left side of the room. To the left side of the dresser was an upholstered chair by the closet door.

I walked to the dresser and opened the drawer. I removed the folded stack of white, neatly ironed handkerchiefs. When I reached in and picked up the folded pairs of socks, I noticed a letter underneath them with the salutation *To my darling* not in my handwriting.

My knees got weak and the fire in my heart turned to ice. I looked past the words to the signature. *Nancy.* Fear, pain, heartbreak and anxieties from the past surged through me. *Not again.* The tightly patched wound in my heart burst open. I was too upset to look at the date or read what it said. Trembling, I sat in the chair and tried to decide what to do next. Should I break up with him again or not say anything? Did he want me to find it? I regained my composure took the letter and went downstairs, without the socks and handkerchiefs.

"Who is Nancy?"

He paled when he saw the letter in my hand.

"Who is Nancy?" I asked again. "How long have you been seeing and writing to her?"

"She lives in Canada and was here last fall visiting her grandmother who lives on Culver Road. We met when I waited on her in the drugstore."

"Was that the only time you saw her?"

"No. She asked me to visit her at her grandmother's house."

"Did you go?"

"A few times until she went back to Toronto and invited me to visit her there."

"Did you?"

"Yes, but I was only there for the day."

"How did you get there?"

"I hitchhiked."

"What! She didn't mean a thing to you, and you hitchhiked to Toronto?"

"She means nothing to me," he said adamantly.

"I don't believe you." I was shouting now. I started to remove his ring from my finger when he grabbed hold of my hand.

"No, I won't let you do this to me again. I love you, I want to marry you, no one else but you. I should have destroyed the letter."

"If she didn't mean anything to you, why did you keep it?"

He yanked the letter from my hand, tore it up and threw it in the trash.

"Take me home! Now," I said.

"No, not until you calm down." He held me in his arms.

"Why would you hurt me again? I asked him when I was finally able to speak. "I've never broken my promise to you since we started going steady. I think I fell in love with you the day you walked on the porch and asked my dad if I could go on a date with you. The love I have in my heart has deepened; you've betrayed it again. Why?"

He said he was sorry, but I'd heard those words before.

"Since we started going steady, have I ever given you a reason to think I've been unfaithful?"

"No, you never have," he said.

"Have you ever thought what could happen if I get lonely, and that loneliness leads me to take an interest in someone else? Think of me in someone else's arms, kissing him and betraying your trust. If you're not sure of your feelings, let's break up. It will hurt, but I'd rather hurt for a little while than wonder if you are seeing other girls behind my back. Maybe we're too young and shouldn't be going steady."

"No, we're not too young; I've loved you for a long time and I'll love you forever," he whispered.

"I love you, too, but you can't keep hurting me this way."

He held my face in his hands and kissed me tenderly. We'd kissed and held each other many times, but this was different. He was leaving and wanted to take our love to the next level.

"I don't want to do this Joe." I said.

He drew away and walked to the door.

"I'll take you home."

Shortly after his parents returned from South America.

Joe loaded his father's pickup truck with the trunk and his luggage and stopped by my house the day before he left to say goodbye.

Once again, torn threads of trust and faithfulness needed mending. Repairing my heart again was going to take time. I wasn't sure how long it would take me to trust him again. I felt jealousy, anger and betrayal. Was he comparing me with others? Were they fulfilling needs I wouldn't or couldn't? This time I struggled accepting his unfaithfulness. I was no longer the naïve little ingénue with her head stuck in the sand or in the clouds. I knew I loved him. I knew I could forgive. What I didn't know was whether or not I was strong enough to forget and more importantly to trust him again.

January 11, 1952

To my darling Mary Ann
I got your letter the other day and was disappointed to find you had not received my letter yet. I guess there must be something wrong with the mail because I only got one letter from you and none from home at all. I hear there is a big storm down around your way, maybe that is why the mail is tied up. No matter what honey, don't ever think I stopped writing to you, you know better than that. I have a regular schedule for writing to you and its set so you will get two letters a week. I won't forget you, don't worry.

Last night I went to the hospital with John to see his mother. When I got back, my roommate told me I had a call from home. I wondered if it was from you or not. If it was from my folks, I know what it's for, to report for my physical. If it were important, they would have called me back.

By the way, have you been behaving yourself? I hope you're not getting into any mischief. I imagine there are a lot of basketball games going on at school. Remember, please don't let me find out any bad things when I get home, because you know I'm going to be away for a long time and plenty of good and bad things can happen. I only hope for the good things so I can make our plans work out soon. Your last letter lacked a little love. Don't forget it's the same me two hundred miles away from you and I love you just as much as always. Every little extra helps to make the day go by faster. Remember when you thought there was something lacking in my letters?

 Be good honey, I love you very much.

 Joe's first letters from college said nothing about Nancy or how I was feeling. It was as though it never happened. Instead, he was concerned about me behaving. That should have been the least of his worries. The double standard at home was now part of my relationship with him. He was a boy and assumed it was acceptable behavior to see other girls even though we were going steady. I, on the other hand, had to remain the chaste, faithful virgin until marriage. I accepted my decision to be so, but I expected him to be faithful, too. His actions spoke louder than his apology and loving words. It was going to take more than a short two weeks to rebuild my trust in him. I knew if I couldn't, I'd never marry him.

January 14, 1952

Hi Honey,
 I better break the news to you in a nice way. Remember what I told you in the letter? Well it came true. I have to report for my physical. So next Wednesday I have to hop on the bus and come home again. I won't mind it too much, because I'll be seeing you. Thursday morning, I have to be at the Draft Board at 7:00am sharp. From there we leave for Buffalo and stay there all day. The nicest part is I won't leave to come back until Sat. That will give me some time to spend with you. I'll make a couple of visits to the recruiting office and see what if any deal they will give me. Don't worry I'm not jumping to any harsh conclusions. I've a couple ideas now that may keep me out for a couple more months anyway. They give you thirty days at least before they call you.

 I found out there is a Colonel in the Army somewhere that needs men who know how to survey. He said he is willing to take guys that have graduated from the Ranger School and put them to work. It's a pretty good deal, about the best for an ordinary guy going into the service. One problem with this deal. You have to enlist and it's not a definite thing. So now, it is a tossup between that and the Navy. The Navy offers you more money and good schooling, but for four years. That's why I have to spend some time inquiring about the whole deal. Let's face it honey it's going to happen no matter what. I'm not promising, but sometime after I am in the service I'll be coming home with a certain something for you. There is no law that says a service man can't be married. Well honey I hope this letter doesn't make you feel too bad. I love you. Be good.

Unfortunately, it didn't work out as Joe had hoped. He came home, went to the draft board, had his physical and went back to school without a deferment. Questions without answers filled the few hours we shared before he had to leave. Our future was uncertain, and we needed to reassure each other we did have a future, regardless of our immediate circumstances. He did make one promise; we were going to be engaged.

There were times he said he was depressed because so much was crammed into an eight-hour day followed by long nights of studying. He called me a few times to discuss his apprehension and concern of making it through the semester. My encouragement and reassurance that he could accomplish his goals helped us to depend on each other, and sharing the burden strengthened our love. I assured him I was still his girl and all was well. He didn't have to worry about our relationship while he was away. His discussing problems with me and resolving them with a positive attitude impressed me.

March 23, 1952

Hi Beautiful,
Well it's Sunday night around 7:30 and just got thru with supper so I thought I would write you and home. Back from the miles of woods and I mean miles we walked. A couple of friends and I went out and set traps for bobcats and the like.

A friend, Johnny got us interested in it. If we do catch anything, we'll make about $25.00 for everyone we catch. That will give us a little more spending money. I've made about six good friends. After supper we do our homework and then get together in one room and talk or play cards. We have a great time at it. We went into town yesterday. That's where I called you from. You sounded surprised when I called. That's the way I wanted it to be. I'm glad you were home or I would have felt down hearted. I didn't give you much of a chance to talk did I, you usually do all the talking. This friend Johnny has a girl in Long Island and he called his girl too. We both felt kind of sad when we got through. I'll call you as much as I can, but last night's call was $2.25, but who cares just as long as I can talk to my "pumpkin." What do you say sweetheart? It's only once every so often. I'll make up with letters in the meantime. Well beautiful, what have you been doing with yourself lately? I'll bet you're having it pretty rough too. You just keep thinking of those songs and before you know it, we'll be back together again. Things are quiet up here so you don't have to worry about me.

Don't forget those pictures you're going to send me. The more I get the better the wall will be decorated with your sweet face. I have to outdo the other guys so I can show them what a great girl I have.

My parents are coming up for Easter weekend. If at all possible, do you think you can come with them? My mother will give you a call when they will pick you up. I hope you can come with them.

Well honey, homework time is coming around so I'll close. Keep those letters coming.

"May the good Lord bless and keep you till we meet again"

I asked my mother if I could go with Joe's parents to Wanakena for Easter weekend. I was surprised when she said I could go. I was also surprised that Joe's parents agreed to my going

Joe's mother called to let me know what time they were picking me up.

I was excited for two reasons. The first was seeing Joe, and the second was the suit I was tailoring in class that I hoped would be finished before Easter. I asked Mr. Mohr if I could work a little faster to complete it for my trip.

"What's left to be done?" he asked.

"Not very much. The jacket needs to be fitted and the shoulder pads put in place."

"I'll do the fitting this period if you're ready."

He asked the class to pay attention to the proper way to fit a tailored jacket. I put on the jacket, buttoned it and Mr. Mohr pinned the shoulder pads in temporarily, so the seams over the bust and at the waist were in line. He smoothed out the shoulders and asked me turn around with my back to the class. He held the center back seam in his hand.

"Pinch the seam between the thumb and forefinger," he said to the class. "Less than an inch can be taken in on one seam; more may have to include darts if the jacket has them. With chalk, mark the area at the tips of your fingers. Do the same along the entire seam."

He asked me to turn and face the class so he could check the fit on the seams over the bust line. It occurred to me if he had to adjust those seams, I would be embarrassed in front of the boys. I stood like a mannequin, turning my blushing face to the side as he looked at the seams on the front of the jacket. I exhaled a sigh of relief when the darts at the side of the bust seams were the only ones that had to be taken in.

"Shouldn't it fit tighter on top?" one of the boys asked.

"What about the waist? Can't it come in more?" said another.

"Every article of clothing needs to have ease for comfort," Mr. Mohr said cracking a smile. There was no problem with the skirt. That was the first and only required fitting. I completed it in time for the trip.

March 31, 1952

Hi Pumpkin,

I am glad I waited to write today because when I went to the mail box I found two letters from my little sweetheart. Those pictures really serve the purpose, but I won't be satisfied until I get a dozen more.

Tomorrow we've a test in Dendrology. I really have to study before I get booted out on my rear. Every day they toss a little more on and we spend Sat. and Sun. making up Survey exercises. Today we took a ten-mile walk (Dendrology class) through the woods trying to identify trees. I could tell a few but I could do better if they were cut and made into furniture. That doesn't come until the next course.

Mr. Dubar (director) took us home from church Sun. He asked us how we like the outside world. What's he trying to be funny? Today he gave us a lecture in class and said, "if we want to get through this course we can't go pounding the pavement on the weekends," meaning keep out of the beer gardens.

How about sending up some cookies sometime. We can't eat between meals, so the cookies will be nice while doing homework. I mean homemade ones of course. OK?
Don't forget I'm waiting for more pictures that you promised.
Well beautiful, test tomorrow so I'd better hit the books. Love you.

Saturday April 12

Joe's parents picked me up early in the morning, and for the entire trip, there was mostly silence. I was glad I brought long my *Seventeen* and *Mademoiselle* magazines to read. We arrived at the college just before lunchtime. Joe said it would be best to register at the Cranberry Lake Inn, have lunch and return to the campus for a tour.

The Oswegatchi River flowed in front of the college. Joe said that in a few weeks they would be taking their canoes on the river to explore different areas of the forest that surround the college. There were scattered patches of snow on the ground, and the buds on the trees would open after a few more days of sunshine.

As we walked through the college building, Joe talked about the subjects taught in each classroom we visited. When we reached his room, I noticed the pictures and poems I'd sent him on the wall. He mentioned there were still some open areas waiting for new ones. We went back to the motel and spent the evening in the lounge talking with his parents. Joe returned to the college and picked us up in the morning to go to church. Joe commented how beautiful I looked in my suit, and couldn't believe that I had made it. He gave us the tour of Star Lake where he and his friends hung out when they had some free time.

We left in the early afternoon. Joe and I didn't have an opportunity to spend any time alone together.

April 16, 1952

Hi Beautiful,

I finally found some time between studying for tests, doing homework and trying to get some sleep, to write to you.

Just in case you didn't realize it, last Sat. night, I really enjoyed being with you. I was so busy talking that I didn't realize how much fun I was missing not being with you. After you're gone then I think of how much fun I could have had and told you how much I love you and miss you. Then again my folks were there, and I couldn't. I am sorry if you didn't have a good time. Had we gone to the movies as I wanted to I could have told you how much I love you and miss you. Oh well, one of these days we'll be back together and then we can make up for lost time. It will sure take plenty of kisses to make up for all the time I've spent up here alone. I suppose someday it will all be worth it, and then we can be together and enjoy our lives. That is the day I'll be looking forward to, and if we keep loving one another maybe our dreams will come true. At night, before I go to sleep I wonder what will happen and how it will all come about. I imagine it will take a lot of hard work, and plenty of hardships, but it will be worth it. What do you think? You don't have to tell me because I know what you will say. You've been with me with every task I've undertaken, and we've come out all right. So we'll just keep plugging along and we'll get there.

Thanks for the books. They helped me a lot. So far my marks have started a slight increase. I hope they keep on rising.

So long for now beautiful, and take good care of yourself because someday I expect you to be my wife.

I took more pictures to send to Joe but didn't get them developed for a while. Grandma, my mother's mother became ill, so my mother decided to move her to our house while she recovered. She slept in my room, and I slept on the couch in the living room. She never learned to speak English, but Mom knew she understood.

I was born in Grandma's house on 76 Woodward Street in Rochester, NY, on July 24, 1935. My brother Michael, (Sonny) was five years older and James, (Jimmy) born two weeks before my second birthday were also born there. We lived in the second floor apartment of the brick two-story house. Grandma lived in the first floor apartment with Mom's sister, Mary and her brothers, Paul and Joseph. Theresa, her married younger sister, lived in Buffalo, NY, and Rose, her older sister who emigrated from Italy to America with Grandma and Grandpa and was married, lived on Hemple Street in the city. Mom, the second oldest, was the only one born in Lyons, NY in 1909. She and Dad were both born the same year.

Our neighborhood was predominately first and second-generation Italian immigrant families. Mount Carmel Catholic church was a five-minute walk from the house. Next door to the church was Falvo's Funeral Home. At the end of the block was North Street where my Dad's family lived. After a visit to their house Dad would take us across the street to Savoia's Italian Pastry Shop for a dish of Spumoni ice cream. Before we left, he would buy a box of assorted butter cookies and a loaf or two of Italian bread to take home.

April 27, 1952

Hi Beautiful,

Just have about 15 minutes to drop you a few lines. I'll write later when I get some time to myself and I'm not so darn tired. All week long, we've been out in acres and acres of land planting little trees. Each man has to plant 400 trees a day for the next week. At night we are so beat we eat supper and go to bed. The last few days it's been so hot I wondered if we were ever going to make it. You have to rip away the bushes, dig a hole and keep on going so that you keep up with the next person. I thought it would be fun, but I found out it is the hardest work I've ever done and that's not all, there's more to come. In between we have to find time to do homework for the next week. The last few days it has been so hot that towards 5:00 I was wondering if I was ever going to make it.

Well I got the bill for room and board for the next 5 weeks so I guess I will be staying for a while. The truck to take us is ready to go. I'll write Sat.

The day of my junior prom was rapidly approaching. I wasn't sure if Joe would be able to take me. When I mentioned my concern to my Dad, he offered to take him back to school if he was able to come home. I wrote and asked Joe about the prom and the offer to be taken back. I waited anxiously for his reply.

April 28, 1952

I love you very much darling; I wish I were home with my honey.

Hi Beautiful,

Every day I realize how much I love you and miss you. I can't wait until I get back with you. It's nice to know that a guy like me can have such a great time with his "honey". We did have wonderful times; what do you say beautiful? Oh well it won't be long before I am back with you again. I can't wait. I guess I'll have to though.

Now that I am finished with planting, I can get back on schedule writing you letters. Don't worry pumpkin you'll get your letters. Don't forget I said I'll always love you and even though I may miss a letter it doesn't mean that I've forgotten you because I can never forget my little honey. I love you too much.

Sat. night we came up the river and stayed at John Merchants cabin. You remember the one who is a friend of the Latimer family. It's a nice log cabin about a mile up the river. We've been doing some fishing and I caught a few trout. We cooked them for breakfast and they were good, especially that we caught them

Yes, honey, I'll take you to your prom. Would it be ok if your dad took two friends, John Merchant and Dick Rollins back with us? It would sure be appreciated. Let me know.

Hey how about some cookies? I could use some even if it's only a few. Well time to hit the books, so lover just keep writing and waiting until I am back with you.

I decided to make my gown for the junior prom. It would cost less, and I could make it in the fabric and color of my choice. I sketched the design, and Mom took me to Brodsky's Fabric Store. I looked in pattern books and found one I could alter to look like my design. It was strapless; the circular cut skirt had no gathered fullness at the waist. All the fullness was at the hemline. The fabric I chose was ice blue organza over taffeta. The fabric, pattern and findings for the gown were less than half the cost of purchasing one. Mom was very happy with my savings. I had three weeks to cut and sew to be ready for the prom.

I took the pattern and fabric to school and asked Mr. Mohr if he would help me alter the pattern and cut it out in class. He said he would. I sewed it at home and my aunt helped with the fittings. There was no way I would have Mr. Mohr fit a strapless gown in front of the boys in class. I modeled it for Mom and Dad, and they said I did a beautiful job.

May 16

Ken called me and said he was going to pick up Joe and his friends at the college. They had classes and couldn't leave until late afternoon.

Around seven thirty, I heard the doorbell ring and went to the door. When I opened it, I saw Joe smiling at me with his arms extended to hug and kiss me.

"Are you hungry?" Mom asked him.

"No, I've eaten already."

"I've made an apple pie if you would like some," Mom continued.

"What time do you want to leave Sunday?" Dad asked.

"Around 7:00 am, if that's okay with you."

I hurried Joe into the kitchen so we could be alone for a little while. I served the pie and between mouthfuls, he kissed me and told me how much he missed me.

"You're growing up," he said.

"You, too."

"I know. My chest is filling out and I have more strength in my arms. Must be the rugged life at school." He finished his pie and we went out to the porch and sat on the glider. I ran my fingers in his hair, stroked his face, and kissed him. I told him I missed him and hated being away from him. He took my hand and kissed it.

"What time do you want me to pick you up tomorrow night?"

"The prom starts at 7:30. How about 7:00?"

"I hope I can get a tuxedo tomorrow. If I can't, I'll have to wear my suit."

"It doesn't matter."

"Are you being a good girl?"

"If you mean faithful, yes, I have been. Are you being a good boy?"

"There's no time for me to be a bad boy. Classes and studying fill every waking moment."

"What about the weekends?"

"If I have time to relax, I spend it with the guys at school. You don't have to worry honey; all the students are male. What keeps me motivated is the knowledge we are going to get engaged and married some day."

We went inside and joined my parents watching TV in the living room. There were no television sets in the college and I was just as happy to sit on the couch next to him as we did when he was home.

Joe walked in the house the night of the prom looking mature and handsome in his formal black tuxedo. "Pumpkin, you look beautiful. Sweetheart roses for my sweetheart," he said handing me a wrist corsage of yellow roses. I pinned a white carnation to his lapel and extended my hand to him, so he could place the corsage on my wrist.

I was so excited to be with him again and so happy thinking about the prom, I didn't remember to ask about my curfew.

I was on cloud nine when I walked into the prom with my college sweetheart. Our friend saw us, came over to say hello. They questioned Joe about college and the draft. We broke away when the band began to play our song. As I danced with Joe, the joy in my heart grew until I could hardly contain it. I wanted to stay in his embrace, feel the softness of his touch and hear him whisper in my ear how much he loved and missed me.

"My young sweetheart is growing up quickly," he said softly.

When I looked at him that night, I saw that he was changing, too. Not his smile or his gaze, but his body. He seemed taller, and his arms, when they held me gently but firmly in his embrace, were strong. We were growing up together. He was 19, not the 16-year-old boy who took me on my first date. I was maturing, too. I would be seventeen this July.

We left the prom and drove to the lake to be alone. He turned off the ignition, and moved the seat back. He moved close to me, put his arms around me and kissed me.

"I love you so much, honey. How good it is to feel you next to me. When I read your poems and look at your pictures, I want to reach out, hold you, and love you."

His kisses were tender and filled with passion. Each one lingered a little longer, while his caresses drew me closer. He gently pushed the stole off my shoulder and with his warm mouth kissed my neck, ears and shoulders. Each kiss was an invitation to the forbidden. His hands holding my face, the longing in his eyes before he kissed me and his words of love were gradually toppling barriers I had built up to prevent the inevitable.

He pressed me closer; I felt the beat of his heart against my chest. I had longed for him so much but I was afraid of what was going to happen next. The conflict of submitting or not began within my head and heart.

"Honey, we have to stop," I said, gently pushing away from him.

"Why?"

"You know why. I love you, but I'm not ready to do this. We have to wait. I want you to make love to me, but as your wife, not your girlfriend, in a car. I've dreamed about our wedding night; I won't spoil that dream."

He fixed his gaze on me with affection.

"I know how you feel. I'm trying to be patient and respect your wishes, but it's not easy for me to control how I feel."

"I think about you making love to me, but after we're married, not now."

"It's a good thing I'm away at school and not with you constantly. I don't think I could handle it if I were home with you all the time."

He moved across the seat and leaned back against the door. I was too young, afraid, and not ready to make a decision that could affect my future or his. I changed the mood by telling him what I wanted to do after graduation.

"I've decided I want to go to Trapagen School of Dress Design in New York City after graduation."

"I don't like the idea of you going to New York alone."

"Why, what's wrong with going there?"

"It's not the place for an innocent girl like you. Where would you live? Is there a campus? Would you have to rent an apartment?"

"I don't have all the information yet, but as soon as I have it, I'll let you know."

"I don't like your being alone there." I sensed his opposition.

"What about you and the draft?" I asked, changing the subject.

"If my number comes up, I won't have any choice but to enlist in the Marines, Navy or Air Force. I hope I can finish college before I'm called. Whatever happens, honey, we're getting engaged and married."

It was past midnight and Joe said he had to get up early the next morning. He took me home and said hello to my parents, who were waiting for us to get home. Dad said he'd see him in the morning. I kissed him good night and went to thinking of all we discussed; ignoring his reaction and comments to my decision about New York.

Joe and his friends arrived at our house the following morning at 6;30. Mom offered them breakfast, they said they'd eaten but would have a cup of coffee. They put their luggage in the car, and when they finished drinking their coffee, Dad said it was time to leave. While I waited for him to come home, I did my homework and added the program and corsage from the prom into the box of mementos in the closet.

When Dad came home, I thanked him for the favor.

"I enjoyed listening to the stories the boys told me," he said. "It's really God's country up there. It was so quiet I felt like I was in church."

"I know what you're talking about. Joe says when he walks between stands of tall pines; it reminds him of walking down the aisle in a cathedral, and the stillness almost reverent, broken only by the chirping of birds."

Dad agreed with his description.

May 21, 1952

Hi Beautiful, (pumpkin),

How's my little doll today? Fine I hope. I am still trying to snap out of it from last Sat. Boy! What a time we had. I am glad I could come home. The prom was nothing extra special; it was being with you that made my dreams come true. Right now, I am looking forward to the Memorial Day long weekend seeing you again.

Last Saturday made me think a lot about how wrongly I treated you. Darling if I have ever done anything to hurt you I am sorry from the bottom of my heart. I say that because I realize what a wonderful girl you are and I will never make things wrong for you again.

Ken is going to pick me up and we'll probably be home in the afternoon, so if you have to march in the parade I suppose it will be all right if my honey is counting on it. But you better be there when I get home or I'll really be nervous. Just in case I didn't express myself, tell your folk thanks a lot, because they not only did me a favor but also did one for the guys.

Your Dad was ribbing us all the way about "God's Country" up here. I take it he doesn't care for it. I don't blame him, but by right, it isn't supposed to be fun up here. It's best it isn't because it keeps us away from temptations. Tomorrow is a Holy day so a bunch of us are going to the 7:00 mass. It will mean getting up at 6:00 and missing breakfast but it will be worth it

So be good until I see you because I love you very much and trust you with all my heart.

The next school function I looked forward to was Junior Day, the day dedicated to eleventh grade students. Girls wore their men's white dress shirts with rolled up sleeves over straight leg, loose-fitting dungarees with four or five inch cuffs on the bottom. The boys also wore dungarees and a white shirt or short sleeve "T" shirt. The lunchroom was almost empty because everyone, including juniors, ate their lunch, took pictures and signed yearbooks on the lawn or at Eddie's hangout; similar to Ritz's, located across the street from the school. A place I visited only once.

One day in eighth grade, my girlfriends and I decided to go there to see what it was like. My brother Sonny, a senior, ate his lunch there often. I no sooner walked in when I felt a heavy hand on my shoulder. I spun around.

"You don't belong here. Go back to the cafeteria in school," my brother, ordered.

"Why?"

"Just go back to the school cafeteria," he said leading me to the door.

Embarrassed, I left, but my girlfriends didn't. When they met me after lunch on the way to class, they asked what happened

"My brother said I didn't belong there," was the only explanation I had to give them.

After school I told my mother what happened. When Sonny came home, she questioned him.

"Mom, most of the guys there are seniors," he said. "I didn't want them getting any ideas about my kid sister. She didn't belong there."

That ended the conversation. I never went back.

We enjoyed wearing pants and a shirt for even one day. Girls couldn't wear slacks or shorts during regular school sessions. We wore blouses or sweaters with straight skirts, full skirts with crinolines, jumpers, or dresses, all with hemlines below mid-calf. Socks were worn with saddle shoes, sneakers or loafers, and stockings and garter belts with our ballerina flats or Mary Jane's. Panty hose didn't exist. Because straight skirts hugged our bodies, they featured pleats or slits in the back or side seams to allow for walking. Wide elastic belts cinched our waists to accentuate our waistlines. It didn't matter if they were a wee bit snug.

Our "cross your heart" Maidenform bras "lifted and separated' what little or what bounty nature had endowed us with in that department. We were conscious of our femininity and attraction but didn't flaunt it. We used it to our advantage to pique the curiosity of members of the opposite sex.

I don't remember a dress code per se, but I do know parents were concerned about the modesty of their daughters and protecting it from any abuse.

Most of the boys wore slacks, shirts and sweaters. Some wore dungarees, but they were in the minority.

During gym classes, we noticed boys looking down into the gym from the second floor open corridor balcony. If they tarried too long, the teacher motioned them to move on. The gym suits provided by the school were hardly worthy to show off your legs. They were sleeveless, medium green cotton with a wrap top and short elasticized bloomer bottoms. Tolerable, but not very convenient when nature called and the entire suit had to be removed.

I tried to keep an optimistic attitude about the future, but there were moments of melancholy, sadness and longing. I had more than enough activities to keep me occupied, but the constant undercurrent of concern for our future diminished the short-lived moments of happiness.

The Korean War was always in the news. One of Joe's friends from school was killed, and Mary Navarra, my girlfriend across the street, lost her brother Vincent. My brother Sonny took his physical, but was rejected because of his rheumatic heart. I kept praying that the war would end before Joe had to serve.

The school year book I ordered had arrived. I reserved a page in it for Joe. Either I could send it to him or he could sign it when he came home for Memorial Day. It fell on Friday this year, which meant that Joe would be home for the weekend. Traditionally, we had a family cookout at Webster Park with aunts, uncles and cousins after the parade. Ken was going to pick up Joe at school and we would have the weekend together. I had to march in the parade, so I couldn't go with Ken.

Dad took me downtown where I was to join the band and other majorettes waiting to enter the parade at a given time. For previous parades, Joe had dropped me off at my designated spot and then driven to the street where the parade ended, parked the car, and walked back to where I was. He walked with the parade to the end to take me home and attend our family picnic. Dad took Joe's place, but he waited for me at the end of the parade

Joe and Ken arrived about 2:00, ready to eat and relax. They decided to go the Genesee Gun Club the following morning for target practice, and when they got back in the afternoon, the three of us would go to Niagara Falls. I was worried about the trip. I wasn't sure I'd be given permission, so I didn't say anything. I told my mother we'd be back later and left

We decided to stay and see the Falls lit up at night with colored lights. It was 1:00 am when I got home. Ken waited for Joe in the car. When I opened the front door, I knew what was coming by the familiar look on my mother's face.

"You did it again. You can forget about taking the ride back to college with Joe in the morning."

Joe tried to explain, but to no avail. He tried to convince her that nothing had happened and apologized for getting me home late.

"She's going to be seventeen in a few weeks. She's not fourteen. When will you allow her to make some of her own decisions?"

His voice was firm and controlled as he tried to make her understand I was growing up and capable of making decisions on my own. She wouldn't listen to him, and I could see his patience turn to frustration. I took his arm, led him to the door and said goodnight. He stopped by the next morning to see if Mom had changed her mind, but the answer was still no. Her control was almost spiteful. Once again, she took away my joy of being with Joe.

June 2, 1952

Hi Beautiful,

Got your letter today, boy was that fast. I didn't expect one until tomorrow. I am glad anyway, because I am lonesome for you.

If there was ever a time I didn't want to leave you, it was Sat. night, especially under those conditions. I don't know what happened, something just came over me and I couldn't help it. Probably it was based on many things. The thought of leaving you, the idea of you not being able to come back with me-being deprived of something I had counted on so much, and you getting balled out three times in a row. They all added up to that stinkin, stupid climax, where I lost my head and said things to your mother I shouldn't have. Your mother will never feel the same toward me again, that I know, but I couldn't see you get all the blame for something that was brewing inside of her. I suppose I'll never know the reason why she picked on you so much. I could see getting home late but the rest I'll never see. You know how strict my mother is; well she made a few alterations so that things would turn out alright for us over the weekend. By right my mother appreciates my company, and she would have liked for me to have been home longer, but never even said a word. Even my father was nice to get along with. As the guys say up here, "that's the way the ball bounces", and there's nothing you or I could have done to change matters. All I can say is I'll regret the day I talked back to your mother, and for your sake I am sorry from the bottom of my heart darling. Sometimes I wish I was never born, and sometimes I wish I was old enough to get married and settle down. Just you and I a million miles away from in- laws. That's the truth. Maybe now you'll understand my theory. Little things like that start arguments and lead to miss understandings. There are probably a million things I could make right but still have no sense or meaning to them. Why is it when you are so far away and not able to be near the one you love you love one another so much more? When I come home, I love you ten times more each time I see you. Like last Thurs. night when I called you and you were just three miles away, it seemed like I was up at school, and there was a big curtain if front of us. Sat. morning when I went to the gun club I couldn't wait to get back to see you. When I did get back you were just like an angel sitting in the garden, never dreaming what was going to happen that night. Then Sun. night I went to bed with the idea that the next day I would wake up and I would be able to go over and see you again, but all my dreams were lost when I woke up and found I was two hundred miles away.

Hey pumpkin, in case you've forgotten it is going on four years we've been going together so let's keep it that way forever. Some day both our dreams will come true, and we can make our plans together.

Well before I run out of words to put in your yearbook, I'd better call it quits. Don't forget I'm calling you Fri. night so be ready. Just in case it makes any difference, I am sorry if any body's feelings were hurt, but so were mine.

Don't ever leave me Pumpkin. Stay as wonderful as you are. Be good until I see you again.

Final exams were the following week. I was passing every subject, except American history. Mr. Clark was a nice teacher, but I just didn't like history. Perhaps if I'd made the same effort in history as I did in English and my other classes, I wouldn't have to spend July and August in summer school.

June 13, 1952

Hi Beautiful,

Day after day I think of that long awaited day in the future when just you and I take off on our own in the direction of California. I don't know it, seems that you and I and California all seem to fit perfectly together. There's something waiting for you and me out there, what it is I don't know, but remember and keep waiting and thinking about it because someday you and I will find it together. Sitting up here makes me think about many things, and that is one of them. It just seems to stick with me. I was talking to Dick Rollins and I told him I was going to California. He said that was a good idea. I said I'm not going alone. I'm going with someone and that someone is you, my wife. Then as fate would have it I had a dream about us; something that we've always longed for, and that was getting married. It seemed so perfect, just you and I together, just as though it was meant to be. I don't think anything will stop us. So beautiful, don't make plans because plans can always be changed by some act of God, but you just keep counting on it and I guarantee that it will happen, so help me! See you soon, and stay as beautiful as you are. Write soon.

Summer school started. For the next two months, I'd be spending the mornings in class. I was glad I had the morning session. Going in the afternoon would have cut the day short.

The walk to school and home was quiet and lonely. When I passed Ritz's I'd think of Joe and the fun we used to have going there after school. I missed listening to him talking about his plans for our future.

June 21, 1952

Hi Beautiful,
Well in about one more week, I'll be back with you again. If everything goes right, I'll be able to enjoy two weeks being home with you.
We are having our final exams starting next Thursday. The survey exam is eight hours long. The others are about 2-4 hours long. So, if I start studying tonight, maybe I'll be able to get everything done. You're lucky your exams are over with; too bad about American History but if you make it up in summer school you'll be able to get back on the ball again. I just hope I pass everything so that I can stay

As for your bathing suit, I imagine your choice will be better. So put all your thoughts together and buy something different. This year for sure we'll go swimming. Maybe sometime we can go at night, just you and I alone. Sounds like fun, what do you say? Right now, I'm sitting here looking at your picture with plenty of thought going through my mind, but I'm not able to put them down on paper!

So beautiful when I come home, you and I are going to have another swell time, but I won't have a good time unless I study so I can pass everything. Be good and I love you very much.

Joe worked with his dad the two weeks he was home while I was in summer school. His dad was a Carpenter Contractor and was building a home on a vacant lot on the same street they lived on. He came over as often as he could after supper. If Ken joined us, we'd go bowling or play miniature golf. Most of the time we stayed at home. We were content to be together sitting on the glider on the porch talking about our future. Joe had definite plans for it. He wanted to get engaged and married. So did I, but I still wanted to go to NY.

The day arrived for him to return to his classes. I had three more weeks of summer school and a history exam to pass.

July 18, 1952

Hi Beautiful,

How's my darling? Boy do I ever miss you. I felt kind of lousy leaving you Sunday; it seemed like a long time before I'd see you again. It was tough trying to get back into the swing again. We've a few new courses, and they're rougher than the other ones. Already we have hour tests coming up and I have to start learning all over again. It's really rough some times when I get in this darn mood. I wonder if it is all worth it. It doesn't seem possible I will ever make it. Right now, I am in such a dam mood that I'd be willing to call it quits. I suppose it's just something inside saying I should keep on going. Maybe after a few more days or another week I'll get back in the mood. Those two weeks' home were great but it sure as hell got me out of the idea of getting back and hitting the books. Some day the day will come when I can settle down and be able to enjoy myself, as I've always dreamed and wanted.

I'm sorry about the goodbye last Sunday, but when you are leaving someone you love as much as I love you; it's difficult to be in a good mood and say goodbye. Its times like that I want to hold you close and say that your mine and always will be. Then I have to come back here and let something like this keep me from my life's desire. I love you. Be good.

I knew how he felt. It seemed to me that our entire time dating was filled with saying good-bye. I hated it and wanted to be with him. Being in love and with him was all that mattered. I, too, couldn't wait until the day we were old enough to get married, to share all the promises we had made. Our young love had many obstacles to overcome. We had to be patient and wait for the future to catch up with our hopes and dreams.

. . .

The curriculum at Wanakena was a two year concentrated study crammed into one. Classes began in January and ended February of the following year. The only breaks were two weeks in the summer and two weeks at Christmas. Discipline was strictly enforced. At that time, it was an all-male student body. Today, the New York State College of Forestry and Environmental Science at Wanakena has expanded and become a two-year co-educational college.

I think I would have had some concern if the college had been co-educational when Joe was there.

July 21, 1952

To my darling,
Hi lover,
Happy Birthday! and the best of everything to my sweetheart. How's if feel to be 17 years old? My goodness

you're getting to be a big girl. If you don't watch out it will be time for you to get married. I hope you can come up this weekend. We've got our canoes out and I'll take you for a ride in mine. Take your bathing suit along and maybe you and I could go swimming in the place I call ours. I am sure no one will be there so you and I can be alone for a few hours. If you want, we can celebrate your birthday and you and I can just let the day go by.

I'm not sure, but maybe for Labor Day weekend I'll be able to come home, but don't count on it because it is only a rumor. If I do, I'll get your gift then. There are no shops here to get my honey something special. It's kind of rough not being in a city where they sell the special thing for someone special. Let's keep our dreams high and don't let anything ever change them. I love you so! I hope you can make it this weekend so we can make some of our dreams come true. Just you and I alone forever. Until then darling, be good and stay as beautiful as you are.

I wrote you a letter last Friday but left it at the cabin. If Mrs. Merchant mailed it on Sunday on her way home, you'll get it. If not my intentions were good.

Happy birthday sweetheart, and be good, because I love you very much. See you soon. I hope.
X... A great big birthday kiss. Good night sweetheart.

Another dream of Joe's for us unfulfilled. I didn't go there for the weekend. I had no way of getting there, and even if I found a way, I knew my parents would say no. It was not the proper thing to do as far as they were concerned, a rule I would have to live with.

My birthday came and went, celebrated without Joe. We continued to write and his letters reflected he'd gotten back into the "swing of things." I did write and ask why he hadn't written as often as he usually did for the last couple of weeks. Summer school was going well; it filled the mornings, leaving me little time to be lonely. Weekends were the most difficult.

Mom took me to Brodsky's Fabric Store to shop for fabric for skirts, jumpers and blouses I'd make for the fall semester.

My desire to sew began when I was about seven years old. I'd cut pieces from outgrown or worn out clothes in Mom's rag bag and draped, pinned, or tied them on my baby and Shirley Temple dolls. Making a pincushion in fifth grade Home Economics class taught me basic hand sewing stitches. I made most of my clothes all through high school. Mom bragged about the money she was saving and took me often to shop for fabric.

Grandma, Mom's mother, gave me her Singer treadle sewing machine when I was twelve or thirteen years old. My first project using it was making a dress, an original design without a pattern from two yards of 36-inch-wide white and yellow checked cotton cinched at the waist with a four-inch yellow patent leather belt. I don't have the dress, but I have a picture of me wearing it taken on our porch steps with my friends. Babe Sortino is to my right, Mary Zangari, my cousin is on my left and Lillian Di Bernardi behind Mary and Margaret Putz behind me.

Sewing took my mind off missing Joe. I looked forward to an occasional phone call from him. When I heard his voice telling me he missed me and loved me, I was content, secure in my love for him. I sent him the package he asked for filled with cookies, candy and Spanish peanuts, his favorite.

One Sunday afternoon we were invited to the Crudeles' house for dinner. Friends of my parents, they lived on a farm in Sodus, NY. Their son John was nineteen. Dad took his 8 mm movie camera and filmed us standing around, smiling, and trying to look casual. After dinner, John asked me to take a walk. We walked down the dirt road to the deck by the pond. Leaning against the wood rail, I was surprised to hear the unmistakable sound of frogs. The sun was starting to set.

John bent down and gave me a quick kiss on the lips.

"What a time to be serenaded by croaking frogs," he said, joking.
"John, I'm going steady with someone."
"I didn't know."
"We've been going steady for a long time."
"No chance for me?"
"No, I'm sorry."
We walked back to the house.

The days were getting shorter. It was still summer, but the nights had cooled down. I wrote to Joe and asked him if he was as lonely as I was. We'd been going steady for almost four years, but the majority of that time we were always saying goodbye. I wondered what it would be like to ignore the clock ticking away our precious minutes together.

I looked into the co-op program of working part time and going to school part time available for junior and senior students. I wrote and told Joe I was considering it. Or, I could take extra tailoring classes that I really enjoyed. After I researched the program, I decided it was better to stay in school. It was to my advantage to take the extra classes in tailoring that would be an asset if I went to New York after graduation.

August 19, 1952

Hi Beautiful,

The nights are really cold up here and when we get up in the morning, it's like stepping on a block of ice. Not like home having a rug to stand on when you get out of bed.

The lake is all misty and cold in the morning when the sun starts to rise. I get up, wash and dress and usually go outside, and look at the sunrise on the lake. All alone and still, without a person around it's a perfect time to think about all the swell times I have spent with you. At night, I sit and look at your picture, thanking the Lord I have you. That picture did something to me. It made me feel you were right here looking at me.

Soon summer school will be over, and you'll be headed back to school as a senior. Just think my honey being a senior. I hope you will be good and not pay attention to any of the big time senior guys. I'm glad you're not taking co-op because it will be better for you to stay in school and not be subject for some of those shrewd operators that are looking for beautiful girls like you. This way I'll have a chance to be back home to take care of my prized possession that I love so much.

I finally got those pictures I took back in March at John's parent's cabin. We look like a bunch of bums but that is the way we enjoy ourselves on weekends. It feels good to stay there, get up and make breakfast. No one around to bother us. I suppose it's just a preview running thru my mind about when we get married; perhaps we can get a cabin in the woods, come up here, and spend a few weeks. "No friends or relations" to bother us, just you and I alone spending our second, third etc. honeymoon together. Sounds like fun but we still have to keep waiting and before we know it we'll be married and enjoying one another's love. "Beloved be faithful and I'll be worthy of you." I mean it hon. I'll see you soon.

Joe and his friend John Merchant (his parents owned the Cranberry Lake Inn where we stayed Easter weekend.) came home together for the Labor Day weekend. John had a girlfriend he wanted to be with and of course, Joe wanted to see me

Before he left, we went out for dinner to celebrate my birthday. Reaching into his pocket, he took out a small box and opened it. It was a ring with my birthstone, a ruby in a gold setting with two tiny diamonds on either side. He took my left hand, removed his school ring and slipped the new one onto my finger.

"The next ring I put on your hand will be your engagement ring," he said.

September 2, 1952

Hi Beautiful,

Well here I am back at school again and what a time I had getting here. All night we traveled and had no sleep at all. The train was two hours late out of Utica and we didn't get into Tupper Lake until 8:00. We took a cab from there to Wanakena

We were in great shape for class the next morning. We started our Timber cruise and on the way back we were caught in the rain. John and I were in the canoes way down the lake when the storm broke. Boy what a place to be when a big one hits. We had to stop once and get on land because it was blowing so hard. By the time we got back to the school it was 6:15, but they still had supper waiting for us.

Thanks hon for being so wonderful over the weekend. It's great to have someone love you so much. It wouldn't be possible unless the feelings were mutual. I can swear they are. Maybe it's all for the best things

don't work our as quickly as one would want them to. I think if each of us continues loving one another there is not a darn thing to worry about. School has probably started by the time you get this letter, and there will be a perfect place to test yourself again. There's no sense in telling you to be good, because I know my darling is just perfect, and nothing will change her in my eyes. This is your last year hon, and it's up to you to make the best of it. I'm glad you didn't cry Monday night because it made me feel better about leaving.

I started this letter last night and tried to finish it this morning. I love you so much. Be good. I miss you.

I hadn't received a letter from Joe in a week, so I wrote and asked him what happened. I included a poem I'd written or him.

Alone Again

Now that you're gone, I'm lonely, lonely as I can be.
Those moments we spent together were wonderful.
Don't you agree?
I feel your hands upon my face, your body close to mine,
Your lips upon my eager mouth, in your embrace entwined.
The longing to be near you, my heart waiting to hear,
"Darling, I love you," whispered softly in my ear.
Your smiles you give me lovingly, the tenderness of your touch,
My sweetheart and my love, I miss you so much.
My love is growing deeper, stronger with each minute,
The day goes by so slowly without you being in it.
The joy within my heart, knowing I'm your one and only,
Shields me from despair, long nights of being lonely.
I'll wait for you my darling until the day when we are one,
Hearts forever joined separations over and done.

September 6, 1952

Hi Beautiful,

So, you thought I didn't write last week. Well in case you don't know, I wrote two letters early so that they would get to you before the week was up. Also, I got one from you last week, but one came today. I don't know what happened. Maybe it was the mailman. Just so long as the letters keep coming I'll know it's alright, so don't let them stop.

Soon we will hop on a bus to West Point. We're going to stay with the cadets, and eat with them. Boy some of their strict rules better not be tried on us or someone will blow their top. You don't have to worry about us going out at night. A lot of the Cadets have tried and not many made it without permission. So, I don't think we will be going very far.

I guess I'll see you definitely for the week of the 27th, but I don't think we're going to have a full week. It is not definite yet. It won't take me long to make up for lost time with you. I would like to spend a full week with you, let alone the rest of my life. Don't forget I'll be coming to school with you and the days I don't I'll be there to pick you up. I have to spend all the time I can with my darling. After that, it will be about two months before I see you again. Two months isn't really too long, but long enough to be away from someone you love. After that, it will be less than two months before I will be home for good. That will be the time we buckle down to business and start thinking about our future. No matter how short it may be from now to February, it's still too long for me.

"Now that you're gone I'm lonely, lonely as I can be, those few moments we spent together were wonderful. Don't you agree"? Remember that quotation? You wrote that, and in my heart I feel the same way, only I can't express it the same way. I do mean it though darling it is lonely. Soon we'll be together again.

Walking into homeroom on the first day as a senior felt wonderful. My classmates laughed and remarked how happy they were to be in their final year. I still had the locker Joe and I shared. His picture on the inside of the door said I love you every morning and goodbye when I went home. It made me feel he was right there beside me. I missed meeting him for lunch and listening to the plans he was making for the day we would be married.

Ken joined the Coast Guard and wrote to me asking why Joe hadn't written to him. I answered saying I would ask why in my next letter

September 20, 1952

Dearest Mary Ann
To my darling, Hi Beautiful,
How is my sweetheart today? Thanks again for the poem. I think you have the ability to be a writer.
Well how does it feel to be back in school again? Don't forget it's your last year.
I nearly froze to death last night. I needed someone like you to keep me warm. I should say I need you to keep me warm like you mentioned in your last letter. I guess the guys would be jealous. Someday I'll take you up on it so watch out.
Don't worry hon, I've got a lot of faith in you and I'm positive I can trust you. But I don't want to take anything for granted. So be a good girl. Every day that goes by I want to be with you more and more. You don't know how much I think about getting married, especially these last few weeks. Maybe I don't show it but I sure do feel it in plenty of ways. It's tough to be away from someone you love. Not many guys are in the same boat that I'm in up here and they don't understand, so it all stays inside of me.
Today during our break, I did a foolish thing. Merchant and I were wrestling and I had my Parker pencil in my pocket Well, John rolled over me and the darn point went into me. It

hurt like the dickens, so I put some stuff on it. This afternoon it started to bother me, so Mr. Dubar sent me to the Doctor. He cleaned it out and gave me a penicillin shot. He said I'd be fine. It's still kind of sore, but I guess I'll live. The dam thing went in pretty far according to the Doc. That goes to show you what a little pencil can do. Trouble is, it got me in the darnest place You figure it out-it was in my pocket. Pretty close but not quite!

It's definite we are leaving for West Point for logging the week of October 13th. Don't worry baby, I'll write from anywhere no matter where I'll be or how far away. That's for sure.

Well doll, here we are at the end of the letter again. So be good, now especially. I love you.

Joe's next few letters were filled with frustrations about his classes. He explained in detail his class in surveying the boundaries of a timber cruise and the eight hours allotted to plot them on a map of the traverse. He had problems completing the map and worked on it until 3:00 am in the morning to have it ready to hand in. I had no idea what he was talking about, but I did know he was upset. Timber cruising, he described as "the process of plotting all trees blown down on a plotted line." He said by the time they'd walked a mile and a half from the starting point, they'd documented more than a hundred trees that had blown down in the last few years, and every tree had to be plotted on the line on the map. I was working hard and studying too. I may not have felt the same degree of frustration, but I needed the tenderness of his letters to help me through the long days. Lately, all of his letters were about his classes and nothing about us. I vacillated whether I should tell him how I felt or keep my feelings to myself. I decided he should know, so I wrote and told him.

September 24, 1952

Hi Beautiful,

Me again, I got your letter today and even though I wrote you last night, I'll write again tonight. The reason is you had me worried. I couldn't realize what I had done. Then it came to me. You don't especially care to listen to me go rambling on about the difficulties I'm having. Instead, you would rather hear me tell you loving things. My conscience said I'd better write to you. After all, I don't want to hurt my honey in any way.

Erase all those sad thoughts and fill them with better things. Perhaps I can help. As for you worrying about me, I suppose it's only natural. If you only knew how much I worry about you. You have to face almost anything when you are in love. Though it may be rough remember darling, we have one another and to tell the truth I like it, in fact I love it. So please beautiful, don't say things in your letter to get me wondering. You know what can happen if one little bad thought creeps into your mind. Another thing, when you keep saying if I don't write you would never answer; Honey, you must be kidding. I hope so anyway, because when two people are in love they don't stop writing because the other missed up on a week. Also, what makes you think I would ever stop writing to you? Maybe it's better for me to get a letter like that. It knocked some sense into me. It also showed me that love is a delicate thing and should be handled that way. So please, forgive me for the things I said. Remember honey, be good. If anything should ever happen that I lose you I don't know what I would do. You know how you feel about me, well beautiful maybe I don't show it or say it but I love you, honest. Thanks for knocking some sense into me, I deserved it.

I'll be home the week of the 25th. I couldn't be home for your birthday but I'll be home for Halloween. I miss you so much now it isn't funny. Only you could ever understand how much I've missed you especially these last few weeks. You know that new song "You Belong to Me". Well it fits us perfectly. Remember honey, no matter where you are or I may *be you belong to me. I'll always love you honey, come hell or high water, so please be good darling. Write soon.*

Part of the curriculum at Wanakena was maintaining phone lines and the thinning and trimming of branches and limbs in stands of trees in areas around the college. Supported by a leather strap attached at his waist and around the trunk of the tree or telephone pole, and his leg braces with metal points on the bottom to jam into the trunk, he climbed, cut, and thinned the trees or repaired phone lines. He boasted that the workout increased the size of his chest and arm muscles.

Most of the last days of September were sunny and moderately warm, a few had temperatures above normal, but the evenings were beginning to cool down. Winter was on its way. It was almost flannel pajama time again. Mom stored summer clothes in the attic, and winter coats hung on the clothesline to remove the smell of mothballs put in pockets to prevent moth damage through the summer months.

Autumn was always a favorite season of mine. The leaves changing color, Mom's apple pies in the oven and the crisp mornings when the rising sun created sparkling shimmering dew in the grass.

September 29, 1952

Hi Beautiful,

How is my lover today? Glad to hear you're not mad at me anymore, but I knew my honey couldn't mean all she said and after all, we do love one another.

I surprised you with all the letters coming so fast. Didn't I? You deserved it, and I think it was worth it. I never expected you to answer so fast.

So, it's getting pretty cold at night back home too, well it looks like you and I have to get together and, get something straight between us. I am ready anytime you are. Maybe the two of us together can keep one another warm. I don't know though, it takes a lot of heat, but I think you have it. The trouble is how long would the heat last? I don't think it would take much effort on my part to keep the "fire" going all night. Sounds good? I know what you will say. But a guy can dream can't he?

Boy yesterday was one day when I practically thought about you every second. It just seemed like I wanted to go home so bad. All our experiences kept running thru my mind. I guess it was because John and I were thinking about the fun we had when we were home with our girlfriends. It wouldn't have taken two minutes for us to take off and head for home. If it wasn't for so much work, we probably would have headed for home and paradise. I use that word paradise with all the meaning from my heart. Only you could understand how much I've missed you. Especially these last few weeks. It seems like it's all burning inside getting ready to explode.

The other night it was cold and the moon was out. It reminded me when we used to go to football games. My darling everything is entering my mind making me more lonesome and wanting to be home with you. So keep your chin up kid and it won't be long.

I read between the lines of this letter. Joe was thinking of our relationship in a more intimate way. It was the second time he wrote even jokingly about having sex. I wasn't ready to commit until we were married. I made a promise to wait until my wedding night; a promise that I intended to keep. My concern was that Joe would understand as he did the night of my junior prom, and not push me to be intimate before we were married.

October 1, 1952

Hi Beautiful,

I sure miss you. Every day the hours pass and here I am waiting and waiting for the time to come when I can get back with you again. I was just thinking about the trip up to Canada with your brother and his wife. You know we should do it more often. I liked it a lot. We seemed like newlyweds traveling around with another couple. It was fun wasn't it doll? Experiences like that don't just happen they have to be planned. I would like to plan a few more weekends like that again.

I don't have to tell you how nice it is up here with the leaves turning. I'd love it if it were at all possible for you to come up. No one ever comes up anymore. We never did get a chance to go for our canoe ride or swimming. There are places where you can just sit, dream, and not a soul to bother you. I know because for the last few weeks when we've been out in the woods all day and sit down for lunch in some deserted spot, well that's the time when all my memories get a chance to get straightened around. That's when I remember that I have someone at home who loves me that I can't wait to get home to see. Now maybe you'll understand why I don't show them to anyone, but inside they are there and at certain moments I have the chance to talk about them. Places like that bring out all the dreams stored up inside me, and when they do start to come out it's pretty hard to hold them back, let alone the emotions that go with them. But all those beautiful emotions have to be locked up until I can get home to you.

Be good, I love you very much.

Joe was right about the weekend trip to Toronto with Sonny and Angie. We had a wonderful time shopping, eating and sightseeing. We decided to stay overnight to see the Falls lit up from the Canadian side. Sonny found a hotel within walking distance and booked two rooms, one for Angie and me and another for him and Joe. He called Mom to let her know our plans. We didn't have pajamas, tooth brushes and toothpaste, so we stopped at a drugstore to buy brushes and paste. Sleeping in our underwear for one night didn't bother us.

The following morning, we had breakfast and headed for home.

Mom raised the roof with Sonny for his decision to stay overnight.

"It's not right for your sister to be away alone overnight with Joe.

"Mom, for heaven's sake, she wasn't alone. We had two rooms at the hotel. She and Angie stayed in one and Joe and I in the other. She was OK. What better chaperones could she have had than her brother and his wife?"

"It's still wrong. What will the neighbors think?"

"The only way the neighbors will know is if you tell them."

He walked out the door. It would seep Mom was more concerned what the nosey neighbors thought about her daughter's flawless reputation.

October 8, 1952

Hi Beautiful,

Another two days have gone by. Another two days less that I have to wait to get home. I got your letter today and it looks like I'd better hurry. According to the letter it seems like my honey really misses me, well I am glad to hear it because I miss you too very much.

Monday we leave for West Point, and about the mail, you had better send it up here. There's really no way for me to receive it while I am down there. I'll write from there but I'll have to wait until I get back to read your letters. Don't think you don't have to write, because I'll be expecting just as many, if not more.   How have the nights been down there?   Pretty cold, I imagine, because it goes down to about 22 degrees up here. Right now I was sitting here daydreaming. I was trying to visualize what it would be like to be home with you. It seems like ages since I've held you in my arms.

Honey, no matter how hard anyone tried; they could never take you away from me. I am so much in love with you they couldn't bribe me with any sort of fortune. I still wouldn't take it, if it meant giving you up. So beautiful, no matter how hard you try, you could never get rid of me because I love you too much.

After school I walked home beneath the canopy of elm trees ablaze with yellow, red and orange leaves that lined our street. The sun filtered through them and cast a soft golden hue on the street. Gentle breezes scattered ankle-deep piles of fallen leaves on lawns, sidewalks and the curbs.

I remembered the autumn days when Joe and I walked home from school together and his conversations about our future. I missed his arm on my shoulder and watching him smile when we laughed together. The walk home seemed longer without him.

Tall matured Elm trees lined our street until late 1949. It was the last year we enjoyed their beauty. Dutch elm disease infested all of the trees. In an attempt to control the infestation trucks often sprayed then with an insecticide. It failed, and all of the trees had to be cut down. Our neighborhood never looked the same.

October 12, 1952

Hi Beautiful,

Here we are at West Point. We arrived here about 4:30 pm yesterday and rode around for about an hour trying to find the place. We all sleep in one big room just like the Army. Last night after chapel, the Cadets marched back to their rooms singing their football songs. It sounded nice when their voices echoed as they walked between the buildings.

This morning we were up at 5:30 and went to breakfast. At 5:45, the bugler started to blow and the band started to play which meant the cadets had to rise and shine. Right now, it's 7:00am and we're supposed to take off at 7:30, so I'll have to hurry or be late. I'll write you again tonight, so don't think I've forgotten you. I'll be home Saturday some time. I am sorry I have to quit, but orders are orders. I can't wait until next weekend. I love you.

Our church held teen dances every Friday night in the recreation hall, and my friends from the neighborhood went to them. My brother Jim was a great dancer and I thought it would be OK if I went and danced with him. When I told Mom I was going, she asked Jim to keep an eye on me. Great. First, my older brother Sonny watched me as a child, and now I had to contend with the younger one doing the same. I danced with him and some of the boys I went to grammar school with. Most of the time I sat with my friends talking and remembering the things we did growing up before going to high school.

We reminisced about riding our bikes to Irondequoit Bay, the long walks to the Dixie Theater on Saturday or Sunday afternoons and meeting at the United Dairy for a soda or sundae. One of them remembered the after school swim program at the Natatorium where Nancy Azzanno and I almost drowned when we jumped into the deep end of the pool thinking it was the shallow and had to be pulled out by the lifeguard. I didn't want to go back in the pool but the lifeguard insisted, and waited until I did. She told me if I didn't, I would always be afraid of the water and not learn how to swim. We joked about the crushes we had on each other in sixth and seventh grade, sitting on my porch playing board and card games and just hanging out.

They asked how Joe was and I told them he was fine and that we were still going steady. I'm not sure which one wanted to know if Joe would be upset about my attending the dances. I said I never went alone, only with my brother and that I would tell Joe about it in my next letter.

October 15, 1952

Hi Beautiful,

It's me again. Right now, it is 8:00pm on a Tuesday night. After supper tonight, we watched the Cadets line up for inspection. What a routine it is. The lower classmen really have it tough. We saw one getting chewed out because he was limping when he was walking. The upperclassman gave him some line about being a disgrace to the outfit and the poor guy just stood there saying "yes sir" and "no sir". The "plebes" can't even talk to one another, and when they eat, they have to eat according to a certain number of counts the Officer in charge is counting off. It's really a life I wouldn't ever enjoy.

I'm wondering about those dances you've gone to. What's happened to my girl that I have so much faith in? I hope I don't get any disappointments when I get home. It seems almost impossible for you to go to a dance even with your brother, and not dance with some other guy. So please beautiful, I know I've been away for such a long time but you have to have faith and wait. It may be hard to pass up temptations but you have to.

If you think I'm talking wrong about what I've just written well that's the time that some changes may be coming over you. I never expected this to happen, so please don't let it be changed. You know beautiful I am in love with you and have all the confidence in the world. I may be too sure of myself but after all honey, I've got to be. If I didn't, where would I be? I just have the feeling that something is wrong. I don't know, maybe you noticed it when I called, but it's just there. I won't be satisfied until I get home. I don't know how I'll find out the answer, but something will happen to prove to me that our love is just as strong as before. So please lover I ask you from the bottom of my heart, please, please be faithful because I love you too much lose you. Until then honey when I see you again.

I couldn't understand why Joe had thoughts about my being faithful to him. I loved him. The boys I talked with knew of my commitment to him and were just friends. His concerns were unfounded. I told Joe he didn't have to worry about me going to the dances at church. I didn't go every Friday night. I explained to him that the *guys*, some of whom he knew, were friends from grammar school. I assured him I was faithful and he should trust me not to do anything to spoil what we had together.

. . .

I was a member of the committee planning the Fall Frolic, the first dance of the season at school. I told Mom I would be late getting home on Friday because I was staying at school to decorate the gym for the following night's dance.

Jim Archer and I went outside on the lawn with another couple to gather leaves to scatter in front of the corn stalks we'd placed near the doors and bleachers.

I was holding a bag of leaves when Jim kissed me. I looked at him.

"Jim, I'm going steady with Joe."

"I know Joe. He lives in my neighborhood; I wanted to kiss you anyway."

I started to walk back to the gym when he took the bag of leaves from my arms and apologized.

We finished decorating about 5:30.

"I'll walk you home," Jim said. "It's late; I don't want you walking home alone."

I introduced Jim to Mom and told her he was a friend of Joe's.

"Thank you for walking Mary Ann home, Jim Would you like a ride home?" Mom asked.

"No, thank you. I can take the bus."

After Jim left, Mom said he was a considerate young man.

October 23, 1952

Hi Beautiful,

I am writing this letter in the morning so I can only write until the bell rings. I want to get it out with today's mail so it can be there Sat. Today's Thursday and it's only a couple of days before I see you again. It makes me think of what happens when the week vacation is up and I probably won't see you until l Christmas. This time it will be worst of all.

If we miss the football game, I'll take you to next week's game. If we go to that one, it'll be almost time to say good-bye again. Let's make the best of this week so we will both have dreams to keep us company after I've left. Just being with you will be enough to satisfy it. Maybe one day when you have off from school we can go to Niagara Falls. Just the two of us going to a place where young couples spend their honeymoon. We'd better watch out or they may mistake us for newly-weds.

Soon it will be Indian summer here and it really is nice. Maybe you could talk your brother into coming up to see the beautiful Adirondacks and I could see you again after I get back. I won't be home for Thanksgiving.

Remember honey, you promised to write me another poem. I was looking at the ones on the wall and it reminded me of the one you were going to send me. I hope you haven't forgotten about it. I think I've also got a picture of you coming too haven't I?

Well, we'll have to save the dreams for later, right now it's time for me to go to class. Until I see you next week darling, be good. I love you.

When Joe came home, Mom told him about Jim walking me home. Why did she tell him? She knew the position I would be in having to explain. Joe questioned me, and I told him we decorated the gym and yes, Jim walked me home. I didn't tell him Jim kissed me. It meant nothing, so why upset him. Imagine my surprise on Monday morning when I saw Joe coming down the hall towards my locker.

"Hi honey, do you know where Jim's locker is?"

"Across the hall. Why do you want to know?"

"I just want to talk to him." He went to Jim's locker.

"Thanks for walking Mary Ann home," I heard him say, "but she's my girl, and I would appreciate your keeping your distance from her."

He walked me to my homeroom and said he would pick me up after school. When I saw Jim, I apologized and said I didn't know Joe was coming to school. "If you were my girl, I would have done the same thing," he said.

Joe picked me up after school every day. We'd stop at Ritz's for a while and then went home. He stayed for supper a couple of times. He did the homework he brought from school during the day. The week flew by, and it was difficult saying goodbye on Sunday knowing we wouldn't see each other until Christmas.

Nov. 3, 1952

Hi Beautiful,

Back at school with dreams about the wonderful week I had with you.

Honey I hated to leave you. You just keep as wonderful as you are and I will keep on loving you. I can't find any faults so I have no reason to ever stop loving you. It's going to be a rough time staying up here until I get home again. I don't ever want to have to leave you again, but I know that the darn service will turn up and spoil our plans for a while. When it is all over and finished we will settle down and get married. We have made it for four years and I am sure we can make it when we get married. Don't worry honey nothing will stop us, we're made for each other and it's going to stay that way. Come hell or high water we are getting married. I'm saving for your ring and I want you to be proud when you wear it. After all you are a beautiful girl and you deserve it. I'm going to make sure when we are married that you get the best of everything. I'm going to spoil you honey because I get a kick giving you nice things as you get when you receive them. Maybe at first it will be difficult but when I get settled down to a good job and good pay you can bet your boots I'm going to take good care of you. We're going to have the nicest home you've ever seen. With your talents and mine, we'll build our dream home together.

Did you ever try putting your first name next to my last name? Mary Ann Marasco, it sounds different but when it's legal, it will fit perfectly. I know you are the one for me; I can give you a long list why, starting many years ago when you were just a small girl, in grade school.

Well beautiful, that's all for now, don't ever forget me, and please write soon.

I wondered what Joe meant when he wrote, "Nothing will stop us. Come hell or high water, we are getting married." That was the second time he'd written that. Who or what circumstances would prevent it? Were his parents still telling him he had to wait or wasn't old enough to make such a decision?

The next time he came home, I was going to ask him how old his parents were when they married. I knew my parents were married at nineteen. If his parents were older, it may have been the reason behind their negative attitude toward our going together.

His comment about my not having any faults to make him stop loving me annoyed me. His "china doll" had her faults, but I did my best to be what he wanted me to be. One day an imperfection would reveal itself; what would he do when it happened? I wasn't going to remain a young girl forever. Would his love for me change, as I grew older? I believed our love would last a lifetime. I wasn't concerned about the physical changes that would happen as we aged.

November 5, 1952

Hi Beautiful,

Getting ready to go to bed laying here with my P J's on and thinking of you as usual. I got your wonderful letter today and was glad to hear you miss me. Three days have gone by since I saw you and the days are dragging already. I wish it were December so it would be time to come and see you again. This time for two whole weeks. It doesn't seem like very long but two weeks is long enough for us to spend together compared to what we've been having.

When I graduate in February I hope to spend at least a couple or three months together. I am sure of having to go into some kind of service. Right now, I'm not sure what is going to happen. I'm sure of one thing though and that is marrying you. Honey I think about that all the time and I try to visualize what it's going to be like. During the day in class, I sit and daydream about it, and sometimes beautiful dreams come to me. If they would all come true I'd be the happiest guy in the world. The day I marry you will be one of those happy days, and I'm sure you feel the same way. You're going to look beautiful walking down the aisle in your wedding gown, but I have to wait until the day we are married to find out just how beautiful you will look. I have no worries. I can guarantee you will be the most beautiful bride there is. After all, you belong to me, and I think you are beautiful. I'm afraid there are a few other guys who think so also. I don't worry though because after going with you for four years I'm sure of your being faithful. I really haven't much to complain about because you haven't gone out with anyone else. Honey I am proud and appreciate what I have and when that lucky day arrives we will both belong to one another.

Right now, I wish I had all of you back in my *arms. Well honey, keep writing and don't ever pause from now until December, because I may start to worry. I love you honey, and no one better change that for us. Good night darling and please be good.*

Joe's concern about "other guys" was unfounded. Who was he talking about? I hadn't thought about anyone else since I started to go steady with him. It was inevitable for me to meet and talk to boys. I didn't lead a cloistered life, but there was no one for him to be concerned about. I loved him and honored my commitment to be faithful to him. Perhaps he thought about the times he was unfaithful and wondered if it would ever happen to me. Whatever it was, he always made a point of telling me to be faithful. Was it guilt?

November 9, 1952

Hi Beautiful,

I got your letter yesterday and was a little worried to find you hadn't gotten mine, but then I read on and found you did get it. I wrote Monday night and it didn't get mailed until Tuesday and it takes a few days to get to you. I can't make them come any faster. This one I'm writing Sunday night and I'll be a hundred kisses you won't get it until Wednesday. Yesterday we had to go to school until 5:00 because of the extra time we had off. It beat the heck out of the weekend. This morning we got up at 5:30 and went deer hunting. We walked for miles and didn't see any deer.

Well honey a week has gone by that draws me closer to you. I wish the time would fly to draw you permanently closer to me. That's the one day I can't wait to see when we will be together again. The night I graduate at Syracuse will be a happy day for both you and me. I always enjoy being with you and that's one thing I'll never get sick of.

We're going to make a success of our marriage that's for sure. Honey, you were made for me and there is no getting out of it. I saw you first and no other guy is going to claim you, not if I can help it. The way things look now, it will take a big fight for me to claim defeat, so honey keep your chin up and keep fighting until I can legally claim you as my own.

As for Christmas vacation, I think I'll be able to work things out to make everything go alright. I also know that we will be able to make something else work out in regard to spending evenings together.

Well beautiful it's time to say goodnight and remember darling no matter what may happen or how you may think, I'll always love you. Good Night.

I knew what he meant about "working things out" while he was home. We never talked about his parents' feelings about our going together. We didn't have to. Respecting their wishes, Joe couldn't be with me as often as he wanted. The holidays were the hardest for him because they expected him to be home with them, not with a girlfriend. They felt we were too young and wanted to keep our time together at a minimum. Our letter writing was the one thing that they had no control over. I sent him another poem.

Thinking of You

I miss you so, my darling, the warmth of your embrace,
The smiles you give me lovingly when you gently kiss my face.
The talks we have together; our future you have planned
Within the perfect framework of His divine hand.

I'm longing for the day when we shall say "I do."
That will be the day, my love; I'll truly belong to you.
No longer will the clock steal minutes from our joy
Without the least regard for the love of a girl and boy.

Hello, good-bye, I'll miss you, no longer will we say.
Time stands still for us alone; we'll keep the world at bay.
Some may say that we're too young to really be in love.
What do they know of destiny? Our love is from above.

God looked into our hearts, and made the fateful choice
For us to meet and fall in love; we listened to His voice.
He chose us for each other and knew we were a pair,
Our hearts combined as one, our love forever shared.

The time has come, my love, for me to say goodnight.
I'll dream sweet dreams of you until the morning light.
Remember I love you, each night for you I'll pray
To be at your side eternally; from you I'll never stray.

November 12, 1952

Hi Beautiful,
Me again. Well I received your letter and the poem I've been waiting for. The poem is wonderful, only a poem you could write. I don't know where you ever got the ability to express in words what others have so much difficulty saying. If I could put my words together in such a manner as that, I'd have no trouble telling you how much I love you. The only way I can do it is in just my simple way and that is, I love you very much. When you put things down on paper, it makes the simplest words turn into words with a hundred beautiful meanings.

Soon it will be Christmas honey, a time of the year that I always look forward to and this year it seems I am looking forward to it more than ever. The reason can be explained very simply. We will have another New Year to ring in together. Another year for the both of us to spend happily together. We are going to see that year when it is born and we are going to be a part of it. Every day of our life will be a part of it. So let's make it a successful and perfect one.

It's been snowing most of the week, and the snow is about six inches. Winter comes early up here. Last weekend they recorded 7 degrees above at one of our weather stations. I think I need you to keep me warm. Wouldn't it be nice if that dream came true? Thanks for not going to the football game. I'm sorry they lost. Honey please be good and remember that I love you very much.

He was lonely, and so was I. I hadn't written as often because I was busy with after school activities, sewing and studying.

November 16, 1952

Hi Beautiful,

I was surprised to get another letter from you yesterday. It made me feel good. Now I know how you feel when you get an extra one from me. Don't worry honey you will still get at least two letters a week from me if not more.

Yes, honey, another week has gone by, but I wish it were only a week until I see you again. I still have to dream for a while until I see you. You're the only one I can enjoy myself with and you will be the only one as far as I'm concerned. The days go by slow and it seems like it's going to be an eternity until I can see you again, but the time still has to go by and soon it will be Saturday morning when I'm hopping into the bus on the way home to my one and only.

I'll finish this last page by telling you how much I love you. I suppose I could start out saying that I love you again and again but I'd be copying your little brother Tommy. No, honey it would take a thousand pages to tell you, but I always try to sum it up at the end of my letter when I sign it "All my love always and forever". Remember honey, love is a word easily written and easily spoken but the meaning cannot be told by a thousand prophets. The meaning I hold in my heart can hardly be expressed, but I try to show it whenever I have a chance. Well beautiful remember I love you very much. Be good and write soon.

I began to feel the tension in his letters. I knew he was worried about the draft and what effect it would have on our future. I wanted to be there to hold him and assure him everything was going to be fine. I did the best I could in writing and called him to hear his voice and tell him that I loved him and prayed for him. It may have helped, but I knew he would be calmer as soon as he knew the results of his exams.

Asking him to attend a dance with me at school seemed so insignificant at the time, but the last occasion we danced together was at my junior prom. Not able to come home for Thanksgiving break added to the stress he was under.

November 19, 1952

Hi Beautiful,

Just got back from talking to you on the phone. It sure was good to hear from you again, even thought it was just for a few minutes. I was beginning to worry about not receiving any letters from you. Just today during class, I said to myself I ought to be getting a letter from you. I was disappointed that I did not get one. Tonight when one of the guys told me I had a phone call, I was wondering if something happened at home. When I heard your voice, I knew it was alright. Let's not make a habit of not writing because I don't want any excuses to start worrying. After all honey with all the work I have to do I find the time to alter my schedule to write letters home to you. I'm not balling you out honey so don't feel hurt. I don't want you thinking wrongly of me either. I'm sure you won't forge me so nothing has changed.

My roommate got his notice for induction into the Army today, but he also got a letter to apply for a deferment. I hope if this happens to me, I can do the same. Never can tell honey, maybe I won't have to go right away. I'd like to stay out as long as possible to spend most of my time home with you. Every time I write a letter, the time gets closer and closer when I'll see you again. Did you know there are only 10 school weeks left until I graduate? Boy that will be a happy day for both of us. I'll probably need a few extra prayers honey, so how about a little help.

How's my honey been? Behaving yourself? I haven't had any of those darn feelings so I guess there is no reason to worry. Be good honey, because I want you perfect when we get married. Well that's all for now. I love you very much.

There was no reason for him to worry about me, but I began to worry about the immediate future. How could we fulfill the hopes, dreams, and plans we had looked forward to since we started to go steady?

I spoke to my mother about my fears. Her simple straightforward answer was,

"It is normal to be concerned about the future, but being overly anxious is not the answer. Having faith and hope are what you need to keep a positive attitude about it. No one can predict what will happen tomorrow. What is meant to be will be. Love will hold and keep it all together."

November 25, 1952

Hi Beautiful,

Just got up after about six hours of sleep. It's now 7:00 in the morning and I feel I am ready to go to bed. Ever since I talked to you last week I've been going like a "madman". I've got so much work to do it isn't funny. It's getting close to the last term so you know they are piling on all the work they possibly can. I can't wait till Dec 20 comes so I can get away from this place for a while. When I come back, I'll have to worry another twenty pounds off whether I graduate or not. I wish I were home with you honey. It's only when you're away from someone you really love that you feel how much you miss them. Now, when I need you most to build up my courage and give me the little push I need I don't have you. I don't have you near me to at least talk to and get some of the troubles off my mind. It may have been hard before, but right now, I am wondering if I'll ever make it through this place. I wish I knew what the score was, and it was Feb. 18, and I was getting ready to graduate; then I would be relieved. That will be the happiest night of our lives, at least one of them anyway honey.

Sometimes when I'm feeling kind of "blue", I look at the poems you wrote. Some of them help, but some only make me want you closer to me. If only my wish could be fulfilled and bring me home to you without any worries left behind from here.

Have a nice Thanksgiving honey; sorry I can't be there to spend it with you. Be good and I love you very much.

Apprehension about passing his finals, graduating, the draft and how it would affect our future, and not able to come home for Thanksgiving must have stretched his patience to the limit. I wanted to be near him, to comfort him. The treadmill of separations that we were on had to slow down and end eventually. We just had to wait.

I woke up Thanksgiving morning with the smell of garlic, parsley, celery, onion and giblets frying in butter. Mom added the sautéed mixture to day old moistened cut up bread seasoned with parmesan cheese, salt, pepper, poultry seasoning and parsley for the turkey stuffing. The twenty-five-pound bird sat in the large oval blue porcelain roaster waiting to be stuffed, trussed, rubbed with butter and put into a low temperature oven to bake. Peeled and quartered white potatoes sat in a pot of water on the kitchen counter until it was time for them to be boiled and mashed. Whole sweet potatoes sliced down the center, filled with brown sugar, butter, and a dash of cinnamon, would join the turkey in the oven. Fresh cranberries simmered on a low burner on the stove. Washed broccoli florets were still in the refrigerator. Mom's apple and pumpkin pies made the day before were on the buffet in the dining room.

November 30, 1952

Hi Beautiful,
A few more weeks and I'll be home with you again. Those weeks will probably be the slowest I have ever spent away from you. It's just loving you so much and miss being with you. That new picture really tops the list of all the beautiful ones from you. I put it in the frame with a lock of your beautiful red hair on the bottom. There are only two words I can think of to describe that picture, "absolutely beautiful"! During the week when things get rough, I picked up your picture and just held it looking at you and dreaming about our wonderful times. Right now, I'm sitting in the laboratory room where I've spent most of my time all week. It seems kind of funny not doing calculations or the like. I prefer doing this any

day. Mom called me Friday night and tried to give me a little pick up; she said my letters seemed a little down hearted. After all, I did spend Thanksgiving away from you and home.

  How's everything in Rochester? We had more snow up here. I hope it's a "white Christmas", when we're together again.

  Well beautiful, that's all for tonight. I have more work to do. So be good and remember darling, I love you very much.

I wrote more this week. I felt his loneliness and knew he was worried about something. I knew when he was ready he would let me know. I was concerned he was burning the candle at both ends, studying for final exams and graduating, compounded by his worry of being drafted.

December 2, 1952

Hi Honey,

  I was surprised today to receive another letter from you. I got your special delivery letter yesterday and another long one today. It seems you're kind of worried about me. Don't worry honey everything is okay now. My letter that you'll get tomorrow will explain it. You ought to know honey I'd never forget about you, but at times, I have to put my memories in a dormant stage so I can concentrate on what I'm doing. Don't think I would ever forget you because I have too many wonderful memories.

  As for the dance, it sounds like a good idea. It will be good to get away from all this darn work for a while. I'll take you to the dance honey you deserve it.

  Honey, will you do me a favor? Every time I look at your picture, I appreciate how beautiful you looked with your hair long. Will you let it grow long for when I come home? It makes you look so much more grown up and it really does something for you.

  Now that I think of it, how are you doing in school? Remember all the plans you had about going on to school. Well don't change them; it always helps to have extra knowledge in some field. Get all you can out of high school honey. Well the days go ticking by and everyone draws me closer to you. One thing I have to go thru and that's the big exams before Christmas. If I pass those then I have a good chance of making it. As for sleeping when I get home-I doubt it. During the day, I'll have some work with me to do and at night, I'll be busy with you. So I won't have much free time. Just the idea of being home with you will suit me just fine. Until then honey, all I can do is hope and dream.   Be good. I love you.

Our maturing together did have advantages. We learned to cope with the changes taking place in our thinking and responsibilities. We adjusted to our "growing pains" with the knowledge we were separate but in the process of becoming one when we married. The hopes and dreams of our future kept the fires of our young love burning in our hearts.

December 7, 1952

Hi Beautiful,
Well two weeks from today and I'll be home again. Boy, it sure will be good. I have a lot to go thru until I see you again. Next week we start studying for a bunch of big exams. Right up until the last day before I leave, I'll be taking exams. These are the big ones and I hope to pass them. I wish these were all over with so I can stop worrying, but I won't until I graduate.
The other day they put a big Christmas tree out in front on the lawn and they're going to decorate it. No matter, it won't seem like Christmas until I am home with you. We will work something out over the holidays. I don't think your folks would mind if we went to church together. As for the other time, don't worry honey we will spend as much time together that is possible. I don't even know what to buy you for Christmas yet. You deserve something nice, but I can't think what you would like. Also, I want to surprise my honey with something she least expects. I'll have to put my brain together to think of something nice for the one I love. Here I am talking

this way and I wish I were saying them to you in person.

I miss you a lot honey. The other day I was daydreaming on my bed when one of the guys asked me what the matter was. I told him I was dreaming about someone I love very much. He said that I shouldn't let my mind think about those things because there is too much to be done. When I come home, I'll take you up on all you ask for, but too soon won't be soon enough. So be good honey, remember I'm longing for the day until I can see you again.

Once again, Joe expressed his concern about the amount of time he would be able to spend with me over the holidays. It wasn't my parents he had to worry about. They wouldn't mind our going to church together. I thought perhaps I might be invited to his house this year, but it never happened.

December 9, 1952

Hi Beautiful,

I'm still at the steady grind, working hard waiting until Saturday so I can take off and get home to you. It's down to just a few more days until I'll be home with you again. They've got our Christmas tree decorated out in front and it looks nice too. Once in a while we get a chance to listen to a few Christmas carols and it's starting to sound like Christmas. The only trouble is that it doesn't feel like it yet.

I dream about you all the time honey you never leave my mind. The last thing before I go to bed and the first thing getting up I have you in my mind. I am always thinking what it will be like when we get married. I am going to baby you so much, that you won't have a chance to be mad at me. No matter what honey we will both have fun just being with one another. Just think honey, for me to go around saying to people that this is my wife "Mary Ann."

By the way, I think two children would be nice to have, after all, I want to keep my wife in as nice a shape as possible. If she has too many to chase around all day long, it won't help any. I was reading in one of the magazines about movie stars going to places to keep in shape. It said they were "figure conscious". That's a pretty good attitude to take don't you think?

Someday we will see all these wonderful things happening and I wish it were soon, but right now, I have more studying to do.

"From you I'd never stray." Be good honey. I love you.

Joe's comments regarding our having only two children bothered me. I came from a large family. My mother and maternal grandmother were not thin. I couldn't help but wonder if I gained weight in the future how he would react.

I never thought about the physical changes that would occur in us as we grew old together. I ignored his vain comments.

Christmas Eve was an important day in our house, and I hoped Joe could be there to relax and socialize with my family and friends at our annual midnight buffet.

December 12, 1952

Hi Beautiful,

Writing a little ahead of time because of a little extra to tell you. I hope you won't mind but Bernie, a friend of mine is coming to Rochester for a few days. I thought it wouldn't be a bad idea for you to meet one of the guys I pal around with. We can go out Saturday night and he will be leaving Sunday to be home on Monday. You didn't mind when Dick came home and I know you will find Bernie just as nice. The only problem is we have to find a date for him. Ask Ken if he knows someone who would like to go on a blind date. Bernie is a good-looking guy so use your own judgment. I'm sure all of us will have a good time. I'll call Wednesday night to get everything straight. Well beautiful, the clock is ticking away and before long no matter what happens I'll be with you again. I enjoy every minute I spend with you, and there is nothing I want more than to be with you, but in order to spend it happily I have to make a success of this place. So just a few more months and I'll know how everything is going to turn out. For your sake and mine I hope it is for the better.

Well beautiful, that's the reason for the extra letter. See you soon honey, and be good, it won't' be long now.

Bernie came home with Joe. Ken found him a date and we went out to dinner. Joe was right about Bernie. He was a good-looking guy.

One evening Dad took out the projector and showed home movies. When the one with John's family flashed across the screen, Joe looked at me.

"Who's the guy you're talking to?"

"John Crudele. A friend of the family. No one to be concerned about." I said.

Joe came over, but not as often as he could have. I didn't expect him for Christmas Eve supper or Christmas Day dinner, but he did say he would be able to come to our Christmas Eve midnight buffet. I had a special surprise for him.

When Joe was home in October, I'd noticed him thumbing through a jewelry catalogue. "I'd like to own one of these," he said, pointing to a sterling silver identification bracelet. I was glad he said that, now I knew what to buy him for Christmas. I went to Hirschberg's Jewelry Store after he left and chose a bracelet I knew he'd like. I asked the sales person what the total charges would be if it were engraved with his name on the top and "All my love always" on the reverse. The cost of the bracelet and engraving was about $20.00, a lot of money for someone without a job or an allowance. It was a purchase I couldn't ask my parents to pay for, but I had an idea. The store had a lay away program. With 10 percent down and weekly payments, I could purchase it. Mom gave me $.50 a day to buy my lunch. I could save it until I had the down payment and make the weekly payments until it was paid for.

I decided to make a dress to wear on Christmas day and the night of my senior banquet, that was coming up in January. I purchased the pattern and fabric, emerald green "Cantoni" velveteen at Brodsky's'. I still have the dress. It is in the large steamer trunk that Joe used when he went to college. My engagement dress, wedding gown, negligée and nightgown, and other "precious memories" are also stored there.

. . . . .

Christmas Eve

After we finished eating, Joe and I went into the living room to exchange gifts. We took our gifts from under the Christmas tree and sat on the couch. He handed me a large, obviously store-wrapped package and I handed him a small box wrapped in silver paper with silver ribbon.

I opened mine first. It was a deep hunter green leather jewelry box engraved with my initials, and it came with a lock and key.
"It's beautiful," I said and put my arms around him and kissed him. "I don't have a jewelry box. Now open yours."

Joe slid the ribbon off the box and removed the paper without tearing it. When he saw the jeweler's name on the lid of the box, he tilted his head and looked at me with the same curiosity as when I'd cut my hair. He opened the box.

"I don't believe this," he said and read the inscription. He kissed me. "I never expected this, Honey."
It was worth all the effort and missed lunches to see his surprised expression when he opened his gift.

I didn't see him at all during the day while he was home. He gave me no valid reason other than he was studying.

January 1953

Before Joe had to leave, we were watching a variety show on television one night. One of the guests had red hair; I don't remember if it was Arlene Dahl or Rita Hayworth, but she was asked if she was Irish. "No, just because I have red hair doesn't mean I'm Irish," she said. After her remark Joe said, "I have another pet name for you. I think I'll call you Irish because of your red hair." Joe returned to school right after the New Year.

January 4, 1953

Hi Irish,

Well I am back again safe and sound and lonely as before. I can't complain though, because as usual I enjoyed myself being home with you. I'm sorry I couldn't have made better use of the time I spent with you. I know you wanted more than I gave you. Pretty soon I'll be home again, for a while at least until the draft notifies me. I only hope I can graduate before they call me. Maybe I wasn't there every minute of the day but I was with you almost every night. My life wouldn't be complete without you honey and that's the way I'm going to spend it, all I can with you. There will be interferences, but when we get back together, we will make up for lost time

Honey, without you I would never have gotten as far as I am now and I don't know how to thank you for all the help you have given me here.

In six more weeks honey I'll be home again with you. I hope and pray that it will be for a long time so we can make up some time lost. Any little time that I spend with you will be worth it, even if it's just for a while. In the meantime, honey just keep making yourself pretty and by the time I get home it would be nice if your hair had grown longer. I have to admit it does look nice that way. You are really sharp all dressed up and I love the way you look. So be good honey, see you soon.

I'd been hesitant to ask him what his parents thought about our going together or about me. He never volunteered any information. Whatever it was, Joe kept it to himself. Perhaps they told him we were too young and I would hinder their plans for his education or the future they envisioned for him. Was this the reason he kept me at a distance from them?

I looked forward to graduation. With good grades in all my classes and no worries about failing, I wrote to Trapagen School of Dress Design in New York City asking for an information packet about their program. While I waited for the information to arrive, I received the inevitable, dreaded letter from Joe.

January 14, 1953

Hi Irish,
I better break it to you in a nice way. Remember I wrote to you about the draft? I received notice I have to report for my physical. Thursday morning, I have to be at the draft board at 7:00am sharp. From there we leave for Buffalo and stay there all day. The nicest part of it is that I won't have to come back until Saturday. That will give me some time to spend with you. In the meantime, I'll make a couple of visits to the recruiting office and see what kind of a deal they will give me. Don't worry; I'm not jumping to any harsh conclusions until I make up my mind. The trouble is they give you thirty days before they call you
I found out there is a Colonel in the Army, somewhere, that wants men who know how to survey. He said he is willing to take guys that have graduated from Ranger School and he will put them to work for him. It's a very good deal, about the best for an ordinary guy going into the service. I am not promising anything but sometime after I'm in the service I'll be coming home with something for you, probably when you are 19. That is if everything turns our okay. There is no law that says a serviceman can't be married.

So honey it looks like next week I'll be seeing you again. Right now, the affairs of the Ranger School are a little mixed up. Was it a waste of time, or wasn't it? Maybe it will help to save my life, who knows. There are many questions to be asked, but they will be answered soon enough, in fact too soon. Honey, I hope this letter doesn't make you feel bad, but it had to happen. I love you.

A chill went through me when I read he had to report to the draft board for his physical. We knew it would happen one day but it was still a shock. As hatchlings pushed from the nest, we were suddenly thrust into the adult world. There was no alternative. We had to grasp and hold tightly to our dreams and plans for the future regardless of the immediate circumstances. With hope, prayer and determination we would work through the uncertain days ahead of us.

My senior banquet at Cutler Union, University of Rochester was January 17. The class prophecy read, "Mary Ann in Paris is setting the style.

I remembered two years earlier when Joe picked me up to go to his senior banquet and the confrontation he had with my mother when we came home late. I didn't have that problem. Dad took me there and picked me up when it was over.

January 18, 1953

Hi Irish,

When I get back here next week, it will only be three more weeks to gradation and that will go by fast. I can't slow down now or it may spoil everything, and I don't want anything to happen this late in the year. Right now, I am going crazy doing a complete set of bookkeeping records. We've only had the darn thing two weeks and we are through the whole cycle. It seems complicated to me but to someone like you who took it for a year in school it doesn't seem difficult. Don't forget I learned the whole works in two weeks in an hour per day. Pretty fast, at least for me.

You and I have some serious talking do about the near future. There are a few matters you and I have to discuss, this way we will both be happier about the whole "stinking" mess coming up soon. In the meantime, there is nothing you or I can do about it except enjoy one another's company. So until next week when I can see you and tell you I love you, be good.

We had only a few hours together. I was in school and Joe was home completing his homework. He said he discussed our future with his parents, who said he was too young even to think of marriage, especially now with military service facing him. He didn't elaborate on the discussion, but I knew they voiced their objections. I didn't question him any further. He had enough unanswered problems.

Joe told me his dad never said a word to him as they drove to the bus station. I told him he may not have said anything, but I was sure he was thinking of the unforeseeable future and didn't want to reveal his apprehension to his son.

January 18, 1953

Hi Irish,
Well here I am back again at school with my memories of you to keep me busy and nothing to look forward to except the future after I get out of the Army. I suppose I should be worrying about graduation but it doesn't mean too much to me anymore. It won't be long before it's all over with and things will just be starting. No matter what, I think whatever happens can't be helped, because I am supposed to do it. It's all planned out for me somewhere. I'll have your picture with me that has accompanied me here at school. Where I go you'll be going too, not only in heart, but almost in reality. I suppose by the time it's all over you'll have outgrown your picture and matured a little more. Stay as beautiful as you are and remember honey you're mine and no one has the right to take

you away, if that is the way it is to be. Maybe it is better that this came along because by the time it is all over with we will be a little wiser and have a little extra money to fall back on even though it may be little.

I won't be home for your graduation but I'll be thinking about you and you'll hear from me regular if not more than regular. So maybe it won't be too bad, maybe it will all turn out and maybe, we will both be happier when it is all through. Those three "maybes" depend a lot on our future or vice versa, so if there is any way to help them along let's try and give them a push. In the meantime, we'll just keep praying and loving one another. I'll see you soon.

Joe had resigned himself to the circumstances ahead of him. His resolve to work through situations he had no control over prepared him for the responsibilities he would encounter in the future. I was disappointed he wouldn't be home for my graduation and senior ball. We rarely had the opportunity to be together on special occasions.

I too had to accept what I had no control over. The only choice was to have patience. I couldn't govern circumstances, but I could control my reactions to them.

January 25, 1953

Hi Irish,

Back again with a couple of pages. I went to see about getting a deferment. He told me that I have to get re- classified before getting my induction papers. The possibilities of a deferment are very slight. The lady at the draft board said, "It's pretty late in the game to get one now." Also, by the time I get one it will be pretty near the end of the school year and the school won't have much to say about it. So, it looks like I'll be going into the Army. I suppose I won't mind too much, it is only two years, and if I can specialize in something, the time will probably go by a lot faster.

Being away from you for another two years is going to be very difficult because I've spent a long year away from you already and I can't see another two. I guess we'll have to take things the way they come. We don't have much to say about it. It will give me time to think about the future, and give me time to settle a few of my hopeful plans. In other words, I'll have a chance to make some money so that I can purchase a few things I want to get. You're involved.

Just think honey in two more years we can start making permanent plans at least ones that will last and not have to be broken up by some sort of intrusion. It's got to be done so I better get out there and help in the whole darn mess. In the meantime, you and I will have to endure and keep hoping and praying for the final day to come rolling around for us to be together always.

The time will go by fast and before you know it, I'll be home to pester you again or maybe you will change your mind about me. You better not let me catch you, or else. Well in the meantime, I've got to study so I'll have to close. Be home pretty soon honey so be good. I love you very much.

I was at a loss what to say to him in my next letter to make him feel better. I wrote, "As long as we love each other, we can make our plans and accomplish them together. My mother always said that we live one day at a time and we are to make the most of each day."

I was beginning to understand the truth in those statements. She'd say them often during the war years if I complained or questioned when the war was going to end. She was a woman on her knees every night reading a chapter of her Bible, a promise she'd made to God if my older brother, who was critically ill got well. He recovered and she fulfilled her promise. "One day at a time" and "This too shall pass" were sayings I heard often in my childhood. Their meanings were clear to me now.

I wanted to be with Joe, and although the future was uncertain, I knew as long as we continued to love and depend on each other, we could face anything. I was lonely and longed for him. I missed his conversations about our future. I wrote and told him not to be concerned about my graduation; we could celebrate it when he came home. The world we lived in as children was rapidly changing and issues we had to face about our future were more important.

February 1, 1953

Hi Irish,

Well here it is the first day of Feb. and in just 17 days I'll be graduating, and best of all I will be seeing you again. I don't want to write about the Army so I'll write about more interesting things. I was rather surprised to get such a long letter from you, even though it was late. I guess it was late because you wrote it in two days. That is what I understood it to read.

Tonight I am in one of those sentimental moods again. Been thinking about you. Maybe it's from looking at your picture and realizing what I've been missing. It's rough to know that you have someone who loves you, but still you can't enjoy one another. Why is that? I don't know. It seems like it just keeps going on and on. When will it end? I wish it were sooner than it's most likely to be. I am getting lonely now and it's going to be worse even sooner than I expected. It makes me mad to know that every day you're growing up and soon you'll be a woman and I won't be around to enjoy it. After all, I am a part of your life and I want to spend my life being with you and knowing every step in your growing.

It seems mean to take someone away, and then if it turns out alright, let him go back and continue where he left off. However, you can't do that because there are two or three years of aging in between. The human body yields to too many temptations, and I don't want that to happen. I want to be around so that I can protect the one I love from any of those temptations. After all, we are put on this earth to fulfill a course of life, and that course of life should be filled with the love of one another, not broken up by some sort of force that removes you at will. If I had my way, things would be different, although they would have their faults, but one's life could be filled with answers to his dreams he always longed for. It will probably take some time before I learn the crude ways of life. Maybe I won't learn, and continue being bitter the way I am now. Nevertheless, honey, though I may be bitter I still hold the same true love that I've learned to value up here, so many miles away from you.

So honey, whether near or far away, I'll always love you the way I love you tonight. I hope I haven't bewildered you with my feelings, but it's the way I feel right now. Any way honey, in the meantime (long time) be good.

Joe poured out his deepest fears and the uncertainty of our future in this letter. It must have been difficult for him to open up the way he did. Normally, he kept his feelings deep within. *Still waters run deep.*

Joe's apprehension about graduation and the draft caused him some anxious moments. I kept writing to let him know it would all work out in due time, not a minute sooner. Our patience was stretched as tightly as a rubber band, but I tried not to show my anxiety in my letters. We could do whatever had to be done, if we did it together.

February 9, 1953
To my darling,
I've been dreaming a lot about you lately. It's the kind of dream I don't appreciate. It seems that every time you are giving me the run-around. When I wake up in the morning, I feel depressed. I hope it hasn't any correlation with real life. Then I look at your picture sitting here on my desk and I know someone as lovely as you who loves me so much couldn't do a thing like that. If I ever get the guy in my dreams that's trying to take you away from me, I'll break his neck. Or maybe give him a talking to, because I may wake up and find myself beating the heck out of my pillow. One of these nights, I'll dream about

our real love, but the trouble is my night goes by too fast and it doesn't give me much time with you. Most of those darn dreams are hard to figure out anyway. I'd prefer to have the real thing, and then I can enjoy it. Someday. We will have a lot of talking to do before I take off so let's plan on making it an enjoyable stay, even if it is for a short time. The next time I see you again I'll probably be in uniform. It looks like an Army uniform unless something turns up.

Well beautiful, the days are growing short and soon I'll be able to share them with you. I don't know what I would do if I didn't have you to come home to. I'm a lucky guy to have such a wonderful girl like you. See you soon honey, write and be good.

Did Joe's dream foresee the future about someone trying to take me from him?

. . .

On February 12, I called him at school to wish him a happy 20th birthday.

"You're not a teenager anymore; you're a man."

"You're going to be 18 in July; does that make you a woman?"

"Probably."

"Does that mean I can make love to you when I get home?"

"What do you think?"

"Knowing what I've known all these years we've gone together, you'll still be stubborn and say no."

I could visualize the expression on his face accompanying that response. Not disappointment, but resignation to the fact it would not happen until the day I said, "I do."

February was a pivotal month for Joe. He turned 20 on the 12th, graduated on the 18th and received his induction notice from the government to report for duty on the 25th. We had only a week after his graduation to be together, not the one or two months he thought he would have after he graduated. I was in school, so we saw each other after classes and in the evening. We said good-bye again, and as I had done so many times in the past, I waited for his first letter to arrive. This time it was different. He was not in college, he was in the Army, and the Korean War was a dark cloud hovering over our future.

He called from Ft. Devans to let me know his 16 weeks of basic training would be at Indiantown Gap, Pennsylvania, and he would write the first chance he got.

February 26, 1953

Hi Beautiful,

Well here I am in the Army. We got here, this morning bright and early from Buffalo. We march or trot every place we go. Tomorrow we get our haircut and instruction about the Army and how we are supposed to act. They gave us more tests, and Monday we took a couple of shots. We may be shipped to Camp DIX in about 10 days. Nobody knows yet. They have us restricted until sometime tonight, and that means that we can't leave the barracks. Don't count on a set amount of letters each week until I get to basic training.

How's my honey doing back home? I hope you're not taking it too hard because I don't mind the life; it's just the idea of not seeing you and my folks. There are rumors we might be home for Easter so keep your chin up and maybe I'll make it. I'm quite sure we might get home before basic training is over, so it won't be too long before I'll see you. Every night I pray my dreams will come true, so you give a little help then maybe we can get what we're hoping for.

They showed us the proper way of making the bed. We have to get up at 4:45am, wash, make our bed and clean up around our bunk by 5:15 am. At first, it will be rough, but we'll get used to it. We have no choice; we have to follow orders.

Honey, you can write to me at the address on the letter, but if you want to catch me, you better write fast.

Well, they'll be calling us soon so I'll close. I love you darling.

Over a week passed and I hadn't received any mail from him. I wasn't upset. I knew when Joe had the time, he would write. I kept writing and waiting for his letter to arrive.

I was impressed he learned how to make a bed the "proper" way by tucking and folding the sheets and blanket tight. I knew that he probably thought, "This is woman's work."

15 March 1953

Hi Beautiful,
I suppose you were wondering if I was going to write to you. When I said I thought I thought I'd have a lot of time this week I was wrong. No kidding honey, I've been on the go 10-12 hours a day and that's no joke. I'm up at 5:00am, fall out for revelry, and then run around the area for about a mile. Then, all sweated up, we fall out for chow. Last Saturday we had a division parade that only comes once a year. All week long, we've been drilling for it. Friday, they got us up early and marched us until 10:00 at night. We had an hour off for each meal.

Early Saturday morning, we marched to the parade grounds, wearing our O Ds, which is our wool dress uniform, boots and a 9 ½ lb. riffle over our arm. If you think that rifle doesn't get heavy after about four hours of sleep, well honey you're wrong. It was a big deal parade with a Brigadier General; most of the officers here are Colonels, Majors and a mess of Lieutenants. We were congratulated by the Major because our Battery ("B") won for the best marching. After chow, we had to move to different barracks because they wanted everyone in alphabetical order.

Gee honey, you have really been writing and I felt like a fool for not getting more mail off to you. I hope you understand that I honestly didn't have time. You know that I write regularly and as soon as things are settled and I get used to the routine I'll be getting more mail off to you. Boy when they had mail call and I got six letters all at once it sure made me feel good. I know how you feel honey only getting a few so tonight I am going to try to make up for lost time. Letters sure do something for a person who is down in the dumps. You must have spent most of your time writing because just about every one of them is packed full of love.

Did you know honey I worry a lot about you? It's not that I don't trust you or any of that stuff, but it's because I'm so far away and I can't be home with you to protect you from any harm that may come along. There are times when I'm thinking about you practically every emotion surfaces. Wouldn't it be nice if I were going to come home for good or for at least a month or so, so that you and I could get engaged? I don't know it I told you before but I am sending $30.00 a month home to be put away. Speaking about coming home, after four weeks of basic training (starting Monday the 16th) we are allowed a 36-hour pass every weekend if we are not pulling a detail. If we do get time off and you are in New York with your parents, I'll come and see you. Don't count on it. I won't be sure until the last minute.

Here is more to go with the above. My best buddy Len is from Rochester. Get this; he is going steady with Sheila, if you remember her. She's also going to be in New York that weekend. So Len and I may take a trip there if we get a pass. If not, I am sure I will be home the following weekend.

I was just looking outside and it's raining now. That sure does give me a funny feeling. Makes me think of many things. I've a lot of memories to think about that happened to you and me in the last five years. When I think about all those wonderful things, you more or less forget what a lousy life you're leading.

So, you like it when I call you "baby". Now that I know that I'll call you baby all the time just to make you feel better. I want you to have the best of everything and I am going to baby you all the time. I do love you and you're supposed to take care of the one you love. I'll call you if I can. In the meantime, keep writing those extra letters and I'll do the same.

I was relieved to hear from him. Reading the rigorous schedule, he followed made me thankful for the year he attended Ranger School. Joe was prepared for the training ahead of him because of the discipline he had acquired there and I was sure he could do anything he set his mind to. I also knew there would be days of discouragement similar to the ones in college; he'd weathered those and he would do the same in the Army. I questioned why he wrote the day and month reversed. "That's how it's done in the military," he responded,

His explanation of going to New York with his "best buddy" who was going steady with Shelia raised a red flag. How could he have a "best friend" in less than a month? When I spoke to Sheila, she said she never had a boyfriend Len. Hmm . . . .

18 March 1953

Hi Beautiful,

Here I am again with a few minutes to write a letter. We just got thru scrubbing down the barracks. It is called a G.I. (general inspection) party. They usually have one at least once a week and if we are bad boys, it comes more often. So far, we've been good boys except for a couple of guys who sounded off at the wrong time.

You spoiled me when I got all those letters in one day, now I am expecting more. I know you're wondering what happened to my mail, but you must have received my last letter by now. I wrote more to make up for not writing. Maybe I didn't express myself enough but no matter what honey, I miss you a lot and I wish it would be soon when I can see you again. As I said before, it's tough being away from someone you love as much as I love you. There is not much you can do with your time off, when you get it, except dream about being home with someone as affectionate as you are. Our First Sergeant is sure trying to make us forget about our home life, but he will really have to go some to make me forget about you. I've been thru deals like this before but I guess I'll manage. I hope you can do the same. I don't want my baby to forget about me as long as I am in this Army. It's no picnic, but someone with as strong a love as ours can really pull thru a deal like this one. There is no doubt about it honey; I'd prefer being home with you anytime. Where else can someone find a person as sweet and loveable to come home to? We were made for one another and no one is going to keep us apart. We can do it honey. One of these days, you and I will be able to get together for good. The sooner the better. I don't know how much more of this being away from one another I can take, but I hope from the bottom of my heart that you will never forget me and always be faithful. I promise to God that I will do the same. There isn't much more a man can do except carry out that promise, and I plan on doing just that. There will be plenty of temptations that may arise, but remember honey I am not here because I want to be. I'd rather be home with you. We have been thru all kinds of experiences before and this is nothing new to us. Our love will get stronger day by day and it will keep us closer together even though we are miles apart. Every night I pray that our love continues to grow deeper and get stronger.

You'll probably hear from others how foolish you are, but remember honey we have our own plans that someday we plan on carrying out. It will be a while yet, that's for sure, but in the meantime just remembers I love you more than anyone ever could and that is from my heart. You know how I feel about you, so don't forget ever.

Be good darling until I see you again.

I had never given Joe reason to think I was unfaithful. I could have dated, but I had no desire to. I was committed to the promise that I would be true to him and one day we would get married. I had male friends in school but that was all they were, just friends. Most of them knew I was going steady and didn't cross the line by asking me out, with the exception of Harvey in homeroom.

I was satisfied with the way things were. I was looking forward to graduation and going on to school. I had my senior picture taken for the yearbook. Now I really knew how short a time it was until graduation.

9 March 1953

Hi Beautiful,
Had a few more minutes tonight so I thought it would be a good time to write to my honey. Right now, our barracks are on fire call. That means they can call us out anytime tonight if they see fit. I just hope they don't decide to around 3:00 in the morning. What a life honey, I wish I was home with you. It didn't take the Army to make me realize my longing for you that was always with me from the day I started to go out with you. The night I left, I felt like crying myself. Really, at that moment it didn't strike me what it would be like to be away from you. I have been away before, but it didn't affect me the same way.

Yesterday I took another test for Officers Candidate School. If I pass, I will be eligible to go to school to become an officer. If I graduate from there it means I will be a second lieutenant with a salary of $328.00 a month, and if I am married, they add another $90.00 to the pay. A lot of "ifs". That's not bad considering I am only making $78.00 a month now. We could get married and I would be allowed to have my wife living with me wherever I am in the states and possibly overseas. It's not a bad idea and if I pull it off I could probably get a good job in the Engineers Corps. By the way, how would you like to have a husband as an officer? Let me know how you feel; after all you are concerned what happens to me. Don't forget I have to pass the test then be accepted to an Officers school. I can always turn it down at the last minute if you or I ever change our mind. I am serious about the whole thing and willing to accept it, if everything turns out right.

What is my honey doing on the home front? I suppose it must be lonely back there by yourself. If you're looking for proper amusement, don't be afraid to take it. Just remember honey it would break my heart to know you have done something wrong while I was away. I have faith in you so don't let me lose it. I can honestly say I've never known you to do anything wrong. Keep it up that way honey-please.

Honey, I'd give anything to be home with you now. In the Army, they say we never had it so good. Well take it from me they are crazy. I'd prefer to be home anytime. Every night when I go to bed I pray that it will be soon when I can see you again. I think the good Lord will take care of you so when I come home I will find you as loveable and wonderful as you were when I left. Do what your conscience tells you to, I'm sure it will be correct. I know what you expect of me and I will do my best to keep you happy. Don't worry honey; you will get the best that is in my power. Someday our dreams will come true, so keep praying honey, keep praying. Until my next letter, there isn't much I can say except I love you.

Reading this letter reminded me how lonely he was. I

longed for the comfort of being in his arms listening to his plans for our future. He seemed so secure talking about it. I understood how lonely he was because I was lonely too. With our faith to keep us strong, we knew we would survive the weeks and possibly months of being apart.

I kept my letters going out to him. He needed encouragement to stay focused, and if it meant I had to write more, I would. I had the time.

Graduation was just around the corner. I knew I had made the right choice to substitute three weekly study hall periods for tailoring classes. There was so much to learn. Cutting and sewing were easy. The inner construction was time consuming. I was amazed how the under collar of a lapel on a jacket was rolled using hand sewn stitches to hold the interfacing in place before the top was attached. Each day was a new learning experience. All that I was taught would be a plus when I followed my dream in fashion design.

23 March 1953

Hi Honey,

I suppose you are wondering again what happened to me. Same old story, we have plenty to do. If I don't fall asleep before I finish this letter, I'll be lucky. I doubt it though; just thinking of you will keep me wide-awake. I wish I could write more often, but honestly honey I don't have the chance. Every night I want to write but there is always something coming up; rifle inspection, barracks inspection, fire call or else they just have us fall out because we may have been slow during the day. If we only had some time to ourselves I could make up a schedule, but we're never sure when they will call us out. One of these days, I'll get used to this darn schedule and things will be easier. In the meantime honey, just bear with me and I promise I'll write whenever I get the chance.

As far as health goes around here, it's not good. Just about everyone has a sore throat or cough, not the kind of cough from a cold, but the kind you get from smoking too many cigarettes. Company "A" has two barracks quarantined for something or another. Last night, right next door they carried someone out with pneumonia. At mess, a guy acted as he was choking on his food. When they took him to the hospital, it was a nervous breakdown. Someone during roll call asked how he was and the lieutenant said, "What, are you married to him?" You can't even ask in this Army. As for me honey, I don't feel too bad, except being tired and beat every night. What I need is some good old-fashioned loving that only you can give. Seems like years since I've had a chance to be in your arms. Those were the days and I'd give anything to be back with you again. Once we are back together, I'll never leave you. The next time I leave for somewhere you'll be at my side. Sounds good, doesn't it honey and I want to make it come true.

Someday I will too, and no lieutenant or first sergeant will stop me. I think about you and I going out, me in my uniform and you at my side; holding on the way you usually do with both hands. I can practically see you in front of me right now looking up at me with your unforgettable smile. If you get some time would you take some new pictures and send them to me? I always like something like that or cookies too.

Lights out in a few seconds, so be good and I love you ever so much.

Almost a week went by before I heard from him again. I wrote to him about my concern for his health and the difficulty he would have keeping up a letter-writing schedule. I didn't want to add to the mounting pressures he faced.

28 March 1953

Hi Beautiful,
Here it is Sunday morning about 9:00 and I feel pretty good because they let us sleep until 7:30 and that is pretty late for us considering yesterday we had to get up at 3:30 am and march 8 miles right after breakfast. We marched to the other side of the Post where we saw a demonstration of all the weaponry that the Infantry uses in combat. We stayed there

until about 10:00 and rode back on the bus, that was a relief after the long hike we took up.

After dinner, they spotted all the guys who needed haircuts and there must have been 100 of them. I spent my whole afternoon there and last night I went to bed early. This afternoon we march in another parade that's why I am taking this time to write to you.

Today is Palm Sunday and here I am stuck here in the Army. Next Sunday is Easter Sunday and honey I am sorry but I'll be right here on this Army Post. Rules and regulations say that we are not allowed off the post until four weeks of basic is completed and Easter Sunday will only be three. The following Sunday I've got the right to go home for a short while, that is, if none of the guys in our Battery (219 guys) don't go AWOL for two more weeks. We will be allowed a long weekend. It means leaving here Friday at noon and not having to be back until Sunday at midnight. Some wise guy will probably ruin it for the rest of us. It will give me a few short hours to spend with you.

I'm giving my hair just two more weeks to grow in to look presentable when I see you. I suppose it won't be all the way in but maybe a little longer than it is now. We're only allowed 1 ½ inches before they tell you to cut it. No more long hair you used to like to run your fingers thru. I hope you won't change your mind when you see me again.

I imagine you have a new Easter outfit. Did you make it or buy it? You write and let me know. I suppose Sunday will be a big day for you but don't forget honey I'll be on this post with nothing to do but go for a walk or to the movies with some of the guys. I'll be thinking of you honey and if it is at all possible I'll call you so I can talk to you for just a while. When you go to church Sunday receive communion and I will too, this way at least it will be almost like receiving it together. We'll both say a prayer for one another and I am sure the good Lord will take care of us. I'll be home the following Sunday and I'll be expecting to see a beautiful angel when I walk thru that door and that angel will be you. I love you truly.

1 April 1953

Hi Beautiful,

Here I am a sloppy mess full of mud from head to toe. I don't think there is one piece of clothing on me you can find a clean spot. We were on the rifle range and it rained all the time we were there. I Went to bed at 11:30, got up at 3:30 this morning, ate breakfast and then marched the 3 miles one-way to the range. When we got there, it started to rain and kept up until we got back. All that time we lay on the ground in the mud. When we returned, we had to clean every piece of equipment we owned. Lucky for us I found a few minutes to write a letter. I know you are wondering what happened to the mail from me, but it is the usual thing honey, just too busy. The days are still going by honey just as empty as the last five weeks. The only thing that I have to keep me going are memories and that pretty picture I have hanging in my locker that has been with me through hell and high water. I wish I were back at school with you on my desk knowing for sure I could come home and see you. I think I may be home for the weekend. I am not sure what time exactly I will be there. I'll just walk in any old time and surprise you. If it's 3:00 in the morning, I'll still knock on your door and make you get out of bed to come down and greet me with open arms.

One of these days I'll be thru with basic training and be allowed to come home whenever I get a chance. I have a better idea; let's get married so that you can come with me wherever I may go except overseas. One of these days, honey I'll make you mine and I'll be as happy as I can be. Then you and I can start to work on our plans of raising a family. Like I said honey two kids and then we can call it quits. Do you think a dainty thing like you can handle a home, two kids, husband and keeping herself pretty? I think you can honey no matter how tiny you are.

We got paid last night honey; it wasn't much but enough to put some away for that certain rainy day. I hope it doesn't take too long to save up enough to buy that something for a special certain someone. It will be a nice ring honey; you can be sure of that. I know you will say that it doesn't make much difference how big it is but the nicer it is the longer it will take. Once you have that ring honey it will be all yours and no one can take it from you ever. The next thing that will come is the wedding band and that will be soon I hope. I love you honey, every bit of you and everything you stand for. The million and one things you stand for is the reason I love you as much as I do, now have been and always will. That's the truth and you know I don't have to keep writing it down on paper to prove it to you. The reason I do is because you love to hear words like that, so I'll keep on saying them just to please my darling future wife.

Have as nice an Easter as you can without me there. If everything goes alright I'll call, so please be around. If not, I'll be very disappointed. Well beautiful, time is getting short and I have to be getting to bed. Be good!

His comment of *two kids and then we can call it quits* bothered me. What would happen if we had three or four? I thought it sounded a bit selfish on his part.

I made my Easter outfit; a navy blue faille coat and light blue taffeta dress. I also made the same coat and dress in a different color for my sister-in-law Angie. Joe sent me a corsage of pink sweetheart roses. They looked beautiful pinned on my coat.

The following week he came home. When he walked in the door, wearing his uniform and the smile that always melted my heart, we embraced and kissed. We didn't care if Mom, Dad and my brothers were watching, we just held on tight. Dad complimented him on his uniform and Mom said he looked handsome.

Joe told them he was taking me out for a ride and we left for Durand Eastman Park. The front seat of the Buick was one piece without a separation in the middle for the gearshift and almost as long as our couch. Joe pushed the seat back, rested his head in my lap and told me his plans for our future while I ran my fingers in his hair. It was short but it didn't matter.

"Five weeks is long time to be away from you," he said.

"I know. I can't wait to get home from school to see if there is a letter from you."

"I want to marry you as soon as possible. If I'm stationed stateside, you can come with me until the time I have a tour where you can't come with me."

"Joe, you know I wanted to go to New York after graduation."

"I plan to give you your diamond in June, and I don't want my future bride in New York alone."

"I thought you said it would be next year when I'm nineteen."

"I changed my mind. I don't know where I'll be a year from now, and I want to marry you as soon as I graduate from OCS."

"I'd like to have the opportunity to go out on my own and do something I enjoy."

"If we get married, how can you go? If my assignment is here in the States, I want you with me and that means no New York."

He sat up put his arms around me and kissed me.

"Now is not the time to worry about it. I love you and want you with me. We've been saying goodbye to each other too long."

I was upset. I knew that once he made up his mind to do something there was little I could do to change it. I agreed to think about what he said.

19 April 1953

Hi Honey,

The time sure goes by fast when you're enjoying being home with the one you love. At first, I was rather disappointed but after we talked things over, I found that you were the same wonderful, loveable Mary Ann you have always been. It was good to be home two weeks in a row. I know one thing the sooner we get married the better I'll like it. Then all our problems of loneliness and wanting will be gone, only to make way for the new ones after we're married.

I enjoyed every minute I've ever spent with you and I know the future will be the same. You're so wonderful to get along with. To me, you're the perfect one for me and I want to keep it that way. You were sweet and understanding Saturday night and I loved you for it. I don't know how anyone could ever get mad at you or doubt your word. It makes me feel good inside to tell you or call you my wife. I love you so much honey. I know you can take care of yourself and you're not weak to the evils of being alone and so beautiful. When I get home, I plan on picking up where I left off. I don't ever want you to get mad at me the way you did last week, it's not that it makes me mad but it's the idea I think you're losing your love for me. I know now it was just a way for you to make me learn my lesson. I'll tell you one thing I have learned and that is I'll never slight you in the least. You don't deserve to be treated that way.

You're probably in bed right now honey and I hope you are dreaming of me. I'm dreaming too, picturing myself lying there next to you, touching your soft, white, warm body. It sends a chill up and down my spine just thinking about it. Right now, I am only dreaming but soon, some day when we are married I won't have to dream anymore. I love you honey and I don't ever want you to forget it. I'll try to show you how much honey, just give me the chance and I'll prove it to you. Maybe not right away, but it will be soon. I think about you all the time honey. The Lord above knows how we feel toward one another and He loves us enough to help us carry out our dreams. Right now that is all they can be, just dreams, but someday they'll come true, and you and I will be together once again.

We've been away from one another for a long time and when that day comes when we can be together always, I am sure we will appreciate one another's love. Just keep praying

You pray for my protection and love and I'll pray for your love and love from me. Just be good honey and stay as faithful and wonderful as you are. I'm sure it won't be in vain. I hope while I was home I managed to settle everything so you don't feel hurt anymore. I don't because you managed to straighten me out. Let me know any time I've done something wrong, so I can fix it before it goes too far.

Be good honey and keep writing. I love you again and again.

There wasn't anything to do. Mom preached often about choices and the responsibility and commitment attached to them. Joe wanted to get married. I did, too, but the dreams and plans I made had to be set aside to do so. I could have said no. I chose to be with him.

I wrote and asked Joe if he could come home for my senior ball on May 26. He said he didn't think he could and felt bad about it. I didn't want to miss it so I asked my brother Jim to be my date. Joe was happy with that decision. I enjoyed dancing with Jim and I knew I would be dancing with him all night at the prom as I had done at the teen dances at church.

I found a Simplicity pattern for my gown. I chose a fabric of fine sheer illusion in ivory and shades of blue. The full skirt was five layers of fabric. The first and second layers were ivory and the remaining three layers were in graduated shades of blue from light to dark. I draped a panel of blue and ivory sheer over the left bust and under the right, reversing the draping to the opposite side. I constructed the fitted bodice onto a long line strapless bra. It fit perfectly. The bra stayed in place so I wouldn't have to spend the evening tugging at the gown to keep it up. The zipper on the gown covered the hooks of the bra.

When the gown was finished, I wanted to see how it looked, but I could only capture the reflection of my upper body in the mirror above the dresser. I decided to take it down. I removed the tray with the matching comb and brush set, put it on the dressing table and set the lamp, Joe's picture and everything else on the bed. I boosted myself onto the dresser, held both sides of the maple-framed mirror and lifted it until I released its wire from the wall hook. Struggling with its weight, I slid it down to the top of the dresser, turned it on its side and leaned it against the wall. I sat down, steadied the mirror with one hand, rolled onto my stomach and eased myself down the front of the dresser until I felt my feet touch the floor. The rest was easy. I slid the mirror to the floor and leaned it against the bed. I put on my gown, hooking the long line bra and closing the zipper as far as I could. It didn't matter. I held the zipper together with my hand as I admired the gown.

It was the final gown I would wear before my wedding gown. My only regret was Joe would not see me wearing it.

One of my graduation gifts from my parents was jewelry, a sterling silver necklace, bracelet and earrings set with oval blue moonstones. Mom gave it to me a little early so I could wear it with my gown. The color of the stones matched the blue of my gown.

Jim and I double dated with Norma Schmidt and her boyfriend Al Smith, who were going steady and planned to be married after graduation. Dad volunteered to be our chauffeur for the evening; he drove us to dinner and the prom. Dancing with my younger brother, almost six feet tall, I realized my sibling rival was the best choice for an escort. I missed dancing the slow dances with Joe; he avoided the fast ones. Jim was a better dancer than Joe was in that regard. We didn't avoid any of them.

My uncle John was a manager at Gitlin's Jewelers, and when he heard Joe wanted to buy me an engagement ring, he offered him the use of his discount. That would give Joe the opportunity to buy a larger diamond at a sizeable savings. I didn't know the budget Joe had to work with, so I suggested he call Uncle John and discuss it with him.

A short time later, he brought home a ring selection in the price range Joe could afford. I would have preferred Joe and I doing it together but he wasn't sure, when he was coming home. If the ring needed sizing, which it did, he wanted it ready for the night he would give it to me. My choice was a solitaire in a white and yellow gold setting. I didn't select my wedding band at the same time. I was waiting to do that with Joe when he came home.

3 June 1953

Hi Beautiful,

Me again. Can't keep away from keeping in touch with you. I'm not sure but I think next week we take off on our two-week bivouac, (you probably can't pronounce it) where we'll be away from civilization for two whole weeks. There won't be any weekend passes. So honey if things don't work out I won't be home for your graduation. Would it be alright if we got engaged when I come home for a number of days after basic training? I'm not saying that we will have to wait until then but just in case, I want you to know ahead of time. I tell you not to worry that soon everything will turn out all right and I tell myself that too because sometimes, I stop and wonder if it will be alright. I don't know if you realize it or not but the day I put that ring on your finger I'll be the happiest and proudest guy in the whole world. That's what I dream about all the time while lying in bed. Maybe you don't believe it but I have all kinds of plans dreamed up in my mind. Things like, how I'll give you the ring, where I'll give it to you, and what I'll say. All I have to do is carry them out and I'll be happy. All I have to do is find out whether or not they are going to issue passes this weekend and if so, can I get one.

Just think, no more having people telling us what to do. We can go where we please and do whatever we please. It's going to be a big change in our lives and I'm sure you and I will be able to accept it and will surely enjoy it. You're going to make a perfect wife for me. I'm sure of that. We're also going to have the nicest kids you ever saw. All these dreams will come true someday, but there are three that can make all this possible, God, you and me. You and I must do our part. Pray to God that he will help both of us to be loyal and faithful and protect us from any evils that may occur. So beautiful there may be temptations, especially this time of year, but remember honey I love you enough to make you my wife. Please, don't spoil it. I couldn't stand any disappointments. Be good!

June 4

Joe called; he had a weekend pass and was coming home Saturday. When I went to school on Friday, I didn't say anything to my friends about Joe coming home or our getting engaged. So many times we'd made plans that for one reason or another never materialized.

I did tell Harvey, a boy in my homeroom who constantly asked me for a date.

"Joe and I are getting engaged this weekend."
"I don't believe you. It won't happen."
"It's true. If I don't get engaged, I'll go out with you."
"It's a deal."

June 6

Sitting on the porch glider, I waited for Joe to arrive. Mom and Dad joined me. Joe's arrival time came and went with no Joe. I worried that something may have happened to him on the way home or that his weekend pass had been cancelled. I went into the house, took off my shoes, and sat on the couch, worried about Joe and what I had foolishly promised Harvey.

Finally, I heard the car pull in the driveway. I put my shoes back on and went out on the porch. Joe ran up the porch steps, picked me up, kissed me, and apologized for being late. We chatted with Mom and Dad for a few minutes before we left. He seemed unusually quiet and didn't say very much as we drove to Durand Eastman Park and walked to an area overlooking Lake Ontario. We leaned against the metal railing and looked out across the lake. The moon glistened on the tips of the waves and the only sound we heard was the splash of the water rushing against the rocks. We embraced, and he held me tight for a few moments before reaching into his jacket pocket. He took out the box with the ring.

"I think we'd better step away from the railing," he said before opening it. "I don't want to drop it in the lake." He opened the box, removed the ring and took my hand.

"Honey, I've waited for this day for almost five years." He slipped the ring on my finger. I looked up into his face and waited for his lips to kiss mine.

He lifted me up off my feet. As he held me against his chest, I looked into his eyes and held his face with my hands as he had so often held mine.

"I love you, Joe."

"I love you, too, my darling, and no one is going to stand in the way of our getting married."

I remembered the words my mother spoke to me when I told her I was going steady with Joe. "The second ring Joe may give you is your engagement ring, your promise to marry him and to remain faithful." The last and final ring was still to come, the one that would bind us "until death parted us forever."

"My house is close by. We'll stop there first to tell my parents," Joe said. His voice was full of excitement as he talked about his plans for us as we drove to his house. We walked in the side door into the kitchen. His parents' were in the living room and came into the kitchen when we walked in. Joe and I stood in front of the kitchen counter.

"Mom, Dad, Mary Ann and I are engaged," Joe said. "I gave her an engagement ring."

I extended my hand to show them my ring.

"It's lovely," said his mother. His dad stood there with folded arms and didn't say anything. It was evident they didn't approve of the decision their son had made without their consent. We stood there for an uncomfortable few moments. I felt the same awkwardness as the time Joe brought me into the kitchen for a glass of water the day I rode my bike there. Joe broke the silence. "We're going to tell her parents."

Joe didn't say anything when we left. I knew he was upset because he didn't hear the congratulations he wanted from his parents. When he gave me the ring, why did he say that no one was going to stand in the way of our getting married? Was he late because he had discussed his plans with them before he picked me up? When we arrived at my house, Mom and Dad were in the living room. Joe stood with his arm around me.

"Dad, I want to marry your daughter. Do I have your permission?"

"Are you sure you can handle her?" Dad asked.

"Yes, I've been working on it for almost five years."

Dad shook his hand. "You have her mother's and my blessing." He opened a bottle of wine and toasted our future and happiness.

Joe called Ken to see if he was home. He was. We arranged to meet at the Quonset, a small restaurant bar in Fairport where Ken's dad played the piano. We spent most of the evening reminiscing about our high school years, the anxieties of exams, the afternoon Mr. Stalker, the boy's advisor, caught them skipping school, and the trips Ken made taking us back and forth from school to Ritz's on his motor bike. He reminded Joe of the punch he gave him when I asked him to be my date for the Sadie Hawkins Dance. Problems we thought were so important then were small compared to the real world we lived in.

Joe came over early Sunday morning. We went to church and spent the day at home. He said he just wanted to relax and spend a quiet day with his fiancé. Looking at him, I noticed that his shoulders had broadened and his hands that held my face when he kissed me were not as soft as they used to be. Carrying a rifle and digging foxholes had roughened his smooth soft hands. The boy I fell in love with was now the man I planned to marry.

Joe left Sunday evening. Monday I went to school and didn't mention the engagement to anyone. Harvey came over to me in homeroom and said I had to go out on a date with him because of the promise I made to him on Friday. I showed him my ring. "I don't believe you did it," he said. I told him I had gone steady with Joe since ninth grade. He kept saying, "I don't believe it." Hearing him, my girlfriends gathered around to see my ring and to ask when the wedding was going to take place. I had no idea when it would be.

Mom and Dad asked if Joe and I had plans about the type of wedding we wanted. I told them it was too early to decide. Dad told me his budget for the wedding expenses. If I exceeded it, Joe and I would have to reimburse the difference to him.

8 June 1953

Hi Beautiful,
Here I am with a new switch, writing to my girl I am now engaged to. I don't know about you, but it makes me feel very happy. We've waited a long time and it finally happened

honey. I love you honey and that is why we're engaged, although it did take us almost five years

Last night I stayed up late and went over to the Orderly room. I typed a letter to that base in California. My chances are rather slim of being stationed with that outfit. It wouldn't be a bad place to be after we are married and you can go with me. I'd like it very much and it would be a secure job in the Army and not have to worry about being shipped out for a period of time. I wouldn't want you to be left alone in the states with bills to pay and no one to turn to. I'd like to find out, if possible what I'd be doing in about a year so we can really make some serious plans. Any plans I make now will be serious ones for our future.

The more I think about it, going to California would be a good place for you and me to settle down, at least for a while. Maybe, we will come back and live in Rochester. I know that is what you want.

Well, beautiful, in about 10 minutes we're going to fall out for Bivouac and we won't be back until Saturday morning. While I am up there, I'll try to get some letters out to you. In order to get this one out tonight I better try to cut it short. I'll keep writing until I think it is almost time to fall out. You just keep thinking about me honey. I've loved you for five years and I'll love you for eternity, remember that honey.

Keep loving me beautiful. Don't forget to study for your exam Friday. Well I made it. Be good and write soon.

I had mixed emotions about living in California. It was something I didn't want to face. I believed Joe wanted to get far away from the influence of his parents. I, on the other hand, wanted to remain near my family. I knew in my heart if Joe really wanted to move to California I would go with him; that is where I belonged. His words about loving me for eternity filled my heart to overflowing with love for him.

17 June 1953

Hi Beautiful,

    Me again, trying to get a few lines out while I have a chance. Got a couple hours off this morning, so it's a good chance to write. We've been on night problems the last three nights and we're all beat. I'm happy so I can't complain too much about anything. I just keep thinking of you and I don't feel bad at all. I'm looking forward to you being able to come down for graduation. I'd like to show you around and let you see what your "honey" has gone thru. You'll probably get tired just riding around in a car. I've covered a lot of ground in the last fourteen weeks and I doubt if I'd like to go thru it again. It will soon be over and supposedly; I'll be a soldier much to my discontent. In other words, you can figure I don't like the Army or anything to do with it right now.

    I wonder how you are being treated now that you're engaged. I suppose all the kids in school were happy about it and teased you, as some of the guys here did to me. It's nice honey to be able to be home and see all the things happening. It won't be long before the time will come when I won't be seeing you for long periods. I know it's going to be harder than it ever was before, but honey I want you to be strong and understand that someday it will be over with and I'll be able to carry out our plans. The plans we've dreamed of for a long time. I trust in the Lord honey, so it's up to Him. With a little help from you and me, I think He will help us. Yesterday you took your last exam and I've been praying for you since last week. So I think by the time you receive this letter you will know all the praying helped. You're through with school honey. It was a long twelve years wasn't it. Now before we can be together it will mean another wait. Just remember honey as long as we stay with it the time is bound to go by. Someday we will be worried about our kids. We'll worry and fret when they get sick, but I won't complain; after being away for so long, I'd rather hear them screaming and yelling than sergeants and the guys. I'd like to relax just like Saturday night (June 6) when we e were so happy, not caring about anyone or anything in the

world except our own feelings.
Well beautiful, that's about it. Write soon. I love you.

My voyage from a naive eighth grader to a graduating engaged senior was ending. How did those five years pass so rapidly without any advance warning? Next month I would be eighteen. Memories converged in my mind like a kaleidoscope; each turn of the cylinder displaying fragmented bits and pieces of the past; my first conversation and date with Joe, going steady, the heartbreak of breaking up, the joy of making up, walking home, proms, final exams and our engagement. Now when I looked in the mirror, I saw the reflection of a young engaged woman. The realization that I would shortly be a wife with responsibilities was unsettling and exciting at the same time. Was I prepared for the responsibility? I believed my love for Joe was strong enough to carry us into the future.

Joe wouldn't be at my graduation; he couldn't get a leave. There was nothing else for me to do but work through the disappointment as I had done without him on other special occasions that he was not able to share with me.

29 June 1953

Hi Beautiful,
Tomorrow is the last day of training and I am glad to see it come. In the morning, we have a four-and-a-half-mile speed march. I hope it's not as hot as it usually is or a lot of guys won't be making it back. Tonight the guys have the usual horseplay of giving the cooks, and cadre showers with all their clothes on. It gives them a chance to get even for all the grief they gave us these past sixteen weeks. I am waiting for them to try to throw our first sergeant into the shower.
Everybody is in good spirits; at least until they get their orders. I am not sure what is going to happen to me. Every day you hear a different story, so I feel it's best to try to forget about it until the time comes. No matter what happens it will affect you in some way. In fact, anything and everything in my

whole life will affect you. I don't want you to be left behind forgotten. That is why you and I have to pull together no matter what happens. We've both told each other the same thing over and over, but let's face it honey things are going to start happening. The only trouble is that these things are going to be serious ones that may affect our lives. We'll both have to be careful honey, that's all we can do. At first, it will be hard like any other ordeal that we've gone thru but we've managed because we love each other and learned to live with them.

I hope someday honey you and I can spend a lifetime together without any interference from anyone. That's a dream isn't it honey, one that you and I have been wishing for, for a long time. We've never been able to enjoy one another's love yet have we honey. It can't be this way all the time, at least I hope not.

There's nothing I can promise you honey, but I can tell you the things that I wish. Take them for what they are because they come from the bottom of my heart. When I tell you, I love you I mean every word of it. How can a guy like me not help loving you? I am glad I saw you first so I would be the only one to enjoy your love and know in my heart when we get married, no one has ever enjoyed or cherished your love the way I will. That's it, honey. Be good and I'll see you soon.

Reading between the lines of Joe's letter, I knew he was trying to express his feelings regarding the fact that we would not be intimate until we were married. It was difficult for me too. I wanted him to love me but it had to wait until we were married.

With 16 weeks of Joe's basic training completed, Joe's parents, sister and I drove to Pennsylvania to attend the ceremony. We stayed at Uncle Frank and Aunt Theresa's house; they were Mary and Ralph's parents. It was a reasonable drive from Indiantown Gap. When Joe paraded by in Battery "B", I couldn't find him. We were sitting on bleachers a short distance from the parade grounds, but it was impossible to find him among the two-hundred plus men. Observing the graduating companies from the Battalion pass in review was an exciting and unforgettable experience. Their precision marching to cadence brought to mind the armed forces marching during WWII with the same esprit de corps. As they passed in review, I noticed their starched uniforms, highly polished brass on their collars and belt buckles, their boots with a perfect "spit" shine." They'd managed to survive sixteen weeks of rigorous disciplined training, something they couldn't have imagined they'd accomplish when they first arrived. After the ceremony, we met some of the "guys" Joe lived with for sixteen weeks. They all had the same comment; "Boy, I'm glad this is over." The looks of relief on their faces were quite evident, but the questions to follow were, "Where to and what next?"

We spent a couple more days at Aunt Theresa and Uncle Frank's house. While we were there, Joe said he was going to ask his cousin Ralph to be in the wedding. I asked Joe what he thought about my asking his sister to be my maid of honor. He said it was a thoughtful gesture.

Aunt Teresa's kitchen was a bit crowded with all of us there at the same time. Uncle Frank and Joe's father were on the porch drinking coffee. His cousins Ralph, Mary and Grace were sitting at the table with his mother and his sister.
Aunt Theresa was at the stove frying bacon. Joe and I were standing near the front window behind his sister sitting at the table.
"Ralph, I'd like you to be in the wedding," Joe said.
"Sure, I'd be happy to. When is it?"

"After I graduate from OCS next year."

I moved to the right of Marigrace's chair and tapped her on the shoulder.

"Marigrace, I'd like you to be my maid of honor."

She turned around and looked at me.

"I'm sure you must have a girlfriend you would rather ask," she said.

I felt the blood rush to my face. I looked at Joe. He saw my embarrassment. Yes, I did have someone else I could have asked. Out of respect, I thought she should have the honor, an error of judgment on my part.

"If you don't want to be my maid of honor, will you be a bridesmaid?" I asked once I regained my composure.

"Yes," she said, and turned back to the conversation at the table.

My suspicion that Joe's family was not in favor of our marriage was confirmed that morning.

12 July 1953

Hi Beautiful,

Another day's work done, my shoes are polished so I'll sit down and write to you. I don't mind working six days of the week but when you have to work on Sunday it's bad. All day today, I stood guard in our tower with a carbine slung on my back and watched prisoners play ball behind the stockade. My feet were sore toward the end of the day. I'm glad I'm leaving this place next Tuesday (14th) going back to Baker battery.

Well beautiful, the good news has finally come officially. I have been selected as a candidate for OCS. To top it all off I have my first choice. I told you when I called I thought I was going to Oklahoma for artillery school but when I went down yesterday much to my surprise I had orders for the Engineers in Virginia. I feel proud of myself. There are a lot of guys who are jealous because they would rather be in the engineers instead of the infantry. Just think honey I'll be able to do what I've been taught. If I'm lucky I will become an officer, I never thought I'd get this far. Maybe there is something good in store for us yet. This week I'll spend my time processing out of this camp and then if all goes right next weekend I should be thru and my fifteen-day leave will begin.

Just think honey, fifteen days' home together. That will be the longest I've spent with you in a long time. While I'm home, we can have our engagement party and make it official with the families and also if you have figured things out, I'll be home for your birthday for the first time in five years. The only drawback, the two weeks will be over and I won't see you for a very long time, but now the circumstances are different. You and I couldn't ask for anything better from the Army honey so let's not complain. I am now R A (regular army) which means an extra year to serve. Those last two years will be as husband and wife. I think that after I graduate from OCS I should be in a position to support a wife. That means we can take our vows soon. Honey we've a lot to be thankful for, and almost everything we've ever wanted we've received. Let's keep praying for the best and never let up. Well kid, keep your chin up and I'll see you soon.

I congratulated Joe on his acceptance to OCS. "You'll look great in a uniform. "I'll be the envy of all the girls walking next to the handsomest officer in the Army," I wrote. I knew the pride that he felt marching on the parade field to cadence and the band playing. I felt the same marching in the Memorial Day parade. Patriotism was a part of our upbringing and began in grade school.

From kindergarten to seventh grade, every morning before class began, we recited the Pledge of Allegiance, and our national anthem was sung at every assembly. In music class we learned the lyrics to "You're a Grand Old Flag," "God Bless America," the songs for each branch of the military and George M Cohan's "Over There," which was written during WWI and sung again during WWII when our country was fighting for the jeopardized existence of the life we enjoyed. As a nation, we were committed to preserving that way of life. We were grounded in the need for everyone, regardless of race, creed or political affiliation, to work together to end the war and bring home loved ones. Every man, woman, and child did what was expected of him, from rationing food and gas to going without bubble gum and stockings, so those we loved in uniform would be provided for. We had pride, respect and honor for those serving and prayed as a nation for their safe return. We both shared this national pride in our country.

In the summertime, my friends and I scoured the fields around our neighborhood to collect milkweed pods in paper sacks. We took them to school where our teacher collected them and gave them to a company that used the silky–tufted seeds inside ripe pods to stuff life jackets for buoyancy. The jackets were sent to military personnel.

For the first time since we started dating, Joe would be home to celebrate my birthday. He made dinner reservations at Carusoe's Italian Restaurant. I was eighteen, old enough to have a drink. Joe ordered wine, and while we waited for dinner, we joked about all the years he wasn't home for previous ones.

Our conversation during dinner included plans for our wedding, the possibility of him going to Korea and getting married after he received his commission.

. . .

I called Norma Schmidt and asked her to be a bridesmaid and Mary Navarra to be my maid of honor. My junior bridesmaids were my cousins, Darlene and Carol Ann, and the flower girl was my cousin, Janice, all daughters of my father's brother, Jim. Joe already had asked his cousin Ralph in Pennsylvania to be a groomsman, Ken to be his best man and my brothers Jim and Paul to be ushers. Tommy, my kid brother, was our ring bearer.

The Korean War ended in July. I was thankful that Joe

wouldn't have to face the danger of a tour of duty there. I wouldn't be able to go with him, but he'd be safe. We could make some definite wedding plans when he came home.

8 August 1953

To my dearest darling,

Hi sweetheart, I just finished talking to you and honey, I enjoyed every minute of it. You don't know how good it felt just to be able to talk to you for that short time. I imagine it was the Lords doing to be able to get you at my mother's house. I was rather disappointed when I called and you were not at home. I suppose you knew I was feeling bad. I was overjoyed just to be able to hear from home. It will probably be a long time before I get a chance to talk to you again, but we have to make the best of it. I suppose it is rather difficult for you to hear all my feelings and not be able to do anything about them. You helped me honey just by talking and writing to me the way you did. I can use every word of encouragement you can give me. You're acting just like the wife I want to have. Don't forget honey the plans we are making will come true.

Every word I said on the phone came from my heart beautiful. If only you knew how true, they were. I am sure you do but over the phone it is rather difficult to express my feelings as deeply as I want to. I know honey by hearing your voice that you love me very much. You wouldn't try to help me as much as you do if you didn't. Won't it be nice someday when we can live happily and live our life the way we want to? Someday in the near future I expect to make you my wife.

Do you remember that day long ago when we first met? I do very plainly, from that day on, we loved one another and in our hearts, we both started to plan our future together. That's why I'm here now honey, to help our future, yours and mine to be a happier one. I'll close now but there will be more letters to you. Be good my darling and keep praying for us.

Reading the plans and promises in Joe's letters kept me close to him and warmed my heart.

Ken was getting married, and Joe wasn't able to get a leave to come home to be his best man. Jerri asked me to be a bridesmaid, and I agreed. I was telling a friend about the wedding when she informed me I needed permission from my church to be in the wedding, because the ceremony was not in a Catholic church. I called the rectory, and she was right. I couldn't participate in a Protestant ceremony.

I hung up the phone. Another law made by man and not by God? How could I back out now without hurting my friends? What was so wrong with being in a wedding in a church of another denomination? It didn't make sense. Why would it be a sin? I decided to be in the wedding and not tell my mother what the priest said. Something else crossed my mind. Traditionally, Ken and Mary would be Godparents to our first-born child. Would the church allow Ken, a non-Catholic, to be Godfather?

6 August 1953

To my dearest darling,

Hi honey, I just received two of your very wonderful letters and enjoyed every minute while reading them. There were upper classmen all over us today. I forgot about it all and thought only of you.

Honey, you can't imagine how rough it is here. It's exactly like West Point and everything is expected to be the same. You eat at rigid attention one bite at a time, not eating before the head of the table does. You walk thru the halls stiff as possible and every time you walk, pass an upper clansman you have to ask, "Sir, may I pass?" After they check you over completely they may let you pass. The checking includes, shined shoes, pressed uniforms, polished buckle, shave, no strings on the uniform, tucked in chin, and clean fingernails. At night, we sleep between sheets, and put the blankets under the mattress to press them. In the morning, the bed is broken down in a strict inspection manner. We get up at 5:30 and from then to 5:50 you must shave, wash and dress with all the requirements on your uniform. We are not allowed to use contractions such as "don't"; we have to say, "do not". So honey maybe now you know some of the reasons why I am lucky I even wrote this letter tonight.

    Everyone here is on the Honor System. When we are asked a question, we are expected to tell the truth. All of our uniforms have to be tailor-fitted. One man went to the tailor and just fitting him and sewing his patches on all his uniforms cost him $35.00. I don't know if I am going to be able to afford that kind of money.

    I love you honey and I don't plan to spoil it by letting you think that I may be forgetting you. Like I said before, I may not graduate from this school but I may be spending my time here in the States and not miles away. You keep praying for the wedding in April and if the good Lord agrees it to be correct, I am sure, it will happen. Don't think for one minute I don't think about you because every time I do a lump comes up in my throat.

    I love you.

I wrote to Joe and offered to sew the patches on his uniforms. The problem with my offer was the period when he would need them and if he could get a pass to come home for me to do them.

We both would have days of loneliness, stress, and discouragement, but we knew we had to keep looking ahead. I wrote how important our letters were to keep us together in mind and heart. Patience was the weft tightly woven into the fabric of our relationship.

12 August 1953

Hi Beautiful,
    Looks like I'll be writing this letter piece by piece, but no matter I am still going to get it written. I've sort of settled down since my last letter, but it is still harder than ever to adjust to the routine. Right now, we are in study hall and we're supposed to be studying. I'm caught up with almost everything.

Maybe the good Lord is helping us along. Last Sunday I went to church and received communion again. It really makes me feel good inside knowing you're in direct contact with Him. I prayed and have faith that He will help us all He can. I imagine this is going to be a hard task trying to pull me thru OCS, but I am trying more than I ever have before. I think He knows our sincere attitude that we both want to get married soon. Don't worry honey He will take care of that. You told me in your last letter you were making your gown for Ken's wedding. Don't you wish we were in Ken's shoes right now?

Oh, those happy days when both of us were so happy not knowing what it was like to be lonely. We're both learning now, much to our disadvantage. You know a thought just came to my mind how jealous I used to be, but now it's different, I have more confidence in you than I've ever had even though I am further away than I've ever been. I think of you as my wife honey. The only thing missing is your wedding band and the happiness that goes along with it. We've talked about it so much that sometime we may get the thought our dream won't come true.

I thought at one time that our dream of being engaged would not happen because of the Army. Now our wedding day looks so much farther away, but before you know it we will be married and going to visit Ken and his wife, having coffee and talking as we used to. We will do exactly what we want without interference from anyone, and I mean anyone. We will make our own decisions and not have to answer to anyone. We'll be happy honey, not because we were meant for each other (we were), but because we appreciate one another and the love we share for each other has been stored up for such a long period of time. Stay with it darling and I will soon be home to hold you in my arms like you have never been held before. Be good honey.

Once again, he stated he would not be answering to, or allowing interference from, anyone regarding his decisions.

They would be his own. Who was he referring to"? What did he mean, "When will it end?"

16 August 1953

Hi Beautiful,

It's Sunday, just got back from church. I am starting to adjust to this place even though it is difficult. All you do in your spare time is fix your wall locker and foot locker display. I suppose there is a reason having to tightly fold and roll your underwear and socks and fit them in neat rows in the top tray of your footlocker, or hang your shirts in the wall locker facing the same way with the arm patches all in line.

Well honey, you sent me quite a few letters. I really appreciate all you are doing for me. I think if I were doing this on my own, it would be rather difficult. All I do is think about you and our wonderful plans and I tell myself I must continue.

Every day goes by with you in my mind honey. I don't think it would be possible for me to allow you to leave my mind for even a minute. I've said it before and I'll say it again, it isn't fair for us to be parted from one another's arms. Honey, how can you keep going and loving someone that you can't share your love with? I know what the answer is, because I go thru it every day. It's hard, but when you love someone deeply as I love you it not too difficult. Especially on weekends, when we used to go out and how about the long weekend I spent at Conesus Lake with you and your family? Do you remember how we enjoyed the time before we went to bed sitting on the dock, the cozy breakfasts, and the snacks we ate just before bed? It was wonderful darling and I wouldn't trade anything in the world for that memory. Yes, darling, now we can remember it all, unaware at the time the happiness we were enjoying.

By the way, how is your beautiful red hair coming along? I'll bet it is nice and long. You must be the sharpest girl in town, but be careful no one attempts to spoil my dreams and love for you. Well honey, this is all for now, be good and take care of yourself.

I remember the weekend Joe came home from college and joined my family at the cottage. We had a wonderful time with one exception; he lost his college ring in the lake.

Another incident occurred after Joe had gone fishing with my brothers. I had an argument with my mother, long forgotten but I left the room and went to lie down. An hour or so passed when Angie came in the room to ask if I wanted anything. She took one look at me and called my mother. I had developed a case of giant hives and had to be rushed to the hospital for a shot of adrenalin. My face looked like a balloon ready to pop; my eyes were swollen shut and my nose was twice its size. Joe came home from fishing and my mother said to him, "If you love her the way she looks, it must be love."

20 August 1953

Hi Beautiful,

Here it is almost the end of another week honey, the time is starting to go by a little faster but it still seems like years since I last saw you. So how are you doing at your job?

You know, every time I've written I've been so down hearted that I never actually told you what the school is like. Well first, of all honey I must say this place is beautiful. The school is located at the north end of the post, the newer section. There are about 15 brick buildings about the size of the Ranger School. There is a building called Humphrey's Hall with three floors of air-conditioned classrooms. There are no barracks or training areas in fact it looks like a college campus with grass, trees, flowers and swimming pools if you have a chance to use them.

I got a letter from mom the other day. She talked about us getting married and how hard it would be getting started and she wished things were not the way they are. Her last lines said, "Let me know ahead of time so I can get a dress, a real nice dress". It made me feel good honey, just to hear her say something like that.

How about a package? Be good baby and keep writing.

I was happy to read what Joe's mother had to say about our getting married. I think Joe was relieved to know she had finally accepted the fact that there was going to be a wedding. I wrote and asked him if we could get married in May instead of April. The weather would be sunny and warmer with less chance of rain.

August 25. 1953

Hi Beautiful,

I ran into a little extra work over the weekend and couldn't get straightened around fast enough to get a letter out to you. I'm writing this letter in one of my classes, that's the only chance I have. I suppose you're wondering what happened to all the letters you used to get every week, but I just got behind this week that's all. Not because I have forgotten you. I guess you must have been a little busy because I didn't get a letter on Saturday or Monday, but I'm sure I'll get one tonight.

Saturday night we left on another bivouac, this one wasn't as bad as the others were. We acted as the aggressors for the seniors. Our job was to keep them busy all night and not give them a chance to sleep. We didn't have much of a chance to sleep ourselves. I didn't mind, it was nice to be away from the area without someone down your neck all the time. We ate breakfast at 4:30am in the field and started back. We got back about 9:00am. I took a shower and went to church but couldn't receive communion. After church they started details on and off until 10.00pm.

That is enough of that. Let's talk a little about you and me. I bet your pretty little head is just filled with thoughts about next spring. If you would rather get married in May, it's alright with me. As far as I'm concerned, you can start making your plans now. The only worry you will have is about the Army and whether or not I will have enough leave time. I graduate 26 January. A little sooner than we planned. If everything turns out, we could wait until May. Keep saving your pennies and I'll promise you marry an officer, with the help of the Lord.

Every night when I go to bed, I dream and when I dream

honey, it is always about you. I think that is what keeps me from getting so lonely. It gives me the chance to see you and be with you almost real, but as always, I wake up. I may be disappointed but not lonely. All I think about is you home without me, going thru every day as a working girl, but engaged. Do you find time going by fast or slow honey? I imagine it must be worse for you because you have too much time to think. Don't let it get you down. Go on happily every day, keep that smile on your face at all times, and don't ever let it be gone.

Well beautiful, keep writing, say hello to your mom and dad and don't forget those pictures. Take care of yourself darling, and be good at all times.

30 August 1953

Hi Beautiful,

Well how is my darling this fine day? Here it is Sunday and another week has gone by. Not fast enough for me, possibly slower for you. It's hot here today, and by the looks of things, it's going to stay hot here for a while. Maybe you will have a chance to come down. Speaking of coming down, at the end of our "plebe" phase when we become juniors they have a party in Washington at one of the hotels. It would be wonderful if you could come. I know it is almost impossible to ask, but maybe you could figure out something from now until then. There is almost no sense in even thinking about it, but if there were some way of your getting here, I think I would be one of the happiest guys in the world. Perhaps your brother and his wife could come and chaperone. It would only be the weekend and wouldn't take much of their time. I know it seems hopeless but talk it over with them and your mother. Until I hear from you definitely, I'll still keep hoping. I could see you Saturday and all day Sunday. That may not seem a long time to you, but it would be a lifetime to me. If you can't make it, I will just forget about it. It would not be the same if you were not there. It would be a disappointment so if there is any way you could come it would mean the world to me.

Today I had off from 1:00 until 7:00 tonight and it is almost that now. I'm in the day room writing to you. I just saw the movie Paradise Island and all thru it I just kept thinking of you and most of the time I had a lump in my throat. Honey, we are going to get married just as soon as we possibly can. You can be sure we are going to get married next spring.

Before I forget honey, just to make it legal, "Will you marry me?" I know I forgot to ask when we got engaged so before I go any further I'd better propose right now. Maybe in years to come we can both sit down and read this letter and smile at the idea of me asking you to be my wife in a letter, but now it is legal. So keep being happy and try not to be too lonely while I am away. Soon we will be able to be with each other.

See what you can do about coming. I love you.

I was anxious about asking permission to go to Washington for the weekend. When I finally found the courage to ask, Mom was astonished I would ask such a thing. An engagement ring on my finger was not a license for me to do whatever I wanted while I lived at home. Her answer was a definite no without question. What was I thinking of, taking a trip alone to meet my fiancé? I knew my mother was thinking about what the neighbors, busybodies who had nothing better to do than tarnish my reputation, would say. No matter how I tried to convince her, she would not budge. I was about to say, "I am engaged to be married, I am not 14, I am not a child, I'm old enough to do what I want." I decided not to plead my case. I knew from experiences my argument would not be considered. Dad didn't respond at all to my request. Mom did all the talking and gave him no chance to voice his opinion. I glanced at him and wondered if his answer would have been the same. My frustration was clearly visible to him, but he knew there was nothing he could do to change her mind.

Monday was Labor Day and we had a family picnic. Dad's sister, Molly, was there, and I asked her opinion about my going to see Joe. I told her about my Mother's refusal to let me go, and she looked squarely at my mother.

"Pauline, don't you trust her?" she asked.

"Yes, I trust her," my mother said.

"Has she given you reason not to trust her?"

"No, it's not her I'm worried about."

"If she were going to do something wrong, she wouldn't have to wait until she went to Washington. I'm sure opportunity is available at home. If you're more concerned what your neighbors will think, why tell them? Think about your daughter."

I loved my aunt for telling my mother what I couldn't. She spoke up for me, said I was old enough to know the difference between right and wrong and that I should be trusted. My mother gave in. I immediately wrote to Joe that I would be in Washington for the party.

9 September 1953

Hi Beautiful,

I received your wonderful letter today and when I say wonderful that was the best yet. After receiving two letters saying "no", I was not going to give up hope. There was something inside me that kept saying she will come. Ever since I found out about the party I prayed a special prayer after communion asking please, let it be possible for you to come down for the party. I had the feeling you were going to but I was glad to read you had no doubt you were coming. It's the nicest thing your mother could have done for you. I remember one other time, she did us a special favor and your Dad took me back to Wanakena after your junior prom. This means a little more honey.

Oh honey, I'll be happy to show you off among all the rest of the girls that will be here. As for meeting you at the airport there may be a problem. If you got here Saturday morning, I could not be there. I could be there in the afternoon to meet you; in fact, I am sure I can. Here is the problem, every day we are inspected for demerits of our areas which includes almost anything from dust on the floor to unauthorized vehicles.

For the whole year, only six demerits are allowed and anything over that you have to start pulling work tours, which could restrict you for a whole weekend. I don't believe our Tactical Officer would do that and secondly I am the one that has the job of recording demerits. So one way or another I will be there Saturday afternoon unless you would rather come to the school instead of meeting me at the hotel. I would prefer the latter. It would be easier for me to find you, than for you to find me. I'll send you the name of the hotel and phone here at school. This way we are sure of getting in touch with one another.

Honey it is now Thursday morning and I have to hurry to get this letter done so I can mail it out to you. I prayed again last night and thanked the Lord for his wonderful favor. I can't tell you what to wear because I haven't been around to see what is in style, so use your own judgment. Thank your mother a special thank-you and tell her I really appreciate what she is doing. I love you.

September 12 was Mom's 44th birthday. Instead of a birthday cake dad bought her a Black Forest chocolate cake at Wojack's bakery on Hudson Avenue. Aunt Mary and Uncle John came over after supper and we went on the porch, cut the cake and enjoyed the birthday celebration. Mom said she didn't want a cake because she was trying to lose weight, but Dad knew better when he bought her favorite.

13 September 1953

Hi Beautiful,

It is Sunday morning about 10:00. I just got back from church and communion breakfast and decided to come to the phone center rather than go back to the barracks and pull detail. Its quiet here no phones to bother you. I read your last letter and was happy to see there were no changes made in our plans.

You asked how much time we would have together. It would be all day Saturday until 2:00am and all day Sunday until 6:30pm. I think the time will be worth it so don't fret your pretty little head.

There is a cool breeze blowing today and it reminds me of the mountains. The leaves haven't changed colors yet but the wind is blowing them off a little at a time. That will probably be our next job, raking the leaves. I hope they hold off until I become a junior so I can supervise the job instead of doing it.

When I think back over the period of time and how long I've been in the Army and away at school, it gives me a funny feeling how long I've been away from you and my family. When I graduate, it will be a year in the service. This time it did seem faster than it did at school. I suspect it wouldn't be fair to compare school with OCS. I shouldn't complain. I chose to come here, and now that I am here, I am going to graduate for you and my own self-satisfaction.

There are times honey I just sit and daydream about you. The time we spent at Conesus Lake seems to come back to me the most. I don't know why, but it must be that we had such a wonderful time together. No matter what I am doing with you, it always seems we are having a good time. I guess It's because I love you so much. Be good honey, I love you.

This wasn't my first experience flying. However, the plane was much larger and safer than the one I took on my first flight. When I was four, my family attended the 1939 New York State World's Fair. The day was clear, cloudless and sunny when we visited many of the pavilions.

As evening approached, my father asked my brother Sonny and me if we would like to take an airplane ride with him to see the Fair's lights at night. My brother said no; I said yes. Dad and I drove to an open field and walked to a mowed strip where the plane was. It was an open bi-plane with one wooden propeller and two seats. Dad lifted me into the seat behind the pilot and climbed in. I stood up behind his shoulder. There were no seat belts.

The pilot raised his arm and made circles with his hand to the man on the ground to start the engine. The man reached up and pulled down on the propeller a couple of times until the engine engaged. We taxied down the grassy field. I was happy, smiling as I stood behind my father's shoulder. That is until we were airborne. The wind blew in my face and hair; I was scared.

    The only sound I heard was the plane's engine. Suddenly, and without warning, the pilot banked hard to the left. My position behind my father shifted. I slid out from behind his shoulder to the end of the seat; my eyes fixed downward the entire length of the wing. I thought I was going fall out as we circled around the Trylon and Perisphere.

    "Daddy, I want to go down," I said repeatedly, almost yelling.
    "Don't be afraid. I'll hold you in my lap," he said, trying to comfort me.
    "I don't like it!"

    The view must have been spectacular but I didn't see a thing because my face was buried deep in his chest.

    I arrived in Washington around noon. Joe wasn't there when I landed. I confirmed my return flight to Rochester on Sunday at 6:00pm, went to baggage claim, picked up my suitcase and waited for him in the lobby. An hour later he came into the terminal, walked quickly toward me and put his arm around me. I felt his quick, soft kiss on my mouth.

    He checked me into the 2400 Hotel in Washington where the party would be held and said he would be back to pick me up about 6:00. He had to be back on post until then. I wasn't prepared to be alone. His letter said we would be together Saturday and Sunday. I knew he had to be on post at night, but I assumed we would be together until then. I locked the door and put a chair beneath the handle.

I looked around the room and noticed how large and lavishly decorated it was. Three walls were painted a pastel shade of peach and the wall behind the bed was papered with an Oriental cherry blossom design. The tailored bedspread in muted shades of peach and grey matched the drapes on the large window. Nightstands on either side of the bed held tall brass lamps with silk pleated shades. A phone and clock were on one nightstand, a radio and an ashtray on the other. I had no idea hotels were this elaborate.

I unpacked and hung up my dress and the suit I was wearing in the closet. I put on my bathrobe and took my makeup case into the bathroom. I read a magazine and touched up my manicure. At 5:00 I freshened up, dabbed some Tabu, the first fragrance Joe had given me, on my wrists, behind my ears and on my shoulders. One of Joe's work responsibilities at Greenberg's Pharmacy was stocking shelves, including those holding cosmetics and perfume. I remembered the night he came over and handed me a Valentine's Day gift wrapped in red and white tissue paper. When I opened it, there was a tube of Max Factor lipstick, a lipstick brush and the perfume. He said the color of the lipstick was for redheads and he liked the smell of the perfume. I approved of his choices.

. . . . .

At 5:30, I heard a knock on the door. I thought it was too early for Joe because he said he would pick me up at 6:00.

"Who is it?"
"Your husband."
"Who?" I asked, laughing."
"Your husband."
I opened the door; Joe came in and kissed me.
"You're wearing the perfume I gave you."
"Yes, I am, and you're early. I have to put on my dress."

"Not yet." He lifted me up into his arms and walked toward the bed. He set me down and sat beside me and kissed me.

"I've missed you, longed to hear your voice tell me how much you love me. My constant desire is to make love to you."

Yes, I knew how he felt. My desire surfaced as he kissed and embraced me. Once more, I was on the threshold of knowing him intimately. This was not sitting in the car with him the night of my junior prom when he wanted to make love to me and I told him we had to wait. The opportunity was here to take advantage of.

The second stage will be fondling and caressing, the third is intimacy reserved between a husband and wife.

Mom's words rang in my ears. Was it the fear she would somehow find out? Whatever it was, it was important for me to wait until the wedding when I could release the passion I'd stored for such a long time without fear or guilt.

I stood up. Joe looked at me.

"We're going to be married in a few months," he said softly.

"I know honey, but we're not married yet. We have to wait."

"I promised that I would never force you to do what I wanted and I won't now."

I took my dress from the closet and changed in the bathroom.

We stayed at the party until 1:00am, dancing and talking to Joe's friends. The evening passed quickly and knowing, he had to report on post before 2:00am; Joe took me to my room.

He said he would see me in the morning for breakfast. I closed the door, put the chair under the handle and went to bed thinking of the wonderful time I had. I thought how easy it would have been to break my promise and let him make love to me. No one but the two of us would know. With the lingering fragrance of Tabu on my pillow, I thought about Joe, his body next to mine. Our wedding day would not come soon enough.

It was after 10:00 when Joe arrived the next morning. He apologized for being late, but he had obligations to meet before he could leave the post. He also had to wait for his friend to pick up his date. The four of us planned to spend the day together. We decided to go out for brunch and drive around Washington, stopping at the Washington Monument, Lincoln Memorial, The Capitol and Mt. Vernon. It was a whirlwind tour to see as much as we could in such a short time. I took some pictures from the car as we drove past historic buildings not open to the public on Sunday.

Joe had to be back on post by 6:00, so we had to say goodbye sooner than planned.

"I'll walk you to the entrance," Joe said. "I have to be

on post the same time your flight leaves." I kissed him and held back tears until I reached the waiting room.

Waiting for my flight to leave, I thought about the countless times Joe and I had said good-bye during the past years, and there were more to come. I daydreamed about our wedding and the two of us making love. My heart was hurting, and I wondered if it would ever stop. Why were our moments of love and joy so rare? When would we be able to spend time together without worry of someone or some circumstance overshadowing our happiness?

My return flight was nothing like the flight down. The sound of thunder confirmed we were in the middle of a storm. Suddenly, flashes of lightning illuminated the dark clouds and torrential rain pounding against the plane. I noticed electrical sparks in the rear of the propellers' housing, and thought we were going to lose an engine. The flight attendant must have noticed my anxiety. She reached across my seat and pulled the shade down on the window to block out the storm. The seat belt and no smoking signs remained on for the entire flight; no one left their seats, not even to go to the restroom. The plane would swing with jerky movements from side to side or rise and drop suddenly. I didn't get sick, but I was afraid. My stomach said hello to my throat more than once. It was pouring when we landed. Dad was waiting with an umbrella as I left the plane and walked toward him.

"How was your flight?"

"Horrible! The storm was so bad I thought I would throw up and never get home."

I took his arm as we walked into the terminal to the baggage area.

"You probably won't want to fly again. Were you afraid as the time we took the plane ride at the World Fair?"

"Yes, but I was four years old, cried, and, you held me until we landed. I felt like crying on this flight, but I'm not four and you weren't there to hold me."

When I arrived home, I looked at my Mother with a clear conscience.

8 September 1953

Hi Beautiful,
You're gone and it seems like a long time since we were together. I can't complain. I wouldn't trade anything in the whole wide world for those two wonderful days.

From the time I saw you until the time we left one another it was just perfect. I felt awful having to leave you all alone at the airport. I kissed you and you turned and went thru the door, and that was the last I saw of you. I'm glad you didn't turn around because it would have made things harder. It was a long ride back and until the airport was out of sight, my eyes kept looking back thinking I would see you and your red hair. It all seems like a dream and here I am back at OCS waking up to the fact I won't see you until Christmas. Yes, honey, it's all like a dream now, but everything is so clear and I know deep down inside that it did happen. You're back home now honey. I clocked every minute of your plane ride; when you got off the plane at 9:30, it was all just as clear as if I were there. At 6:30, I was on the parade field thinking about you getting on the plane. It was turning to dusk, and the sky looked beautiful. That glowing pink, shining through the scattered grey clouds, left there by the happiness and few minutes' sadness of the day. One minute the sky was glowing with wonderful beams of sunshine, then shadows fell and finally darkness came. How well it related to our own day, a day of happiness spent, and at the airport where the last spark of laughter, love and enjoyment was felt and finally darkness and the long ride back to camp alone, alone again until far off Christmas.

Not all is lost. I still have memories, and I think I am capable of weathering the storm. After all, it's not that we haven't been separated before. You have your job to fulfill and I have mine. Someday our highways of happiness will cross and combine into a super highway of marriage and success, and then no man will stand in our way. Together both of us can make a success of life. When we are apart, we are walking in the sea of loneliness. We prayed to be with one another and the good Lord answered our prayers. Now we are sorry to leave one another. Thank you again honey for coming and thank your mom and dad for their permission.

Now let's finish up with you. How did it feel going back? I'll bet all the girls at work were full of questions. You probably spent every break talking about Washington. Did you enjoy the plane trip back? If I know you, you were too wrapped up in thoughts and didn't wake up until you got to Rochester. Keep writing. Good night my love.

Of all the letters Joe has written this is one I hold most dear. He was almost poetic in his description and comparison of the evening sky to our last moments together. None before or after compared to this emotional description of the love in his heart for our future and me.

Making plans for the wedding included the purchase of a wedding gown and veil. I had a picture in my mind of what I wanted to wear. Occasionally after work, I went to bridal shops and tried on a few gowns. Those I liked were too expensive. Why not design the gown and make it myself?

I sketched the gown that I wanted; a fitted bodice with a dropped waistline, square neckline and love point long sleeves. The skirt with a chapel train would be softly gathered at the waist with fullness at the hemline. Fabric-covered buttons on the sleeves and back bodice completed the design I wanted to wear. I believed a simple design made in the most elegant of fabrics would be the best choice.

I went to Brodsky's Fabric Store and looked in pattern books for wedding gowns. Turning the pages, I saw a pattern similar to the design I drew. With a few alterations, I could make my gown for much less money than those I tried on in the bridal shops.

My fabric choice was lace over satin. The sales person suggested the ivory Alanson or the silk Chantilly with a scalloped edge because of my complexion and red hair. I chose the delicately patterned Chantilly with the scalloped edge to use at the hemline and trim the neckline. I asked the salesperson to hold it until I discussed it with my mother.

When I talked to Mom, she said making the gown was a good idea, and if I needed help Aunt Mary would be happy to lend a hand. Her only concern was the ivory lace instead of white lace. I compromised and used white satin for the lining. The contrast highlighted and defined the fine delicate pattern of the Chantilly. We purchased the fabric and the pattern, which I altered and put away until we set the wedding date.

October 4, 1953

Hi Honey,

Here it is Sunday and I have time to write. Boy, things were fouled up this week and I didn't have a chance to. Last Wednesday they made me section leader and my head hasn't stopped spinning yet. What a job that was taking care of the class with 39 men in it. I was relieved of it at 12:00 this afternoon.

Guess what? I met three fellows here that graduated from Ranger School. It sure made me feel good to see those guys again. The other day I was marching the class to get our bus when I heard someone in another class (plebe) call my name; I nearly fell over when I saw who it was. It wasn't any of the guys I hung around with though. Being Rangers I guess they all qualified for OCS.

Well back to the duties of being a junior. I've really taken an interest in these new plebes and I'm doing all I can to shape them up. The poor guys have only been here for a week and they don't know what is happening. They can't understand how all the work can be done in so short a time. I spent all last night and this afternoon helping them. I had a pass too but instead of using it, I went to the store and bought them a whole mess of stuff that they needed. On the way back I stopped and had dinner with one of my friends. It felt good to be able to get out and eat like that once in a while. I'm their study hall mentor and it's my job to see they keep it quiet and also I am supposed to answer any of their questions they may ask me. You would be surprised if you heard some of them. I do the best I can.

How are you doing honey? It has been a week since we last saw one another but to me it seems like years. You wait so long for something dear to you and then before you know it the time has come and passed so quickly that it all seems like a dream. We should have taken more pictures because some day we can look back and remember all those beautiful experiences. Mom wrote and told me you went there last week. I'm sorry she couldn't find those biology notes. They are there somewhere.

Well honey, I've talked a little about a lot of things but not enough about us. Remember honey I do love you no matter what or anything that may happen. Keep writing and be good.

I wrote and told him I was going to make my gown and bride's maids' gowns. Joe's mother said she would make his sister's gown to take some of the burden off my shoulders. Mom said she would have a local dressmaker make hers.

16 October 1953

Hi Beautiful,

Just got back from bivouac and I feel knocked out. We left early Sat morning and got back Sunday. It was an overnight problem with the juniors and seniors on the defense with the plebes attacking us all night. It was warm in the daytime but at night it sure gets cold. We were machine gunners and our foxhole was rather large so we had a little more room to spread out but that ground was still hard. It got cold so we got into our sleeping bags and waited for them to come. They sent out patrols all night trying to keep us awake.

About 4:00 am, they threw everything they had at us, including tear gas. At first, I thought it was fog, but then I smelled something sweet and my eyes started to burn and I started to choke so I had to put on my gas mask. We ate our breakfast, filled in our foxholes, rolled our packs and started the long march home. When we got back, we had all the equipment, rifles and other guns to clean. We had been lying in that dried clay and it was just like powder and got all over everything, including our clothes. Now you know where my money goes-to clean all my clothes.

The other night while lying in the foxhole, I was thinking about the good old days and the night of our engagement party. Oh how I loved you that night. I was feeling good I'll admit, but I still knew that girl with the red hair was the most wonderful girl in the world.

These autumn days remind me when I used to walk you home from school. It also reminds me of the football games we went to sometimes. It may have seemed I didn't want to go to them honey, but it sure was fun. Remember when I used to play football for the Durand's? Or how about the time we went on the hayride, it was around this time of year, or even Halloween when we had some good times together. Yes honey, this sure is a mystic season. It brings back all the wonderful memories we used to share together. Someday I'll live a life of "forever autumns" and they will be spent with you.

I'd been grounded because of that hayride. I told my mother we were going to a movie, but when we got home, she saw a piece of hay in my hair. I don't know what she had against hayrides, but it was another activity I couldn't participate in.

18 October 1953

Hi Honey,

Today I received your long awaited letter. I was beginning to wonder if you were too busy or something. I shouldn't complain you are doing good things not bad. You must be quite busy with all your sewing. Letters reflect quite a lot of how a person feels even though they are not written down on paper. It is hard for me to visualize what does go on at home and I am in no place to say how you will spend your time.

Maybe if I spent a little more time trying to get more letters out to you, or at least regularly even thought I am taking time during a study hall and classes, then maybe I could expect to get more letters in return. I think our biggest problem now is that we are both in a lazy mood where we haven't anything really interesting to put into our letters to make them appealing to read. That may not be the reason and it does not necessarily reflect my attitude or feelings but we both have to do something about our letter writing.

I am not scolding you but both of us for just writing letters. You know yourself, at least I do, when you get a letter you are really waiting for, you expect it to be more than we are just doing fine and how much we love each other. After two years of letter writing, I guess we both ran out of the method of writing that interesting letter that leaves you with the feelings that I used to experience at school, that we were the happiest people in the world. We always had something to put in our letters because the Sunday before we had just seen each other and had a wonderful time together. Now, our being together is few and far between and our letters lack the basic feeling necessary to establish that motivating factor which build up or ego and make us look forward to each day with a new life. I think we both should sit and analyze our letters. Truthfully honey they are lacking that certain something. Aren't they? I have a long stay in the Army and it's going to involve a lot of *letter writing to keep us both close and loving one another. So what do you say we throw out the old method of writing and start all over again? It may mean a little more effort on each other's part but let's take that little extra time to get those interesting letters in the mail to one who is waiting for them with an eager heart.*

Honey, I've attempted to figure out our situation in a short time. Maybe it has done some good and maybe it hasn't. I know one thing, someone had to start and if takes me till "lights out" I'll try. Honey even though I may complain in these letters remember it comes from the heart to benefit our love for one another. I keep thinking all the time and have that feeling that you are mine. You aren't forgetting your lover who is so far away, longing for the day when we can be together, are you? Those wonderful times we shared a few months back still go thru my mind. It's something that keeps me going. Thanks honey for all those wonderful times. We may be far apart honey, but I can feel you and see you as if you were here in my arms. How I long to be holding you, looking into those wonderful eyes and you with your head tilted back, looking up at me with your eager heart and lips waiting for that long awaited kiss. That is what I picture when we meet again. That is something I look forward to more than I ever did before in my life. There would be nothing to come home to if you weren't there. So honey, let me keep those feelings that someday I'll be home again and we can be happy as we were so long ago.

Remember honey, let's both keep writing a little extra and it will make our days go faster. I love you.

Perhaps I was a little slack on romance in my letters. I was working during the day and planning our wedding in the evening. I shared those plans in my letters to Joe. There were a few times when Joe was in college I felt a lack of love and tenderness in his letters and he understood. I guess it was my turn to reciprocate. He wanted to read about the love I had in my heart for him, my longing for him; and to be re-assured we were going to be together to fulfill our hopes and dreams.

Being absorbed in what I was doing, I didn't realize he was depressed and had doubts about his progress in OCS.

2 November 1953

Hi Beautiful,

Another month and time keeps going by day by day. I said in my last letter that I thought it would be nice to put something new in our letters. Well I probably put something new in this letter tonight but I am not satisfied.

Maybe you have noticed and maybe you haven't, but I've been down in the dumps these past few weeks. There is a very good reason for all this and it really makes me feel lousy. It seems that every time I strive for a certain goal I have the worst difficulty reaching it.

You and I have been praying for me to make it thru this school to become a 2nd lieutenant. Since I came into the junior phase things have not been going so well, mainly academics. I have a passing average but it should be higher. Remember when I was a plebe and I wrote and told you about the board and the action they take if a person is deficient? If you are, you are called before the board to review your case. If they think you are capable and have fallen down somewhere along the line they give you a "turn back" which may mean turned back from six to twelve weeks. On the other hand, it they think you won't make it you are dropped out completely. I may have to go before the board next week. If I were turned back honey it would be an awful blow to me. It could be another six or twelve weeks and I couldn't graduate until May sometime. If it were six weeks, it would be March. So you see honey I've lost a lot of my ambition and it has the hell knocked out of me thinking and worrying about those dam academics. I haven't given up hope, but believe me it's hard to understand. The reason I haven't given up is because I keep thinking to myself I'll make it and if this is a period of suffering and worry I am really living the part. I hope this doesn't make you feel as bad as it does me because if I were turned back I would not graduate in time for us to be married when planned, but honey I am the one that has to go thru it all over again. It would take a lot of courage and if I had to, I could do it. I have initiative to go on, but now it is very difficult and I will keep going if I know that you are still behind me and want me to go thru it all again if I need to.

I am still the same Joe honey and I do love you as much as before, just somewhat discouraged. Maybe next time you hear from me I'll have something better or worse to tell you. Be good and keep your chin up.

I knew Joe was upset and under stress. When he was discouraged at school, I wrote more often to assure him that everything was going to work out. He didn't want to disappoint me if he were set back six weeks. What if writing letters to me interfered with his studies? I wanted to tell him he could write whenever he had the time and not be concerned about keeping his promise of two letters a week. I thought a phone call would relieve some of his stress and the pressure. Hearing his voice would help me, too. This was another hurdle we would face together.

8 November 1953

Hi Honey,

It sure was good to talk to you on the phone Saturday night. It's been such a long time since we have spoken to one another. It made me happy to tell you that everything is going to be alright and soon I'll be a senior. Not only that but I'll be home for Christmas and we will be together again, happy in each other's arms.

It also makes me think of the days to come when I'll be a 2nd lieutenant and shipped far away from you. What are you going to do when you probably won't see me for a long time? In a few months, graduation will take place, and I may be stationed far away from you. What do we do then honey? Eventually I will have to go overseas and leave you home alone again. Right now, I'm thinking about the time right after graduation from Ranger school getting ready to leave for the Army, when your dad and mine talked to me about being an officer. I had no intentions whatsoever about becoming one. Look at me now, doing exactly what I said I wasn't going to do.

Is it for the better? I think it is honey, and I would give anything to have those lieutenant bars on my shoulders.

Every night I pray that I'll make it through this school, and I say, "Please dear Lord let me graduate not only for my sake but for Mary Ann's also". It would spoil many plans if I don't make it but remember honey I am trying especially for your sake and our future life together. The other day I filled out papers starting the process to become an officer. For the first time I signed my name as a second lieutenant and it really makes you feel good inside to know that you'll be an officer, and you'll be respected for what you stand for; an officer of the United States Army, an Army that has been the greatest since it started and has not been defeated. That is another reason that makes me keep on going and trying. You never told me how you feel about me becoming an officer. Does it mean as much to you as it does to me? I hope you'll feel proud, as I will be walking down the street, your arm in mine going out to dinner or even going to get our marriage license.

Well honey, things are coming to a close, write soon. I love you very much. Send a package if you think about it.

I thought of what Joe was doing for our future, and I couldn't imagine the pressures and frustrations he was experiencing. I was proud of him becoming an officer. He would have some interesting stories to tell our children about his experiences in the military, being stranded in a flood in Kansas or running out of gas when he crossed the desert in California.

I sent him a $25.00 money order, so he could use it to buy himself Thanksgiving dinner or keep it on hand for an emergency. He was paid once a month, so he could use it when he ran low on funds.

19 November 1953

Hi Beautiful,

    Today I received your little note and just sat down to read it. Honey you sure surprised the heck out of me. I never expected to receive a money order from you. I'll tell you one thing honey it helps near the end of the month. I'll save it for Thanksgiving and go out and buy dinner.

    Tomorrow we become seniors and receive our new brass. They will be castles worn on both collars. As juniors, we wore two U.S. pins. The other night four of us moved from the junior squad room to a senior squad room. Within the room was a small single room where one man slept and the three other men slept in the open area. I was lucky because I was assigned the single room. My room is twice the size of the one I had at Ranger School and I like the idea of living in a room all my own. No one around to bother you. We have to keep the room in "inspection order". We have a rubber tile floor and every morning from 0630-0700 we get down and hand paste wax the floor and hand buff it with Turkish towels, the brass is polished, windows washed and everything dusted. When we leave in the morning at 0745 the place is "standing tall; wall lockers opened, bedding rolled neatly and book cases dusted with books aligned. I'll make a good husband after going through 22 weeks of this sort of training. The only thing missing in the room now is a radio to play at night. We were thinking of getting a wall clock but we figured that was going a little too far. If we started that, we would soon want a television set in here and that wouldn't go. Tomorrow morning as usual we have an inspection, a complete inspection, with open footlockers and all. One good thing, everybody works together and we are all one big happy family here. After all, we are seniors now and we can get away with a little more than the plebe or junior can. We are the "top dogs" now.

    They told us today how much time we have coming for our Christmas leave. Getting 15 days leave before I am only eligible for 12 days. That is still a good vacation honey. We can't complain and I'll be satisfied to have that time to spend with you. Although it may spoil our New Years together, so chin up and be thankful no matter what happens. You'll be working during most of the time I am home but I will be with you every chance I get. Remember when I used to pick you up after work, or we had lunch together? We'll be doing more of that soon honey.

As for Christmas honey, if possible I'd like to have you over my parent's house for one of the meals. We might go out alone somewhere and enjoy being together. I've just been informed I've got to stand a formation at 9:25 tonight so I'd better hurry, I've got about six minutes. Besides that, I have to get my footlocker in shape so I'll rush a little. Maybe someday, you will realize how little free time I have. Until then honey, be good and I'm looking forward to the Thanksgiving package you promised to send. I'll never stop loving you.

I sent him a package with his favorite snacks to munch on when he was studying, writing, or relaxing. I tried to express my loneliness without him and the longing to be with him again. I was trying to do what he asked, but he wasn't writing the words I wanted to hear. I needed to read the passion he felt in his heart and his desire to be near me to pull me through my lonely days and nights.

There were moments during this period when I questioned my decision not to go to New York. Something was missing, and I couldn't explain what it was that was bothering me. I loved Joe and wanted to marry him, but I also wanted to go on to school. His plan to be married after his commission from OCS prevented my doing so. I was unable to voice my frustration. It just wasn't done. I relinquished my dream by agreeing to his for the two of us. I let him know that I'd go to his house for Christmas Day dinner, the day I knew that his mother would want.

23 November 1953

Hi Beautiful,

I was glad to hear from you today. In fact, it even made my stomach feel good. I enjoy something from home especially during study hall. Good thing there are only four of us in this room, but there are some who always stop in to see what you got from home and you can't turn them away. I doubt it will last until the end of the week. I also got a package from mom, she sent up homemade cookies so that will also help out. No matter how long they last, I appreciate what you send and it will also help Thanksgiving Day to go by a little better.

This morning we got our new plebes and they look like a good crew. Saturday we became seniors and we had a big ceremony for the plebes who became juniors. It really makes you feel good to know all these men shaped up because of our hard work. Once they get that junior brass pinned on they look and act like future officers. We have our new plebes and it is up to us as seniors to make sure they get the best training to become seniors and officers.

Well honey, how are you doing? Just a few more weeks and I'll be home. I don't know about you, but I am looking forward to those days' home with you. It will be great to be with you and the folks at Christmas. I didn't think I would be home this Christmas. If I weren't so lucky, I would probably be in Korea or some other forgotten place. I am thankful to be here in the states especially at Christmas. You keep praying for both of us kid and I am sure that things will be alright. Someday soon, we will be able to live the life that I dream about every night.

I wish it were graduation day, and you were here to pin my bars on and we were ready to go home for a few days. I'll write again tonight. Boy, being a senior keeps you busy. For you I have to make it thru this school so I'll cut it a little short.

Be good and have a nice Thanksgiving. I'll be thinking about you as always.

This was the second Thanksgiving in a row that Joe would not be able to come home. There was so much we had to be thankful for, our engagement, our wedding, the end of the Korean War and Joe's graduation from OCS in January.

26 November 1953

Hi Honey,

Today is Thanksgiving and most of the day I thought about Christmas and being home with you. I guess it's the holiday spirit that set me in the mood, but I sure did feel it. It won't be long now and I'll be home with you. I am really going to enjoy myself for those few days. Besides that, my Dad bought a new car and it will be fun to take you for a ride in it. In fact, I will probably have the car most of the time taking you out to one place or another. I would really like to go dancing. I guess it's just the idea that you are so tiny and easy to move around. The real reason is you know how to dance so well and I enjoy dancing with you.

One of those nights, I'd like to spend with Ken and Jerri. It seems you haven't seen them since I left. They were such good friends and we did have a lot of fun together. We'll have to ask them all about married life and get a few pointers. I really don't think it will be necessary because we are capable of handling it on our own. Just the idea of getting married soon keeps me thinking all the time.

Honey we will be happy, I know that. We were meant for each other from the first day I saw you in grade school. Oh honey, how I wish I could put the next ring on your finger so that I can call you my wife. Honey that day seems so far away and yet we both have so much confidence in that day. I can see you in your wedding gown waiting for the moment we can call each other husband and wife.

Tomorrow is my dad's birthday and I did want to send him a card but because of the holiday, mail was not picked up so he won't get it in time. When you see him remind him that I was thinking of him and soon I'll be home to drive his new car. Kind of a nice birthday present he bought himself isn't it. Let's see how good a shape he can keep it in without me at home to take care of it for him.

Well honey it's about time to go to bed, and I hope I can dream about you. Remember, keep your chin up because before long I'll be home sharing your love.

We never did much dancing all of the years we were married. We danced at weddings, Regimental Balls, and a few New Year's Eve parties, but never went to dinner and dancing as Joe had promised.

While shopping for a birthday card for Joe's Dad at Daw's Drug Store I glanced at the other types of cards in the rack. I noticed one asking someone to write, and another with a lovely verse about missing someone. I purchased both of them to send to Joe.

I was surprised when I received a letter and read his feelings about the cards I had sent him.

Read this letter with an open heart. Remember throughout the letter that I love you very much and soon you will be my wife.

9 December 1953

Hi Honey,

Saturday I received two cards from you, which I thought were rather nice, but had no meaning what so ever. I suppose I could try to understand the thought behind them but that would only tend to get me started off on the wrong foot. In other words, jump to conclusions. The first one I opened was the small one and it told me to write to that long lost friend. The next one was larger and was supposed to make a nice impression, but it didn't. It made things worse for me. I read them, threw them in the wastebasket without another thought, and went on to read a letter from Ken, which contained more interesting information and made me feel more like wanting to get home soon.

I know honey when you get just about this far along in this letter that you'll be about ready to hit the ceiling. I can't say that I blame you, because I would feel the same way.

Truthfully honey I couldn't see the purpose behind those two cards. Remember when I used to write from school and tell you how perfect I wanted you to stay, and how I never expected *anything out of the ordinary to happen? Well I suppose you have grown up and things like that should be expected.*

Saturday while I was on Guard duty, I started to think about you and those cards. It hit me all of a sudden that this is not the same Mary Ann I knew six months ago. What's happened? That question went over and over in my mind and I just couldn't find the answer. I came to the conclusion that nothing actually was wrong as far as being faithful but just the idea that the young love we once had was stronger with affection than the one we have now.

Our love for each other is true and strong but it has changed into a "companionship love," one that shouldn't be obtained for another ten to twenty years. We feel affection for one another but we can't express it and now it seems dormant, a shell has grown around it and it won't be broken until we meet again. Honey, if you are the same Mary Ann I once knew I am sure you feel the same.

Do you remember that little saying I used to say to you in high school? I used to say that, "I would like to put you in a test tube and put you away until it was time to get married." Well honey that is almost being done, yet I am not sure you are really closed up tight in that test tube.

Truthfully, I don't know. Could it be because I am away and without me you have come to find out life could be more interesting than I could ever have shown you? Then I think, it can't be, not my Mary Ann. Honey if I could be home with you, put my hands on your face, and look into your eyes and softly say, "I love you," and hear you say that you understand and love me, and kiss, my worries would be gone.

Be that Mary Ann honey; don't try to change in any way. Be that affectionate one, be the one that smiles when she is happy and cries on my shoulder when she is sad; but most of all honey be my Mary Ann, please, don't change. I love you.

I didn't understand his attitude. Why would he think my love for him had changed? It hadn't. I was expressing how I felt. I hadn't meant for him to react the way he did. The cards were of no real consequence. I assured him I was the same girl he knew but physically and emotionally I was changing. I was growing up, but that didn't affect my love for him. Our young love blossomed. It was maturing into the relationship needed to withstand a lifetime of inevitable trials and disappointments.

My trust in Joe was torn apart a few times, but I forgave him and forgot the pain because I loved him. Almost every letter he wrote he told me to "be good". Why? I didn't understand his constant reminder. The fourth grader with long curls he admired and the eighth grader he flirted with had matured into the woman he was going to marry in the very near future. We grew up together and would grow old together. Changes in our physical appearance were inevitable, but I believed we'd share the love in our hearts for a lifetime.

I tried to express my loneliness without him and the longing to be with him again. I was trying to do what he asked, but he wasn't writing the words I wanted to hear. I needed to read the passion he felt in his heart and his desire to be near me to pull me through my lonely days and nights. It was one of the topics to be discussed when he came home. The second was to decide the type of wedding we wanted, the date and his financial responsibilities.

Joe had mentioned in his letters he wanted to get married soon after he graduated from OCS in January. Getting married in the winter was not my choice. I hoped we could change the date to early spring.

Christmas Eve

Joe and I were sitting on the couch when the doorbell rang. I answered the door. Friends of my parents had stopped by to wish them a Merry Christmas. With them was their son

Tony on leave from the service for the holidays. Mom said we were about to have coffee and asked them to join us. She introduced them and their son to everyone. Tony's warm personality became apparent when he easily joined in the conversations while having coffee.

"Have you graduated from high school?" Tony asked me.
"Yes, I have."
"Are you going to go college, or are you working?"
"Working. I planned on going to New York for fashion design, but Joe gave me my engagement ring and said he didn't like the idea of his future bride being in New York alone."
"He's right. Have you set the date for your wedding?"
"Early spring. After Joe graduates from OCS."
"Do you know where you will be stationed after you graduate? Will Mary Ann be able to be with you?" Tony asked Joe, as I headed to the kitchen to get the coffee pot.
Why was Tony asking Joe such personal questions? We'd never met.
"I have no idea where I'll be assigned, but she can come with me if it's anywhere but Korea."
"Wouldn't it be better to get married after you're out of the Army?"

Tony was still asking questions when I returned, and Joe was answering them.
"If the Korean War didn't end, I'd agree with you, but there are only a few tours where she couldn't be with me, and being an officer, I'm in a better position financially to take care of her. We've been separated too long; I want her with me."

We finished our coffee, and as Tony left with his parents, he said he was very glad to have met me. I returned the compliment and walked back into the living room to sit with Joe.

Mom started to prepare for the midnight buffet. She removed the sliced eggplant, partially cooked artichoke hearts, burdock, cauliflower and broccoli florets from the refrigerator and set them on the kitchen counter next to the stove. Her largest frying pan was placed over a low flame, the bottom coated with olive oil. Into one of two large bowls, she beat together eggs, parsley, basil, garlic, and grated Parmesan cheese. Flour, salt, pepper and baking powder were sifted together in the other. The sliced eggplant and partially cooked vegetables were dredged in the flour, dipped into the seasoned egg batter and fried to a golden brown. The platters of cooked vegetables were covered and set on the kitchen counter out of the reach of those wanting a "taste" before midnight. A baking sheet of pierced chestnuts waited to be roasted with the stuffed mushrooms.

One by one, family members migrated to the kitchen as the aromas of cooked food filtered through the house. My brothers broke off a piece of Italian bread and dipped it into the sauce or lifted the cover on the vegetable platters and took a piece. Around 11:00, the Italian sausage was fried and the mushrooms and chestnuts went into the oven to bake. Mom kept a watchful eye on the kettle of sauce and meatballs on the stove. There had to be enough to make the lasagna for Christmas Day.

Mom put the first of many dishes on the table. The hand-painted Italian fruit platter piled high with oranges, pomegranates, grapes, pears, bananas, tangerines and apples was placed in the center of the table. A bowl of black olives was followed by one of cracked Italian green olives tossed with celery cut in small pieces, sliced red onion, finely sliced garlic, hot red pepper, with an oil and vinegar dressing. Last was the tossed salad greens with cut tomatoes, cucumbers, carrots and celery seasoned with olive oil, oregano, garlic powder, basil and a dash of wine vinegar. Italian bread and rolls, platters of fried vegetables, stuffed mushrooms, chestnuts and Italian sausage completed the buffet dishes placed on the table. Assorted Italian pastries waited in the kitchen until coffee and desert time.

Decks of playing cards were placed on the table after every one had eaten and the table cleared. The men played poker while the women enjoyed a second cup of coffee and sweets.

Joe and I sat on the couch and discussed our letter writing. We agreed to work on adding the love and passion needed to keep our love strong. He said he would pick me up to have Christmas dinner at his parent's house. It would be the first time I was invited there for the holiday.

. . . . .

Joe's leave whizzed by, and before we knew it, he was on his way back to Fort Belvoir. He wasn't able to be home for New Year's Eve; the first we'd miss since going steady. On New Year's Day, he called and said when the clock struck midnight, he thought of all the New Year's we shared. "I really missed those long kisses," he said. I did, too. Our wedding was five months away.

January 1954

7 January 1954

Hi Honey,

Yesterday I received your letter and I can truthfully say that I enjoyed reading a letter like that. Just hearing you're making plans for the wedding and feeling so happy made me feel good inside too. I think we both needed a little jolt to straighten us around. I only hope our plans work out as nicely as we want them to. Honey I really love you and someday our wedding will be the foundation of how I feel about you. I got a letter from my Mom and she said when I get home I'd better get together with her and start making plans for the wedding and not run off like I did the last time without saying anything at all. I am sorry honey but I swear everything will turn out alright. We can make all our plans and then see everyone we have to. I am glad you are picking out the best for our wedding even though the orchids alone will cost $100, but if that is what you want you will have it.

I guess you are anxious to get started on our plans and I am too baby, as soon as I get home, again I want to talk to your folks. Maybe my folks will realize that I couldn't possibly have made plans when I was home for Christmas because I didn't know if I was even going to graduate or where my orders would take me. Now I have more information and my plans can be more stable.

What do you think of your honey soon becoming an officer? Honey you have a date for the first night I am home. You and I alone are going out to celebrate my graduation and our future success. I'll take you to the best night spot there is in Rochester so start looking around and see what you can find. Don't let me stop for one minute while I am home honey. I Want to keep going with you at my side. I love you and I'll be home soon to prove it. See you soon Rusty and be good.

I was working on the guest list for the wedding when the phone rang. The voice sounded familiar.

"Hello, how are you?" Tony said.
"I'm fine." *Why is he calling me?*
"I've been thinking about you since Christmas."
"I'm flattered."
"Do you think I could see you?"
"No, Tony."
"Why not?"
"I'm engaged to be married."
"You're not married yet."
"I will be."
"Are you sure?"
"Yes I'm sure. Thank you for calling, Tony."

I hung up the phone.

Joe asked me to attend his graduation and pin on his bars. My mother said no, and it was final. Nothing would move her this time. There was no Aunt Molly around to serve as my ally and persuade her to change her mind. Joe was receiving his commission as a 2nd Lieutenant. Why couldn't she understand how much this meant to both of us? Why was she being so stubborn? I wouldn't be going alone. I'd be with his parents and sister.

It was such an important event that I asked my father if I could go, even though my mother had already said no. He said I could go. When she heard he had agreed with me, she became angry with him for saying yes and at me for asking him after she said no. Nothing Dad said would change her mind; all it did was fuel an argument between them that got out of hand. I gave in to her decision, asked them to stop arguing and went to my bedroom to write to Joe that I wouldn't be able to attend the ceremony.

There was little conversation with my mother for the next week. I was angry, depressed and felt like a caged rabbit. I felt my mother was flexing her control beyond reason. I was not a child; I was a young woman getting married in a few months. I struggled to find the courage and strength to break loose from her tether. Her attitude was almost vindictive.

I received a few more phone calls from Tony. He asked again if he could see me. I said no, reminding him, I was engaged to be married. I looked forward to Joe coming home, especially since Tony was flattering me with sweet words and phrases. I needed to hear Joe's voice speak words of love, be held in his arms and kiss him, to be reassured in my heart and mind that nothing had changed.

Joe was commissioned and came home on a weekend pass after graduation. I told him about Tony's phone calls. He was angry and upset with me.

"Why didn't you just hang up?"

"I didn't want to be rude."

"He must have thought there was a possibility you would go out with him."

"You're assuming I encouraged him to call. Why would you accuse me of something I have no control over?"

He was not convinced. I was angry at his accusation. In five years, I'd never given him reason to believe I was unfaithful. Now circumstances beyond my control created a situation I wasn't prepared to understand or answer. Where was his support now that I needed it? Why was he so quick to accuse and judge me unfairly? Suddenly, I was completely out of the test tube he had kept me in. I handed him my ring and told him to go home and think about what he said to me. I called Mary, my maid of honor. She came over. When I told her what happened, she said we'd be back together in no time. The next morning Joe called and asked me to go out for dinner.

The drive to the Triton Restaurant was quiet, neither one of us attempting to talk about the night before.
"You look beautiful honey," Joe said.
I said nothing, and the silence continued.
As we looked at each other across the table, I saw the boy who once stood by my locker telling me he wanted me back after I returned his class ring.
"I'm sorry for the way I acted last night. I don't know what came over me. All I knew was someone was trying to take you from me, and I couldn't let that happen."
Joe reached across the table and took my hand. The waiter brought the menu and asked if we would like to order a drink before dinner. We said yes and ordered wine.
"I have no control what a person does or says, Joe. This is the first time I've ever had this happen to me."
"I never had cause to worry if you loved me. I knew you did."
"I'll admit I was flattered by his persistence and his attention."

The waiter brought our wine and asked if we were ready to order. We said we would need a few more minutes to decide.
"There was never a doubt in my mind you loved me; it was my fear of losing you. I shouldn't be angry with you. I should be angry with Tony who knows you're engaged and is trying to take you from me. Forgive me?"
I looked into his eyes and nodded. He slipped the ring onto my finger, and we ordered dinner.
He left for his assignment at Fort Leonard Wood and I went back to planning our wedding.

5 February 1954

Hi Beautiful,

Well her I am in Fort Leonard Wood in my new room sitting at my desk writing to you for the first time as a 2/LT. Yesterday when I arrived, I reported in at Post Headquarters. They told me to sign a lot of papers and gave me a temporary place to sleep until assigned. This morning I woke up at 6:00 to start the long day of processing. We ate breakfast at the Officers mess and the food was very good. They even serve you at your table. That cost us .45 cents, wasn't too bad. From there we reported to G1 who was a captain and he squared us away in our assignment. Two of us were assigned to the same Battalion as platoon leaders. We reported to our Battalion and met our Bn.Co. who assigned us to our respective companies.

I met my Co commander who is a 1st/LT and a graduate from West Point. He explained everything about the company and what its job was. This is when I found out some good news concerning you. In a couple of weeks, we are leaving for temporary duty to Wisconsin, where we have a training assignment. There is an Army Post there that has been closed for some time and we are to go up and reconstruct roads and bridges. We will probably return here sometime in May after we have completed our job up there. It had me worried about our getting married.

I also told him about our plans and he seemed to think fifteen days would not be hard to get and he was sure he could arrange for me to get a leave. I also talked to the Bn. Commander and he said if it was all right with my Co. Commander who is a Lt. Col., he wouldn't interfere. He also told me about bringing you down here to live. They have living quarters for officers and their wives and they're not bad. Right now things look very good for us honey, just keep your fingers crossed and pray for the best. I'll keep you posted.

I have your picture here in front of me and I wish it were you. Don't forget to write because I'll worry. So long for now.

I wrote the following letter to him soon after he left. Among Joe's letters were a few of mine.

February 15, 1954
Hello my darling,
It's late and I'm in bed thinking of you, wishing we were married and you were here next to me. Not much longer.
I'm sorry about what happened. I was hurt but love has to hurt once in a while to grow stronger. I was thinking about the first time I saw you. Your smile is something else honey. One smile from you would melt any girl's heart. Too bad, you're mine. Honey, I know you are telling me you love me by the way you look at me. You don't have to say a word. Your eyes say it all, and sometimes more. That must be the language of love. Just a look from you is enough to let me know what you are thinking. I can read your mind. More than you know.
After our first date my mother said "still waters run deep" when I told her how nice you were but you seemed quiet. Now I know what she meant. You don't show your feelings on the outside, you keep them deep within and only bring them to the surface when you need to. I will have to remember that in the future in case I upset you and you don't say anything.
Honey, I'm so content when you hold me in your arms. I want you to always hold me and tell me you love me. I need to hear you say it. When we sit on the couch and you rest your head in my lap, I love running my fingers through your hair or massaging your forehead when you have a headache. I want it to be like that always. Your mouth is so soft when you kiss me I can feel my heart beat. I can only imagine how your making love to me will feel. The passion we have stored inside will be everything we have only dreamed and imagined. I love you so much I can't picture my life and future without you. You always said that we were made for one another and I know that it's true. You are my first love and nothing can change that. We may be young but the love we feel for each other is real. We've loved each other for a long time and we will love each other for all eternity. God brought us together for a purpose and our

love will last our lifetime and beyond. You won't lose me to someone else. Remember the song "You Belong to Me?" Well one of the lyrics is "Just remember darling all the while, you belong to me." I love you so and belong to you my darling. Time to go to sleep and dream of you.

All my love always and forever,
Mary Ann

p.s. Sonny and Angie had a baby boy. Michael

Mom and Dad were new grandparents and Dad was full of pride that his first grandchild was named after him.

17 February 1954

Hi Honey,

Well here, it is a week since I've been here and every day that goes by gets me closer and closer to being your husband. Honest honey the long weekend we had set me thinking about getting married and I was hoping that next weekend I would be heading toward Rochester to get married to you. I was also thinking about what happened over the weekend. I never doubted your love whatsoever and I never will.

How well I know because now more than ever honey I wish you were with me. I say that because someday soon, we will be parted from one another not as my fiancé but as my wife, and I dread that day. That is why I want so much to get married in May before the time comes when I will have to leave, and be afraid I would lose you to someone else. Not because you didn't love me but people are human and you already know what can happen from these temptations. How well I know! Maybe now you'll understand when I say May 22 will never come soon enough for me or you'll realize the feeling that continually enters my mind and makes me think about you so much more. I worry honey; sure, I worry but to think that I once lost you thru my own dam, stupid neglect only makes me wonder repeatedly if I am slighting you in any way.

The way we had fun together when I was home could be a lifetime if I would only use the head once in a while. I am happy when you are happy honey and I know for sure that you were happy at the Triton when we had dinner. I saw a girl sitting across the table so fair and beautiful that someday would be my wife and bear my children and I said to God just like I say every night now, thank you that she has come back and does love me. Yes honey, I appreciate what I've got and always loved but too many times took you for granted. Not anymore. I'm going to make you the happiest wife you could possibly be. Like I've said before but never had the sense to cherish it I love you honey with all my heart and soon I am going to make you my wife. Until then I can only dream about you. So honey stay happy and don't ever doubt me because I am yours, really I am. Be good and may the good Lord bless and keep you.

23 February 1954

Hi, Honey,

Today I received your first letter since I've been back and I could tell my wonderful Mary Ann wrote that letter with all her heat. When I read the letter, it made me feel so wonderful inside, just as if you were there in person saying all those things to me. Just the type of letter I expect to receive when we are married. A letter like that makes it so much easier to write an answer to, without much sitting around wondering what to say next.

I am glad to hear Sonny and Angie had their baby. I told you she was going to have a boy. Does he have red hair like Sonny? If so I hope, it is a sign our children will too. Since I predicted their baby to be a boy, I'll do the same for ours someday. I hope it will be a girl with red hair as pretty and wavy as your own. Don't think I'm saying that to be nice honey, because it is the truth. I want her to remind me of you. This is only a short note because I have a lot to do, but I'll catch up with another letter tomorrow. I miss you.

May the good Lord bless and keep you for me alone.

Why did he add "for me alone"?

I worked on my wedding gown and finalized most of the plans and purchases for the wedding. I was going to carry the prayer book I used at my Confirmation. From Schumm Florist I ordered white orchids and stephanotis attached to the top, and a small bouquet of white roses to be placed at the altar of the Blessed Mary during the wedding ceremony. The cakes for the breakfast and reception were ordered from Mangione's Bakery. The Florentine Club was reserved for the continental breakfast after the ceremony and evening reception. Everything was falling into place without any problem. Locating a photographer was my last major concern.

I went to Scrantom's Stationery to browse through sample books of wedding invitations, response and thank you cards. A white invitation with an embossed orchid on the cover and black script lettering was my choice. They would have to be ready for mailing six weeks before the wedding.

Tony called again.

"Have you changed your mind about seeing me?"
"No, I haven't."
"I want to tell you how I feel about you?"
"I'm flattered, Tony, but I'm marrying Joe.

He changed the subject and we talked for a few minutes about his being discharged from the Army at the end of March.

7 March 1954

Hi Honey,

Right now, I am in no-man's land on my way to Camp, Mc Coy Wis. Here are the details so you won't worry about me. In about a week our battalion is scheduled to move to Mc Coy for temporary duty that I've already told you about. Well it seems they needed an advance party to leave ahead of time to travel the route and note any outstanding difficulties before the convoy headed this way. 14 enlisted men and I were picked today to set up camp before they arrive. I am the officer in charge and right now I am at the hotel 250 miles en route to Mc Coy. We travel about 35 miles per hour so you can see it is going to take quite a while to reach our destination. It will take us until Saturday night to arrive. Yesterday I received your letter and was very glad to see that things are going along very smoothly as far as Tony is concerned. I'll leave it up to you. I trust you honey and I know you will not spoil our future plans. I would certainly love to have you come down and get married, but I am willing to wait for May 22nd. I know it must be rough on you getting everything prepared.

Here is something I hope will make you happy. The other day I had dinner with my Company Commander, he asked when I was getting married and I told him May 22nd. I then asked him for a leave and he said definitely that he would give me about 12 days leave unless something unorthodox came up. He seemed pleased, but still wanted us to have a military wedding.

Another thing, when we get married, I am bringing you with me for the rest of my time in the states. We will live on post in a prefabricated bungalow for $66.00 a month and they are not bad. I hope you will like them and we can spend our honeymoon wherever you would like.

Everything sounds good, and I hope nothing happens. I'll send you the Priest's address soon. Be good and may the good Lord bless and keep you for me.

The thought of a military wedding was something I did consider. I talked it over with Mom and she was concerned about the inconvenience and travel expenses for family and friends. I called Joe's mother and asked her opinion. She also thought the added expense for her relatives living in Pennsylvania and New Jersey might prevent them from attending. We all agreed it would be best to have the wedding at home.

8 March 1954

Hi Darling,

I miss you very much and I am very lonely right now. The only good thing about this place is when I leave I will be coming home to get married to the most wonderful girl in the world. When I take you back with me, I am sure you will like it here. It will only be for a short time and then I'll take you to Fort Leonard Wood. The scenery here is beautiful and it would be a nice trip for us on the way back especially for a newly married couple.

I spent the afternoon polishing our car. I have to keep it in good shape, because this car is going to bring me home to get married. Maybe after we are married, we could buy one of the new Ford convertibles. We'll get a dark-green one, it will look sharp with your hair, or maybe a yellow one. How about that?

I was just looking at your picture and you sure have been to a lot of places. I can't have you with me all the time but your picture will. You've been in Missouri, Iowa, Minnesota and Wisconsin in the last four days. I was wishing you were beside me while I was making the trip. The radio playing, you sitting beside me with your head on my shoulder and if you might be asleep, my worrying if you were alright, and trying not to disturb you. That's what went thru my mind as I traveled each long day. What I am missing will never be made up. Well honey, I have a lot of work to do so this will be a short letter even though I'm my own boss for another week or so. I love you.

A break in the weather gave Mom the perfect opportunity for spring-cleaning. She asked me to wash the small windows on the side of the house. I leaned the ladder against the house, climbed up and began cleaning the windows.

"Be careful, beautiful, you might fall off the ladder."

I knew that voice and turned around to see Tony smiling and walking toward me.

"How are you and how is Joe? Where is he stationed?"

"I'm fine, Joe's stationed at Ft. Leonard Wood, but he is temporarily at Camp McCoy Wisconsin." *Why the butterflies in my stomach?*

"Have you set a wedding date?"

"Yes, it's May 22nd." I was nervous. I didn't want my mother to see us talking.

"I really can't talk to you, Tony. I don't feel like explaining your being here to my parents, especially my mother. She would really be upset with me."

"I understand. I don't want you to get in trouble because of me."

He said goodbye. I continued washing the windows with mixed emotions and butterflies in my stomach.

When I wrote to Joe, I told him about seeing Tony and his questions about our plans. I didn't tell him how I felt. How could I when I didn't understand what was happening myself? I loved Joe, and I was going to marry him in two months.

Joe's letters for the next two weeks were full of information of getting the Post ready and not having time to do much of anything.

10 March 1954

To my future wife,

Hi honey, it is now 9:00 pm and I've just finished a day's work, and so far every day has been the same with a half hour off for meals.

During our breaks, I have a chance to think about the near future and it helps make the time go by a little faster. I guess every man here knows about our plans. I feel proud showing them your picture but I have to remind them you are getting married soon.

I haven't received any mail since I've been here. You're probably sending them to Ft. Leonard Wood. I hope nothing has happened in the meantime to change our plans. I keep writing and don't even know if the letters are getting to you. Mail your letters to Camp Mc Coy; they will probably get here a lot faster.

I expect to receive around $42.00 for my expenses coming up here. I'll send it to you and you can use it for some of the expenses I will be involved with. When we get married, we will be receiving about $350.00 a month. I am sure we can survive on this healthy sum. As far as leaving you home after we are married, I've decided that I'd rather have you with me because some day we may be separated for a very long period.

At night when I come home from work, I think about you a lot. Especially when I go to bed, I say to myself soon you will be here with me, talking to me instead of everything being so quiet. What must be going on in your mind every day? Do you worry the way I do that everything will be alright and not have something happen at the last minute?

The last letter I received from you told me what happened when Tony talked to you. I couldn't quite understand what happened. Did you see much of him at all and what did you tell him about our plans? What did he have to say in return? He probably told you he will never be able to find a girl as nice as you are and might as well give up. Honey he could never love and appreciate you the way I love you. I only wish that I were there with you to take care of you and show you how happy we could be.

Well honey that should just about do it. I love you very much. May the good Lord bless and keep you for me.

Reading the amount of income we would be living on seemed like a lot of money then. The average yearly income in the country at that time was $3960. Gasoline was 22 cents a gallon, average rent was $85 a month, bread was .17 cents a loaf, fresh ground hamburger was .55 cents a pound, milk .92 cents a gallon and you could purchase ten pounds of sugar for .85 cents. The only problem I thought I'd have is budgeting, because Joe would be paid once a month.

I wanted to have my driver's license before I married. When I turned sixteen, I applied for a learner's permit to drive, anticipating my parents or older brother would teach me. I asked often, but my requests were ignored. My brother was married and didn't have the time and Dad and Mom weren't too thrilled with the idea of my driving the family car. One Sunday my mother's brother Paul, a favorite uncle, stopped in for a short visit. I told him I'd had my permit for over a year, but I couldn't get anyone to teach me how to drive. He said he would take me for a lesson in his new car, a 1954 Studebaker with a standard shift on the steering wheel column.

He drove us to the public market, empty of vendors on Sunday, and told me to get behind the wheel. He demonstrated where first, second, third and reverse gears were, and the coordination using the clutch while shifting gears. He also taught me the use of hand signals (No automatic turn signals at that time.) For about an hour, I started, stopped, backed up, parallel parked and did a three-point turn. It was a lot to remember in one short hour.

"OK, you're ready to go into traffic," Uncle Paul said.
"You mean the street. Now?"
"Yes."
"Are you sure I can do this?"
"Yes, I'm sure."

The traffic was minimal, but his confidence in me was beyond my comprehension. I followed all his instructions, drove home and strutted in the house with the announcement I had driven home from the public market. My uncle praised my driving ability, so I assumed I would get the rest of the instruction from Mom or Dad. It never happened. I continued to take the bus or they drove me wherever I had to go. The permit was valid for two years and would expire in June of '54, one month after the wedding. I lost all hope of surprising Joe with my license before we were married.

Tony's mother called my mother to see if I had time to do an alteration for her. My heart jumped in my throat.

"I'm too busy; I don't think I'll have the time," I said.

"It's only a skirt," Mom said.

"I have the invitations to write."

"We can do them together with Aunt Mary on Saturday after your gown fitting. If the three of us do them, we can finish them in a short time."

I had run out of excuses.

. . . . .

"Would you like a cup of coffee before you mark my skirt?" Tony's mother asked. I said it would be better after I marked the hem. I relaxed when I didn't see Tony. I marked the skirt, and we went into the kitchen to have a cup of coffee.

"Perhaps Tony would like to join us," his mom said. "Would you go to his room and ask him?"

Why didn't she go to his room and ask him? Did he already know I was here? She told me where his room was. I knocked lightly on the closed door.

"Come in."

Opening the door slowly, I saw Tony on his bed, his back to me. I hesitated for a moment and walked across the room, but I don't remember what it looked like. I gently tapped him on his shoulder. He turned around.

"Good morning," he said, as he sat up. I was about to tell him to come and have a cup of coffee, but I never had the chance to get the sentence out of my mouth. He stood up, took me in his arms and kissed me.

"I'd like to wake up every morning kissing you," he said with a smile as I drew away, blushing from his unexpected kiss.

"Your mother wants to know if you want a cup of coffee."

I left the room and went back to the kitchen.

His mother must have noticed I was blushing, but she didn't let on. Tony joined us but there wasn't time for any conversation. I said I had to leave.

I was anxious about what had happened. I wasn't expecting or prepared for the emotions that followed Tony's kiss. I didn't know what to do or how to explain my feelings after it.

31 March 1954

Hi Honey,

I was expecting a letter from you, but I have not received one for at least a week. It's rough here and it would be nice to get even a page from you saying everything is alright. I worry honey and now I have so many plans that I wouldn't want them spoiled.

There is probably some small reason why I have not received any mail but being here away from you makes each day seem like a lifetime. Come to think of it, I haven't received any mail from my folks either. Maybe the address is fouled up. I just hope you are getting my letters right on schedule, but then of course I probably have more time to myself than you do.

Have you seen Ken and Jerri? I am sure they are busy with their new baby. I plan to write them and let Ken know I still want him to be my best man. Maybe the expense will be too much for them now that they have a baby. If Kenny feels he can't do it, I will understand. Have you and Mary got all your plans squared away as for as the wedding is concerned. Tell her hello for me she can't possibly go on the honeymoon with us. Speaking of honeymoons honey, you never really said how you would feel being away from home for the first time. I imagine it will probably bother you for a while. That is why I want to keep you occupied so you won't be lonely. As far as I'm concerned it won't bother me because I've been away a long time, and then again, I'll have you and that is all I want. What do you plan to bring back with you honey? There are a few household things we ought to take plus personal things.

Well I've run out of words, because I am so down in the dumps but a letter from you tomorrow will make me feel a lot happier. So be good darling and remember I love you.

I couldn't handle what was happening to me. I was going to marry the man I'd always loved, now I had feelings for another. One I had spoken to on the phone and kissed only once. It was unfair to Joe. He trusted me and I never gave him reason not to in five years.

3 April 1954

To my darling future wife,
Hi Rusty,

Another weekend of sadness and thoughts of you has about finished, but not too many more before I will be able to see you once again. This time my darling, it will be a lifetime of happiness that we will share together. I don't know what would ever become of me if you should ever leave me. All that I could ever possibly hope for would be that you love me more than you ever dreamed of, and it will always be that way in the future. There is something that I always dream about. That is the day when I would get married. To realize that now, only makes me want to more and more. What more could I ask than to be married to someone like you. There could be no other as perfect as you are, and no one understands me the way you do. I have no complaints honey, all I can say is thank God that I found you, and we are getting married. I'll make you happy darling, and if at all possible, we will have that home that we have always dreamed of. We can raise our children in a nice place and give them the best. I only hope we can do as much or more than our parents have done for us. If we are lucky to have a little girl, I hope she has red hair as pretty as her mother, and I'll let her be with you always so that she can grow up and make someone a wonderful wife like her mother has done for me. I hope that I can live to see and enjoy all this with you darling. Maybe the Lord has other things planned for us, but if not I hope He lets me do all the things in my power to make you the happiest wife that you could possibly be.

The weather has finally changed for the better and now April showers are doing their part to bring May flowers. Let it rain honey, soon it will be May. Time is going by fast but still not as fast as I hoped it would. Soon the trees will be blooming and everything will be beautiful. A perfect time for a honeymoon. Can you see us traveling across the country honey, you at my side without a care or worry in the world? When you get tired, you'll rest your soft little head on my shoulder. When it comes time to stop, we will pull up at the nicest motel and relax for the evening. One big trip, stopping to see anything worthwhile and taking pictures to have for those sentimental days in the future. I hope these last few days apart are making you happier instead of scared. After five years darling I don't believe that you or I could doubt the Lords blessing, so bear with me and I'll be home soon. Bye for now and be good.

My wedding gown was almost finished. My aunt was concerned because of the weight I was losing. Each time I tried on the gown, it had to be taken in. She asked if I was worried about anything. How could I explain to her what I was going through when I couldn't explain it to myself? I loved Joe, but I felt guilty about my attraction to Tony. I wondered if Joe experienced the same frustration when he had been involved with the other girls.

I hadn't received any letters from Joe for a week.

9 April 1954

To my future wife,
Hi Honey,

I suppose by this time you are wondering what happened to you your lover. No honey I haven't forgotten you, I have a legal excuse why I didn't write. Last Monday night we had a terrible electrical storm and the darn lightning struck the chimney of the BOQ and knocked out our lights and ruined our heating system. It scared us a little but luckily, it didn't start a fire. Wednesday night they decided everyone should move out of the BOQ into another one. That took up most of my time transporting all my belongings. Thursday night we had a tactics problem from 8 until 1800 and when I got back, I didn't feel much like doing anything. Here it is Friday, the night I used to go out with you, writing home instead.

Well next weekend is Easter Sunday, another that I've missed away from home. I am going to send you the surprise I've been waiting for. I hope you like it honey. I did when I first saw it. I knew right then it was made purposely for you. It was going to be a wedding present but I just can't wait until I give it to you, so next week I'll send it out. I'll have to think of something else to give you when we get married. As yet, I have no idea whatsoever. If I ask you what you want, you will only beat around the bush and not tell me a darn thing.

I found out another bit of information as far as our financial conditions are concerned. When I take you from Rochester to camp, I'm allowed six cents a mile that turns out to be $60.00, enough for our first months' rent.

Well I am anxious to see what kind of surprise you have in store for me when I get home. I'd be satisfied with just the words "I do" from your lips honey. Take care of yourself and be good. I love you.

On Sunday, I attended the first of my three bridal showers. The excitement of spending the day with friends and family blocked out my inner turmoil. A sheer negligee and nightgown with embroidered inserts in the waist and hemline was my mother's final addition to my trousseau. Her other purchases included lingerie, nightgowns, a suit, dresses and accessories.

When I was thirteen, she asked me to pick a pattern for my sterling silver tableware. My choice was Queen's Lace by International Sterling. For my birthdays, Christmas, graduation and engagement, she purchased a place setting until I had service for twelve. She filled my cedar chest with beautiful cutwork, embroidered or tatted trimmed sheets and pillowcases dresser scarves and linen dishtowels. She wanted me to have what she didn't have when she married.

The wedding was three weeks away. Everything was in place. No loose ends to worry about. I relaxed and thought about the day Joe would come home. My relaxation was short lived. My mother had her pink lace dress made by a local dressmaker because I was busy with my gown and the bridesmaids' gowns.

"Mom, you're not going to wear that dress to the reception," I said when she tried it on for me. "It's poorly constructed and doesn't fit you properly. The hem is uneven, the waistline is too long and the neckline doesn't lie flat."

I took it apart and restyled it to fit her full figure, not accentuate it. When she put it on, she had to admit it was perfect and she said how fortunate she was to have a "designer" in the house.

Wedding Day Morning

"Wake up, sleepy head, it's your wedding day," Mom said raising the window shade. The sun burst into the room filling every corner with its brilliance and warmth. "Is rain in the weather forecast for today?" I asked.
"No, the weather report is for clear and sunny skies. Your prayers have been answered."
The smell of fresh brewed coffee filled the bedroom. Regrettably, I couldn't have any. Because I was receiving communion at the ceremony, I had to fast.

Hooked over the top of the door and supported by a padded hanger, my exquisite ivory Chantilly Lace gown waited patiently for the moment it would be taken down from its lofty perch and shown off to friends and family. Its square neck and long sleeve buttoned bodice was dwarfed by the bouffant skirt attached to it. The scalloped hem of the chapel train barely kissed the floor. Traditionally, the gown was not seen by anyone until the ceremony. My mother and Aunt Mary, who assisted me with sewing and fittings, were sworn to secrecy about what it looked like. Months had passed since I drew the design, purchased the fabric, cut, sewed and survived untold fittings for it to reach this day. It would be revealed when I took my father's arm and walked down the aisle of Church of the Annunciation to marry Joe.

Fine, delicate French silk lace that trimmed the veil worn by my mother now trimmed the edge of my silk illusion fingertip veil. It rested gently across the top of the bedroom chair, modestly covering the "Merry Widow" long line bra, stockings and lace trimmed panties folded on the seat cushion. I glanced at the picture of Joe in his uniform taken the day of his graduation from Officer Candidate School. His smile seemed to say, "We made it, honey. The day has arrived we planned and dreamed about for the last five years."

"Thank you for the day, Lord," I whispered. "There were moments I doubted I'd be getting married today."

I sat up, dangled my legs over the edge of the bed and removed the hairpins from the pin curl that didn't stay in. Fortunately, the only one that came loose during the night. I grabbed my robe, went into the bathroom and took a bath.

I removed the hairpins from my pin-curled hair, and ran my fingers through the tight curls to loosen them before I went into the kitchen.

Dad and my brothers Jim, Paul and Tommy were milling around partially dressed in their tuxedos. Sonny walked in, poured himself a cup of coffee and joined in their conversation. He looked at me and smiled an intuitive smile that only an older brother can give his now grown up kid sister. Watching my younger brothers, I thought of the days when Paul and Tommy were little and my job as older sister was to keep an eye on them. Paul was the last to be born at home and Tommy was the first to be born in a hospital. The morning Paul was born my grandmother came into my bedroom, woke me up and took me into my mother's bedroom to see the new baby. Paul slept quietly on a pillow in Mom's large oval wicker laundry basket. I wanted a sister. Now I had three brothers. My responsibility during the summer was to stay with Paul until he fell asleep for his afternoon nap. I didn't appreciate it cutting into my playtime.

I devised a method for him to fall asleep quickly. I crawled under his crib, took hold of the spring and gently raised and lowered it in a rocking motion. He fell asleep in a matter of minutes.

By the time Paul was walking, he was always going into the street. Mom punished him, but that didn't stop him. Frustrated, she tied one end of a clothesline around his waist and attached the other end to the porch column to curtail his dangerous habit. It restricted him to the curb. Rose Fiammi, our next-door neighbor, told my mother she was heartless doing so. Rose had one child, a son.

"I'd rather be heartless and know he's safe from being run over by a bus or car," she told her.

Looking at Tommy I smiled when I remembered the quarters Joe bribed him with to leave the living room so we could be alone. Mom sent him in there to "chaperone" us. He came and went every fifteen or twenty minutes knowing he could earn another quarter if he stayed in the room too long.

I basked in the sunshine, memories, happiness and laughter around me. Suddenly, the realization this moment would not be happening if two weeks earlier I had made the decision to postpone the wedding. I took a deep sigh and joined the conversation. Mom joined us a few minutes later in her navy blue ankle length organza dress, minus her shoes.

"Where are your shoes?" Dad asked.
"In the bedroom. I'll put them on before we leave."

The florist arrived with the bridesmaids' bouquets, my mother's corsage and my prayer book. Long streamers of white satin ribbon cascaded from the white orchids, lilies of the valley and stephanotis that adorned the top.

I went into the bedroom, put on my undergarments, combed my hair, put on my make up and went back into the living room. Voices and conversations began to escalate as the minutes rapidly ticked by. Mary, my maid of honor, arrived shortly before the photographer. She took me aside.
"I think it's time to put on your gown."
"I think so, too."
She reached up, lifted the hanger off the door, closed it and laid the gown across the bed. I put on my stockings, hooked them to the garters attached at the bottom of the bra and adjusted the tension of the elastic to keep them from sagging around my ankles. I was about to step into my gown when the phone rang. It continued to ring. I slipped into my robe and went into the hall to answer it.

"Hello."
"Are you sure you know what you're doing?" Tony asked, after a long pause.
I wasn't expecting his call . . .

"Yes Tony, I'm sure."
"Are you sure?"

My thoughts raced back to the roller coaster ride of the previous five weeks, an innocent infatuation that took me to the brink of postponing my wedding.

April 12

The day arrived for the wedding invitations to be addressed and mailed. I called Aunt Mary and asked if she could help address them. She said she would be happy to.

Mom and I took the invitations to her house. Aunt Mary took charge. Mom and I watched as she organized the invitations, response cards and the envelopes in the middle of the table. She divided the guest list among the three of us.

"I filled the pens with black ink; they must be written in black," she stated. The name of the guest was written on the inside envelope and the full address on the one, it went into. Once the ink dried, we stuffed, sealed and were ready to affix postage.

"I think I'll send one to Joe. I wonder what his reaction will be when he opens the envelope and sees an invitation to his own wedding."

15 April 1954

Hi Rusty,

I think I'll get used to calling you Rusty; It always seemed to please you. I was glad I waited until today to write to you. When I opened your letter, I thought it was an Easter card, I never expected a wedding invitation. No kidding honey, that actually thrilled me. When I saw it I busted out with joy, and I made darn sure everyone else had a chance to see it before the novelty wore off. That's the closest thing I have felt about how soon I was getting married. It really made me happy to be able to read your name and mine on the announcement. Just about, everyone that saw it joked about getting an invitation to my own wedding. You know something. I think I will come to that wedding. Seriously, I wouldn't miss it for the world.

Yesterday I had my blood test taken. When I get the results, I'll send it to you to take to Doctor Phillips who will make out the certificate for New York State. The way I understand it, New York won't recognize our paper work unless it is made on one of their certificates. Not a problem though the doctor can transfer the results to his copy which will be sufficient. Let me know if you find out anything contrary.

Well I guess you know by now what the surprise was that I sent you. Hope you like it honey, just one of the tokens to show how much I love you. I hope your surprise for me does turn out because I do want you to have your driver's license when we get married. It will help lessen the problem living on Post and give you a chance to get out more often in your spare time.

Glad to see that your gown is done. I'll bet it's beautiful. Don't worry about me being sleepy the day we get married. That will be the farthest thing from my mind. I'll be home a couple of days before the wedding.

As for your writing, yes, I worry but I know the delay is for a good reason. All I ask is just be good because I am looking forward to that day. My calendar is filling up now. Just 32 more days and I'll leave. Till then, I'll be thinking of you always.

That's it for now sweet. Soon I will be home and in your arms. I love you.

Joe's gift was an engraved gold Cross-and chain. I decided to wear it with my wedding gown.

A law at that time required a blood test be taken by the bride and groom a month before the wedding to make sure they were free of any venereal disease such as syphilis. After WWII, many servicemen returned home from overseas infected which caused a national epidemic. The law treated the individual to prevent the disease from being transmitted to an un suspecting partner.

"All I ask is you just be good." Joe had an uncanny sixth sense. I was trying to be good, but I was experiencing feelings I couldn't explain. I was looking forward to my wedding; yet I was confused about my attraction to Tony. How could one kiss from someone I hardly knew create the confusion I was experiencing.

18 April 1954

Hi Rusty,
I'll bet you're the happy one after the shower Sunday. Mom wrote and told me all about it. She started her letter by saying, "Today I went to a shower given in honor of my son's future wife Mary Ann." That sure sounded wonderful honey and I bet you were queen of the ball too. I hear you received some very nice gifts. I wish I could have been around just to see your face as you opened them. I suppose you already know that they are giving you one next weekend too. Sure is a busy life for my little darling. Just 20 more days and I'll be leaving. Every time I think of it, it makes me feel good all over. I suppose you are too excited to think about it, but I have plenty of time to dream what if would be like to be there with you.

How are the expenses? I suppose they are building up by this time. Payday is Friday and I'll send another $30.00 dollars to pay some of my expenses. Your ring and the flowers are the main things to think about at present. When I get home, I'll pay for the others right away. If I am correct, it will be the ring, flowers, Priest, gifts, and license. I do not want any financial problems that will hold us back at the start. If we use our heads, we can have a wonderful honeymoon.

What plans have you made for immediately after the reception? Do you still want to go to Aunt Mary's to change and get ready to leave? Also, where do you want to stay the first night? I don't think we will get too far before it gets late, or do you want to start right out and get a hotel room. Let me know because I am leaving it all up to you. Anything that makes you happy will do the same for me.

That's about it, write as often as you can. I know you're busy but the waiting seems longer when I don't hear from you. I love you honey and please, be good.

I found it difficult many nights to fall into a sound, restful sleep with so much on my mind about the wedding and Tony. I woke up often for no apparent reason. On one of those nights, I went into the kitchen for a glass of milk. As I sipped my milk, I walked into the living room to look out the window into a clear, full moon night. It was as light as early dawn.

A car stopped in front of the house. I was turning away when I noticed the door open. Getting out of the car was a familiar face. Tony. He looked toward the window, and when he saw me, he motioned for me to come outside. I smiled, shook my head, mouthed the word "no" and showed him the ring on my left hand. He kept motioning for me to come outside, but I wouldn't. My parents were asleep. If they woke up and found me outside with him, I'd have heck to pay for being out there. What a field day the neighbors would have if they saw me sitting on the stoop with him at two o'clock in the morning. Tony motioned he was going to call me on the phone. What if the phone woke up my parents? How would I muffle its ring? I covered the phone with a blanket and pillow from my bed. I opened the sliding door of the closet and sat on the floor. The phone cord just reached inside. With the blanket, pillow and phone in my lap, I closed the door and waited; startled anyway when it rang. I picked it up.

"Hello."

"I have to talk to you," Tony said.

"Are you crazy? Do you know how much trouble I'll be in if my parents find out I'm on the phone at this hour talking to you?"

"I have to see you alone."

"You know I won't agree to that."

"You've never dated anyone but Joe. How can you be

sure he is the one you should marry."

"I've told you before Tony that I've been in love with Joe since high school. I'm sure."

"What happens if you get married and realize you've made a mistake?"

"That's an unfair question."

"Why?"

"Because I don't have the answer. I don't want to discuss this now Tony. I have to go. My parents might wake up, and I'm not ready for any confrontation with them."

I said goodbye and hung up the phone.

Another sleepless night.

3 May 1954

Hi Rusty,

  The month of May has finally come around and I am sure glad to see it. Just two more weeks or fourteen more days and I'll be leaving this place headed to Rochester to marry the most wonderful girl in the world. I suppose these last two weeks are going to be the hardest. As yet, I'm not nervous about leaving; it is just the idea of waiting that has me down. Every day the same thing over and over again, coming home at night to find nothing and always having you on my mind. Weekends are worse instead of better.

  How is everything going at home? Any worries or troubles yet? Did you check with the doctor whether or not New York will accept the certificate the Army gives me and will any of the paper work have to be transferred?

  I received a letter from Kenny Saturday and he said he still would like to be my best man. He said they ordered their tuxedo and brought one of my suits along for my size. He asked if we had any plans on having children right away. I don't think I've ever heard you say whether or not you want to right away. As far as I'm concerned, I'd just as soon. Like your mother said though, "let nature take its course." I guess that is the best way.

Just a paragraph now before I close to tell you what's in my heart. Darling I miss you very much and the day I can be with you will never be soon enough, and when it does come, it will last forever. Honey when I think I almost lost you it makes me hurt all over. No need for the test tube now. You belong to me and no one else. Be good darling, very soon I'll be home and in your arms.

His letters added to my frustration. I loved him but I was torn between his love and the disturbing emotions I felt for Tony.

Mary called Friday afternoon and asked me to go with her to the church dance.

"Come with me. You haven't been there in weeks. We can sit and talk about the wedding with the girls. You don't have to dance if you don't want to."

"I'll call you back."

I asked my brother Jim if he was going. He said yes. I called Mary and said I'd go.

Talking with the girls, I saw Tony come in. He saw me and walked toward the table. *How did he know I was here?*

"Hi."

"What are you doing here?" I asked.

"I want you to take a ride with me."

"OK. I'll meet you outside."

I looked for my brother and asked him and Mary to join me. When we got in the car, Tony was upset and told me that he wanted to see me alone.

"I'm engaged Tony; it wouldn't look right if someone saw me alone in the car with you."

We drove around for about fifteen minutes making conversation of no importance. I turned around to make a comment to Mary and Jim gave me a "What the hell are you doing?" look. I asked Tony to take us back to the dance.

Walking home after the dance Mary said, "Tony has a crush on you."

"I know."

5 May 1954

Hi Rusty,

    Today I received another of those wonderful letters from my future wife. First, I could tell by the size of it you must have put a lot of feeling in it and it touched my heart. I'm sorry if I scolded you for not writing but I didn't have the intention to, it's nice to hear from you whenever I can. Don't let it worry you because I understand the situation you must be in. I'm glad to hear you enjoyed yourself with all the showers they are giving you. At least it helps make your time go by faster.

    I received a wonderful letter from your mom. I think we've really come to understand one another. I know we both have something in common and that is, we both love the same girl very much. She really expressed her love for you in the letter. I realize now how many times I was wrong and I'm sure I'll love your folks. I think your mom and dad will make us happy and she doesn't have to worry about interfering with us. I expect things to go just as they should without interference from anyone.

    As for the home we will have at Ft. Leonard Wood, I am sure you'll like it and both of us can really make it cozy. From what I hear, they are nice, just right for a young couple like us. Did you check with the doctor about the blood test?

    Well darling another few minutes of being with you is over. Thank you for the nice letter and God bless and keep you. Keep up the good work and be patient. I'll try to do the same.

    Until very soon, goodnight, and I love you.

I was surprised to read that Joe had received a letter from my Mother. She never mentioned she had written to him.

I ached inside when I read his letters. His trust and love were tearing me apart. I loved him and I wanted to marry him, but someone I hardly knew was chipping away at the foundation of my love for him. I remembered what Joe had written in one of his letters. *I'm dreaming a lot about you, but it's the kind of dream I don't appreciate. If I ever get the guy in my dream that's trying to take you away from me, I'll break his neck.*

With the possibility of his dream coming true, I decided to think only about the wedding. I thought if I concentrated on the wedding and Joe I could forget my confused thoughts. I was trying to pull myself together to get on with the future I had dreamed of since I was a young girl.

Walking home from school one day, Joe said to me, *I want to put you in a test tube and keep you there until the day we are married so no one else can take you away from me.* I was the specimen he wanted to preserve intact until he married me. When Tony came into my life, the cork stopper of that imaginary test tube was jarred loose. I had been freed to discover the world outside its confinement. I didn't know what to do.

That Saturday night as I walked to Annunciation Church to go to confession, a car pulled up in front of me. In it was Tony and he asked if I would go with him just this one time. I was a safe distance from home and I knew no one would know, so I agreed. He drove to an area near the airport where cars with families were parked to watch the planes take off and land. He turned off the car and kissed me.

"My grandfather told me to go out with a lot of girls and say I love you only to the one I want to marry."

"I hardly know you Tony. I'm getting married in two weeks."

"You can't! You care for me. I know you do. You should wait before you make the wrong decision."

"I don't know what has happened. Yes, I do have feelings for you but I love Joe too. I can't throw away the last five years because you suddenly came into my life."

He tried to persuade me to wait. I asked him to drop me off where he'd picked me up. When I made my confession, I almost told the priest what happened. I didn't get much sleep that night. There had been one love in my life and that was Joe. I'd been faithful to him all the years we were together. No one had ever been able to change the way I loved him. Along came Tony. Now there was indecision.

After dinner on Sunday, I went next door to my brother's house and confided in him. I didn't say there was someone else; I just said I wasn't sure I wanted to get married. I asked him to talk to Mom for me; I couldn't tell her. He said it would be all right and left.

When he returned, he said Mom wanted to see me. I went home. Mom said if I wasn't sure, it was best to wait.

How was I going to tell Joe I wanted to postpone the wedding?

The next morning, I went into the kitchen around 6:45. Dad had gone to work and Mom was standing near the kitchen sink washing dishes. I poured a cup of coffee and sat at the table.

"Mary Ann, there isn't anyone else changing your mind, is there?" Mom asked.

"Yes," I said. She spun around.

"Who?"

"Tony."

Her face turned ashen and she slumped to the floor. I panicked and ran next door to get my brother. When we walked in the door, Mom was trying to get up. My sister-in-law slapped my face.

"**What did you do to her?**" she asked.
"**I told her the reason I didn't want to get married**."

I grabbed my sweater, ran to the church rectory, rang the bell and knocked on the door at the same time. Father Simonetti opened the door.

"I can't get married," I said, crying.

He directed me into his office.

"Would you like a cup of coffee?"

"Yes." He asked the housekeeper to bring me one and handed me a box of tissues.

"I'll be right back. I have to put on my collar; I wasn't expecting anyone so early in the morning."

I dried my eyes and sipped my coffee. *How do I tell him why I didn't want to get married?*

When Father returned, he went to his filing cabinet, took out a folder and placed it on his desk.

"This is your marriage license. Right now, it is only a piece of paper. I can tear it up. It has no meaning or value until you and your husband sign it. Once it is signed and witnessed, it is binding for life. Why don't you want to marry Joe?"

"It's not that I don't want to marry him Father. The problem is I think I care for someone else, too."

"Tell me what's going on."

"I've been faithful to Joe since the day we went steady five years ago. Everything was fine until this past Christmas when friends of my parents came over with their son and we were introduced. We talked on the phone, and he kissed me a couple of times. How can I marry Joe when I suddenly have feelings for him too?"

"**That** was the extent of your relationship with him?"

"Yes, Father. Nothing more."

He held the marriage license in his hand. "If you sign it and you're not sure, you're making a serious mistake. I think we need talk to your parents." He drove me home just as Mom was leaving to pick up Dad. She'd called him after I left.

Before she said anything, Father asked her to come back to the rectory so he could talk to the both of us together.

Mom and I sat down; Father explained to her that nothing she should worry about had happened. The issue was my uncertainty about marrying Joe.

"Mary Ann is engaged and shouldn't have responded to his advances," Mom said.

Father looked at me for a moment and turned toward my mother.

"Part of this problem Pauline stems from her obedience to the rules you set at the age of 14 when she first started to go steady with Joe."

"I told her about being faithful, and if she wanted to be with others, she should give back Joe's ring. Was I wrong?"

"No, but following your rules and Joe's, she didn't have the opportunity to be with other boys. It wasn't until Tony came into her life and persisted in winning her over that she finally had the opportunity to compare. Unfortunately, it happened at a most inopportune time, and now she is trying to decide what to do."

"I want her to be sure. If it means we have to postpone the wedding, we will. I don't want her to get married and find out later that she married the wrong person."

"Mary Ann, you never said you didn't love Joe," Father said to me as we left the rectory.

"I love him, Father."

"If you saw Joe, would you know?"

"Joe is in Wisconsin. How could I see him?"

Mom looked at me. "Would you know if you saw him?" she asked. I said yes.

We went home; she called Dad and told him they had something to discuss about the wedding. She went to pick him up.

. . . . .

Walking in the door, Dad motioned for me to sit at the dining room table. His face was serious, not angry as I had imagined it would be under the circumstances. He said he was going to make reservations for Mom and me to fly to Wisconsin. After I saw Joe, if I decided I didn't want to marry him, the wedding would be postponed. I had to make up my own mind; he didn't want to influence my decision.

Two days later Mom and I were on a flight to La Crosse, Wisconsin. I didn't let Joe know I was coming. I didn't want him to know about the flight that would affect the rest of our lives until I could see him in person and discuss what was happening.

We asked the taxi driver where the nearest hotel was. He said the La Crosse Hotel was nearby. We checked in. I looked up the number for Camp Mc Coy in the phone book and couldn't find a listing. I dialed the operator. She connected me to the switchboard on post. I was surprised when a male voice answered. I told him I was trying to locate Lt. Marasco and all I had was an address on an envelope. He put me on hold; after a few minutes I heard,

"Lt. Marasco, Sir."
"Hello, Lt."
"Mary Ann, is that you?"
"Yes."
"Where are you?"
"I'm in La Crosse at the hotel. I had to see you."
"I'll be there in 20 minutes."

Mom was sitting in a chair on the other side of the room not saying a word, but the rosary that was in her hand when we left was still there. I hadn't stopped to think about her feelings. I was thinking about my own. I loved Joe, and I thought I loved Tony. I was at a crossroad, deciding who would be my husband.

A divorce down the road was not an option for me.

While I waited for Joe, I wondered how I was going to explain why I was here. No answers, only questions. It seemed more like 20 hours than 20 minutes until I saw his car come down the street. He parked the car. As he started to walk toward the hotel with that distinct stride of his, I didn't see an officer in uniform, I saw the sixteen-year-old boy who walked up the street to take me out on my first date. The one who stole my heart that I remained chaste for and wanted to spend my life with *until death do us part.* The loneliness, longing and love I felt for him poured through me.

"Joe is here, Mom." I rushed down the steps through the lobby and out the door. I ran as fast as I could down the street to meet him. I couldn't wait to feel his arms embrace me and his lips kiss me with the passion I'd been missing since he left. He asked who was with me. I said Mom.

"Let's go talk to Mom," he said as we walked to the hotel.

"Hi, Mom," Joe said, and kissed her. "What's going on?"

"She isn't sure she wants to marry you."

"I've waited for her all my life. I have her now, and we're going to get married. Is it all right if I take her for a ride?"

"Yes, it's all right."

. . .

We left and drove to an area overlooking the quiet little town. He turned off the motor, put his arms around me and kissed me.

"What happened since I left to make you feel you're not sure you want to marry me?" he asked.

"Where should I start?"

"At the beginning of your indecision."

"I received more phone calls from Tony."

"What did he want, and what did you say?"

"The same things he said before. He cared for me and wanted me to go out with him. I told him I was engaged, but he kept saying I wasn't married yet."

"What else happened?"

"He continued to call and wanted to see me alone. I wrote you about the day he came over when I was washing windows and asked about you and our wedding date."

"I remember."

"After he left, I felt uneasy and I had butterflies in my stomach."

"Is there more?"

"Yes. I did an alteration for his mother, and went to his house. He kissed me."

"And?"

"He said he'd like to wake up every morning kissing me."

"Did you kiss him more than once?"

"Yes."

"Were you ever alone with him?"

"A couple of times."

"Did anyone else know what was going on?"

"No! How could I talk to anyone when I didn't know myself what was happening?"

"When did you think you weren't sure about getting married?"

"Last Saturday evening. On my way to church to go to confession, Tony pulled up and asked me to go for a ride. We parked at the airport. He told me he loved me and wanted to marry me. I told him it was impossible. We never went out or spent any time together. We kissed a few times and talked on the phone. He told me he knew what he wanted, that I cared for him, and not to make the mistake of marrying the wrong person.

. . . . .

Joe turned on the radio and tuned to a station broadcasting the romantic songs we enjoyed listening to while going steady. He adjusted the seat as far back as it would go and turned toward me.

. . .

"Honey, if someone tells you often enough how much he cares for you and the one you love has been away for some time and you're lonely, it's natural for you to be flattered or infatuated with him."

"I don't understand why I feel the way I do, Joe. I've never loved anyone but you."

He held my face with his hands and looked at me.

"You were lonely, honey, and he is telling you what you would normally hear from me. I wasn't there to kiss you or say those loving words to you. I write them in my letters, but hearing them and reading them are as different as night and day. I don't blame him for wanting you. He's loved you for a couple of months; I've loved you for years."

"Why would he affect me so deeply?"

"His constant attention caused your infatuation with him. Our love has grown all these years. It has survived interference and objections from others, and we still love each other. Our love is strong and deep enough to keep us together. I've loved you for a long time. I almost lost you twice, and I won't let it happen again."

"Is this what you experienced with Nancy and others?"

"Probably, but I never stopped loving you."

"I never stopped loving you either, but how can I love you and feel the way I do about Tony?"

"I don't have the answer, and I don't care. I'm not letting you go. I couldn't put my finger on it, but I had the feeling that something was wrong. A little voice inside kept telling me I had to get home to you. I kept praying for you to be good. I wrote it at the end of my letters, didn't I?"

"Yes, you wrote it in almost all of your letters."

"I'm going to try and get my leave advanced by a week so I can drive you and Mom home. I don't want you home without me any longer."

We drove back to the hotel and I told Mom my decision and the possibility that Joe would be driving us home. She called Dad to let him know my decision and the change of plans.

Mom and I talked for a little while after Joe left. She said she tried to instill in me the values I would live with all my life and the reason she was so harsh so often was to teach me responsibility for the choices and decisions I would make in the future. This was the first of them.

Joe called in the morning and that said his Commanding Officer had given him permission to leave. The advance would cut into our honeymoon, but it didn't matter.

When we got home, Joe said hello to Dad. They smiled at each other. Dad hugged me.

After Joe left, I went to my room to change my clothes and returned to the kitchen. Dad and I sat at the table.

"Have you made the right decision?" he asked.
"Yes. Why are you asking?"
"While you were gone, I had a visit from Tony and his father. He told me his son's intentions were honorable. I told him you had to make up your own mind; the decision was yours."
"I've made the right decision. I was infatuated with Tony, but I love Joe."
"I know your mother has told you what mothers are supposed to tell daughters, but I think you should know a few more things from my point of view as a man."

Dad had never said much to me about my relationship with Joe. He treated him as his son, not my boyfriend. He hesitated, as if he were trying to put his thoughts and sentences in proper sequence and not be embarrassed by what he had to say to me.

"First, put your pride in your pocket and sit on it; pride will ruin a marriage if you think only of yourself. It's all right to admit you were wrong.

"If Joe's tired from working all day and wants to fall asleep on the couch, let him, it's better if he falls asleep on yours than on someone else's.

"Put on some perfume in the morning before he leaves. There are women in the world he works with who look and smell good. You want him to remember your fragrance not theirs.

"Kiss him goodbye when he leaves for work.

"Freshen the way you look before he comes home and greet him when he walks in with a kiss.

"Making love should be spontaneous. If he wants to make love to you and you're busy doing something else or cooking, lower the heat on the stove and turn it up in the bedroom.

"Don't tell him your problems the minute he walks in the door. He has his too. Wait until both of you have time to talk quietly; he'll listen then.

"Don't' go to bed angry.

"Talk to each other. Your children will grow up and leave. If you haven't talked to one another while they're growing up, you won't be able to have a conversation after they leave.

"Be a mother to his children, his wife in the house and his mistress in the bedroom."

It was a lot to digest in one sitting. I knew what to do in every instance except the last. What does a mistress do that a wife doesn't? I had no experience to draw from to know the difference. I would have to depend on Joe to teach me.

On Friday night before the wedding, Joe went to his bachelor dinner with my brothers, my dad, his dad, his cousin

Ralph and Ken. When they returned a few hours later, they said Joe was determined not to drink too much. He didn't want a hangover on his wedding day.

He was not drunk, but he was feeling good when he took me into the kitchen away from everyone, held me in his arms and said, "Tonight I'm kissing you as my fiancé; tomorrow night I am going to make passionate love to you as my wife." Ken said good night and told Joe he would see him at the church in the morning. Joe left with his dad and cousin.

"This is your last night as my little girl," Dad said, as I was getting ready to go to bed. "Tomorrow you'll be a married woman."

. . . . .

I heard Tony ask again.

"Are you sure?"
"Yes, Tony, I'm sure. I'm sorry if I hurt you."
"I love you. If you ever need me, I'll be waiting."
I said goodbye and put the phone on the receiver.

I went back into the bedroom, looked out the window and then at Mary holding my gown.

"Is something wrong?" she asked.
"No, nothing is wrong."

I stepped into my gown. Mary buttoned the back while I buttoned the sleeves. She handed me my veil. I slid the combs on the headpiece into my hair and adjusted it. The photographer tapped on the bedroom door and said that he wanted to take some pictures before we left. I looked at my reflection in the mirror, picked up the train of my gown and walked into the living room.

About 9:45 Dad said, "We have to be at the church by 10:00. if we don't leave now, she'll be late for her wedding." Mom handed me my prayer book, and we walked out the door.

On the arm of my father walking down the aisle toward the altar, I saw only Joe waiting for me. Soon the promise we made to each other and patiently prayed and longed for would be fulfilled.

After pledging our vows, Father Simonetti announced that we were going to place a bouquet of white roses at the shrine of the Virgin Mary in dedication of our marriage. It was the first time it had been done in the church. Father said we started a tradition that became part of the wedding ceremony of many couples in the years that followed.

Following the ceremony, a nuptial kiss was not permitted. I took Joe's arm when Father Simonetti introduced us as Mr. and Mrs. Joseph Marasco. We smiled at everyone as we walked down the aisle toward the opened doors at the front of the church. When we reached the end of the aisle, Joe stopped and turned to face me. He put his hands on my shoulders, looked in my eyes and whispered, "My darling wife," and kissed me.

The day had been a blur of emotional highs. It was over before we knew it. Exhausted, we left the reception about 9:00pm. Joe had said if I was too tired, we could sleep and he would make love to me in the morning. I hadn't waited all these years to be too tired for him to make love to me.

We were staying at Aunt Mary's because it was a brand new house, and they offered it to us for our first night together

. . . . .

I asked Joe to unbutton the back of my gown while I unbuttoned the sleeves. He took off his jacket, tie, and walked toward me. I could feel his fingers nervously removing each button loop. He kissed me when I stepped out of my gown.

"Honey, why don't you shower first," I said. He took his pajamas and went into the bathroom. While he was showering, I folded the bedspread to the end of the bed and removed my negligée and nightgown from my suitcase, and took the perfumed soap, talc and bottle of Tabu perfume he gave me from my makeup case.

When Joe came out of the bathroom, I noticed he'd shaved. I put my arms around him.

"I don't know what that scent is that you're wearing, but I can't wait to get close to your body to smell it again."

I kissed him and went into the bathroom to shower. I closed the door behind me.

I had instructions for what not to do; but no one had ever discussed or instructed me on what I should do.

I slipped into my nightgown and negligée, dabbed Tabu on my neck shoulders and wrists and started to brush my hair. I opened the door to the bedroom and walked to the bed. I set the brush down on the nightstand. Joe was sitting on the bed with two pillows behind his back, his eyes fixed on me from the moment I came into the room. He moved to the middle of the bed. I sat next to him. I kissed him while I unbuttoned his pajama top and took it off. I stood up and removed my negligée and nightgown. He didn't say a word.

"Are you too tired to make love to me?" I asked.

He took me in his arms and kissed me.

"You're trembling," Joe said.

"I can't help it. I don't want to disappoint you."

"I love you, baby. You won't disappoint me, but I don't want to hurt you."

The discomfort of the first time was forgotten when Joe gently kissed and caressed my face, neck, shoulders and other formerly forbidden parts of my body. I didn't bridle the passion I felt in Washington or the night of my junior prom. The first time Joe made love to me, I was his wife. A promise fulfilled.

Getting into bed, we found the top sheet was too short to stretch out. We looked at the bottom of the sheet and discovered it was folded, "short sheeted" and scattered in between the folds were white sugarcoated almonds. Removing the almonds and unfolding the sheet, we knew it had to be Mom, Aunt Mary or both who'd made the bed. We didn't expect a practical joke to be played on us.

"What a way to start a honeymoon," Joe said.

Falling asleep in his arms was everything I had imagined.

After breakfast, we dressed and opened the gifts we received at the reception. The car was in the garage and packed with our new life. Electric coffee pot, toaster, frying pan, boxed china, flatware and linens were in the trunk. Our luggage was on the back seat.

We drove to my parents' house to say goodbye. I handed the almonds to Mom. She smiled and said her mother had done the same thing to her and Dad on their wedding night. Joe asked dad if there was a balance on the expenses for the wedding. Dad said there was. Joe took the amount from the wedding deposit envelope and handed it to him.

"Would you deposit the rest in our savings account?" he asked.

Dad said yes, and he put the money Joe gave him back into the envelope.

"Why did you do that?" Joe asked.

"Because you were responsible enough to reimburse the debt, I have the option of cancelling it."

He handed the envelope to Mom and told her to take care of it. We hugged them both, said thank you and left. We went to Joe's house, took pictures, said goodbye and started the long drive to Camp McCoy, Wisconsin.

We checked into Jane's Motel in Sparta, a small town a short distance from post. There were no quarters there for married personnel. I brought in the electric coffee pot, frying pan and toaster and set them on the small table in the room. I stored dishes, tablecloth, and flat wear in the nightstand drawers. The motel changed the sheets and towels every other day. There was no refrigerator in the room, but the weather was cold enough to keep the milk, orange juice and eggs on the windowsill to stay fresh. Two weeks later, the orders came for Joe's return to Fort Leonard Wood. Once again, he was advance party for the convoy; this time I was with him, so the trip back would not be as not as lonely.

We packed the linens and appliances in the trunk and our suitcases on the back seat of the car. We left cups, coffee pot, sugar, cereal and milk on the windowsill to have breakfast before we left. Joe set the alarm for 5:00am so we would have ample time to shower, dress and be on our way before the convoy left. For some reason the alarm didn't go off. Joe woke up, saw the time and woke me up.

"Mary Ann, wake up. The alarm didn't go off and the convoy is on the road!"

Joe got dressed but I didn't have a chance to. I was busy putting the cups, dishes, coffee pot, and small cooler in the trunk of the car.

"I'll dress in the car," I said grabbing my clothes as I rushed out the door. He handed me a map and told me the route the convoy was taking.

"Find a way to get ahead of them. They can't be that far ahead of us.

I opened the map and located roads that would eventually get us ahead of the convoy. Some of them were narrow, unpaved and passed through cow pastures. In the middle of navigating, I had to get dressed. I didn't take notice if anyone on the road was watching me. It was quite a maneuver to put on underwear, a half-slip and hook a bra under a bathrobe. I didn't bother with the garter belt and stockings. I slipped my arms out of the robe sleeves and into my blouse, took off the robe, buttoned the blouse and pulled on my skirt. Our back road plan to get ahead of the convoy took about half an hour, but we did it.

Once we were far enough ahead, we stopped in a restaurant and had breakfast. Joe took his ditty bag into the men's room and shaved.

Our temporary housing at Ft. Leonard Wood was a two-room apartment in a converted Bachelor Officer's Quarters. The bedroom contained two army cots, a chest of drawers, a lamp and a chair. After our first night, I pushed the cots together and covered them with a bedspread, which didn't make them any more uncomfortable to sleep on. A door from the bedroom opened into a bathroom we shared with the couple on the other side. Potentially embarrassing if you forgot to lock their door. The other room served as a kitchen, dining, and living area. A two-burner hot plate sat on the grey counter top next to the refrigerator, and another small dark brown cabinet with a sink and drain board completed the kitchen. In front of the windows was an overstuffed brown mohair sofa, matching chair and end table with a lamp. A maple table and two chairs served as our dining area. I did the best I could to brighten the room with a colorful tablecloth, and flowers. It was almost impossible to bring any warmth to the dull cream painted walls and dark brown furnishings.

One afternoon I was sitting on the bench in the recreation area when an older man in uniform sat on the bench across from me. He opened the conversation asking how long we had been on post. I told him we just arrived. He said he also just checked in and his wife would be joining him shortly. I told him Joe had graduated from OCS in February and we were on our honeymoon. He joked about spending a honeymoon on a military post. I said it didn't matter; we were together. It was almost time for me to make supper; I invited him to join us. He accepted. When Joe came home, I told him we were having company for supper. He asked who it was.
"I don't remember his name."
"What rank was he?"
"I don't know."

"What brass was on his uniform?"
"Silver eagles."
"You invited a Colonel to supper?"
"He said he was alone, waiting for his wife to join him."

I made spaghetti and meatballs, tossed salad and chocolate pudding pie for desert.

The Colonel arrived in civilian clothes. He introduced himself to Joe not as Colonel, but by first and last name. The ice was broken and Joe felt at ease.

A few days later, I received a bouquet of flowers and a thank you note from him.

Shortly after, Joe took me for a drive off post to an area called Devil's Elbow. We pulled into the driveway of a private home. He held my hand and led me to the side of the house that had a walk out basement. He opened the door to a furnished apartment with kitchen, living room, bedroom and bath. He said his housing allowance would pay the rent and he liked the privacy we would have there. The landlord had agreed to a month-to-month rental. Joe said the apartment would be cool in the hot Missouri summer. We packed our belongings and moved in.

I called my dad on June 16 to wish him a happy 45th birthday. A few days later I received a letter from my mother.

June 16 or it should be 17,
it's 1:15 AM

Dear Mary Ann & Joe,
It was wonderful hearing your voice again. Thanks for calling Dad on his birthday. (He had tears in his eyes). That was the nicest thing you could have given him. I was glad to hear you found a new place but I didn't understand the rest. Is Joe going to be stationed in California or what? I haven't said anything so don't worry. May the Lord watch over both of you. I haven't lost any weight but I don't eat as much bread, the

weather is too warm anyway. If Dad has to work on the 4th I might come down with the kids before. Then Dad can fly down to meet us. As I said, no plans are being made, you remember every time I planned on us going for a good time something happens. So God willing when the time comes we'll just leave. Angie and I sat and talked about you until 1:00AM. She sends her love with a kiss from the baby and Sonny. Paul turns the radio on full blast every morning and dances around the living room.

Please take good care of yourself and Joe. God bless you both. Good night, I miss you.

Love Mom

I still didn't have a driver's license. I needed to get one so I could take the car to go shopping. We asked our landlord where I could apply for one, and he gave us directions to a nearby grocery store. We thought it was a rather odd place to get an application, but we drove there.

It was a small, quaint building with white clapboard siding and one large front window. The wooden screen door squeaked when we opened it; inside was a wide worn planked oak floor. The store's inventory included bread, cereal, cold cuts, flour, milk, canned fruits, vegetables, and other basic staples. We walked up to the counter and spoke to the man behind it.

"Can we apply for a driver's license here?" Joe asked.

"Go to the wire cage office at the back of the store," he said motioning with his hand. We found the small caged office with an opening for customers to speak through.

"My wife would like to apply for a driver's license," Joe said to the man behind the cage.

"Fill out this application and bring it back to me."

"Can I fill it out now?" I asked.

"Yes you can."

I filled it out and handed it back to him.

"It will take about a week to ten days before you hear from the license bureau."

I assumed he meant I would have an appointment for my road test.

I was surprised when I opened the letter from the license bureau a week later and found my license instead of an appointment for a road test. I couldn't wait for Joe to get home to tell him.

"My driver's license came in the mail today."
"You mean your appointment for your road test."
"No. My license."
"They sent you a license without taking a road test?"
"Yes."
"I can't believe it. That would never happen at home."
"I couldn't believe it either. I'm glad I had that lesson from Uncle Paul."
"I'll let you drive to the post a few times so you'll know how to get there and gain more confidence on the road. Once on post, I'll show you where the Commissary and PX are located. I want you to be careful driving on Route 66. It's notorious for accidents. The days when I car pool, you can have the car. Just be careful."

. . . . .

Mom, Dad, and my brothers Tom and Paul visited us for the Fourth of July holiday. When they arrived, I made some lemonade. Dad and the boys went outside to look round. No sooner did they walk out the door than Mom started.

"There's a rumor in the neighborhood you had an affair with Tony before you were married."

I looked at her in disbelief.

"What on earth are you talking about? How could you believe such a vicious rumor? If you who raised me question my innocence, how can I defend myself?"

"I'm as upset as you are, but that's what I heard,"

"Why would you believe such a lie?"

I slammed my glass of lemonade on the kitchen table. As I paced from the kitchen to the living room, my thoughts raced back to the years of obedience saying no to sex before marriage. My morals came from my Mother. Before I was twelve years old, I knew what a virgin was and I had to be one when I married. Her warnings filled my head.

"If you let a boy fondle you, he will brag that he went further and your reputation will be ruined.
You have sex and a baby after you marry, not before.
Sex is not love.
There are places for girls who make a mistake. They are sent to homes for unwed mothers and in most cases give their babies up for adoption.
The burden of virginity is your responsibility."

She preached until I was fully indoctrinated to her will. Now she confronted me with a malicious rumor.

I loved my mother but suddenly I was able to respond to the accusation without fear. I stood in front of her and looked directly at her.

"The only person I have to account to is the man I married; he knows the truth. I didn't take your instructions lightly, Mom; I adhered to them and struggled with them often while dating Joe. I wanted to break the rules, but I didn't because I was afraid, respected you, Dad and myself. I valued my reputation and knew if I made a mistake and got pregnant, not only would my reputation be ruined but everyone in the family, and my child would have to endure the whispers and rumors of my mistake. I was infatuated with Tony. That's all there was to it. Why would you believe the lie about me?"

I didn't give her a chance to answer.

"What is an affair, Mom? Tony calling me on the phone, the one night I sat with him on the front stoop. Going for a ride in the car with Mary and Jim, or the one time alone when he told me he knew I cared for him and I should wait to be sure before I married the wrong person. That is what your nosy neighbors saw or heard and assumed more because of their small evil minds. There was no intimacy. If I were going to have an affair, it would be in secret, not visible to the whole neighborhood, especially ours."

Dad heard our continued arguing and hurried in. He asked what was going on. I told him. He glared at my mother.
"Why didn't you keep your mouth shut and your opinions of busybody neighbors to yourself? They hide behind closed curtains to watch what's going on in the neighborhood, waiting to find something or someone to pull apart. They have nothing better to do with their time and are probably guilty themselves of what they're rumoring about."

For the remainder of their visit, things were strained between my mother and me. I reflected on all the years I dated Joe, about her instructions and my obedience following them. Why would she succumb to such vile gossip and not defend my innocence? She of all people knew better. I loved and respected my parents; however, that day I cut the maternal apron string. I was suddenly aware I no longer needed her permission or feared her disapproval. My decisions were my own. I was accountable only to my husband and myself.

Joe and I were happy but the day arrived when he received orders for a new assignment. He said he wouldn't know where he was going until he reported to Patrick Air Force Base in California. He felt it could be Korea. The war had ended, but there was still a need for our military to serve there. I was thankful he wouldn't be fighting but the separation was for a year, and would be more difficult than all the others. For the next year, we would be holding and loving each other through our letters. We packed the car and headed for home.

I wanted to look for an apartment, but Dad said I could live at home rent-free while Joe was gone. Joe thought it was a good idea too. The money I saved and the allotment he sent home might be enough to put a down payment on a house when he returned.

I agreed, but I knew it wouldn't be easy. I was accustomed to making my own decisions with accountability only to Joe. That was going to change radically when I moved back home, considering the history with my mother and her restrictions. I consoled myself that it was only for a year before Joe and I would start our own family. Joe hoped I would pregnant before he left, but it was not to be.

Mom and Dad made plans to take a trip to New York city for a few days to celebrate their 25th wedding anniversary on September 3rd, and Mom's birthday on September 12th.

It would be the first time they went away alone since their honeymoon in Niagara Falls. The night before they left Dad took her to dinner. She wore the pink lace dress that she wore at my wedding reception.

2 September 1954

Hi Honey,

    Here is the first letter to start a possible year's chain of letters. Maybe you are wondering what I meant by "possible", well there is a chance you might be with me in a few months. I guess if we pray we may be able to enjoy being together in Japan. What I have been told officially so far is they are pulling all units out of Korea and moving them to Japan. Well tomorrow, the 4th I am leaving here and taking a bus to Travis Air Force Base where I'll board a plane and fly to Japan. It will take about 36 hours and we will probably make two stops. One in Honolulu and one in Okinawa. It will not be as nice as a trip to Rochester, but it is better than 14 days on the ocean. As I said in the beginning, there might be a chance that you will be joining me in a few months. If so, we will probably get a home in Japan and buy some furniture. The only expensive things are the appliances. If it works out, I am thinking about having the car brought over with you.

    How did you make out with your job? Any news yet? Even though there is a chance, you might have to quit in four months I'd take it anyway and make a little money so we can still save. I know this is a question that has been answered no before, but is there a chance you might be pregnant? If not, we will have to wait until I get back from overseas to settle down and try. I called home tonight and they said you were out with dad. I'll call again before I leave and let you know the news ahead of time. I've enclosed my temporary address. You can write and I'll get them when I get there. I miss you. Write honey please. Until next time.

After Joe left, I had an interview with Bob McGraw, the manager at C I T Credit, and he hired me the same day. My job was collecting payments at the counter. Working outside the house was the best way to help time pass quickly and gave me the opportunity to save towards the goals Joe and I set. I was out of the house and could maintain some sort of independence.

7 September 1954

Hi Honey,

I am still in the states. Just like the Army, hurry up and wait. They moved us out of Parks Friday and said that in 48 hours we would be out of Travis flying to Japan. I expect to get out either tonight or tomorrow. There is a slim chance I can be stationed in Japan. If so, you can join me. It would be nice if we could be together there.

Do you miss me as much as I miss you? I suppose at times it's hard for you to say that I was the best thing that ever happened to you. Whatever I may have done to you to hurt you honey I am sorry for it all. If you only knew how much I want to take you in my arms and tell you how sorry I was then you might believe me. Many times, I was just too stubborn to let myself go, even if I wanted to. I love you honey and though we might have quarrels I would not trade anything in the world for you.

I've loved you and fought hard and long to keep you, maybe at times not long or hard enough.

I've done wrong and at times like this, I wish you were here so I could tell you and make you feel you belong to me. Honey, take my word for it if a year goes by and we don't see one another I'll know what I've missed and what it means to have a wife that loves you and willing to accept the separation. I'll suffer, I know I will, but to make it easier and go by faster I will have to make myself a little colder toward my own feelings because the only thing I have will be your letters and our memories. Write and let me hear from you often. I love you!

I was puzzled about his feelings and thoughts about hurting me in the past. Were there other instances I didn't know about? My wounded heart healed because I loved him and that's what mattered. What happened in the past was not important. We had our love, each other and our future together.

He said not to count on my joining him in Japan, but I did think about the possibility of being with him and not facing a long separation. I wanted him to know whatever the future held in store, we would face it together.

12 September 1954

Hi Honey,

Here I am in Japan. We arrived Saturday morning and landed in Tokyo International Airport. On our way across, we stopped in Hawaii for about six hours. It was beautiful. I had a chance to take some pictures and Waikiki beach. From there we went to Wake Island, which took another 9 hours.

Yesterday we went to Tokyo; it really is amazing the way they do business there. The shops are in front and their living quarters are in the back. Things are very expensive, 360 yen to one American dollar. The workmanship is beautiful. I bought you one present so far and I have my eye on a black, eggshell china tea set. I think you will like it.

Tomorrow I go for my assignment, I pray it's not Korea, but there is still the possibility it could happen honey. Don't worry if it does happen honey because it will only be for 12 months and I can stand it if you can. As far as what might happen in the near future, I can't say for sure.

I miss you darling and I hope you understand how deep my love is for you. The white orchid I sent you brought back all the memories of our wedding. I know some people may say that gifts can't take the place of the one you love, but remember honey I love you and the gifts I send you are my way of saying how much I appreciate you for being my wonderful wife. I'll remember you exactly that way. We may not see one another for quite some time but remember a good marriage bond is stronger than anything in the world is if the ties of love hold it together. Since I can't really express my love in letters, the best thing is to remember all our wonderful times, and I'll supplement them with a few gifts now and then. Remember, the most I can be away is 15 months unless something unforeseen may happen. So pray honey we may soon be together again.

One day I came home from work and Mom and Dad said they'd been looking at new houses. I didn't pursue the reason for their decision, but I had my suspicions. The contractor said it would be finished in about four months.

"Where is the tract of homes you're looking at?" I asked.

"The subdivision is off Empire Blvd. about twenty minutes from here. It's near a bus line, but it would take you about 15 minutes to walk to the bus stop," Dad said.

"That's not a problem in good weather. When it's cold or raining, I'll drive the car to work."

After supper, we drove to the subdivision. The homes were large, on landscaped lawns and quiet streets. The move was inevitable.

16 September 1954

My Dearest Wife,

This is the first letter from Korea, as you probably knew from the address on the envelope. For me to start telling you exactly what Korea is like would be hard to put in writing. Unlike any other place, that I have seen in the world this is the worst. We landed at an airbase called K-16 about two miles south of Seoul. From there, I hopped on a 2½-ton truck and rode about 25 miles south to this airbase called K-55. What the numbers stand for I don't know. Headquarters of the 934th J.A.G. is located here and I am waiting for further assignment within the group. I don't know if I'll stay at this base or not. As far as living conditions are concerned, they are the least putting it bluntly. Three of us live together in one tent about the size of a kitchen. The inside is finished in wood, mahogany at that, and a canvas cover on the outside. The tents are in a line up and down a mud street and everything including the mess hall is typically in the "field." It's not bad. When you settle down with a group of fellows in the same situation, you manage to get along. One way to look at it there is no war going on over here.

Now how about yourself beautiful. The mail hasn't

caught up with me, so I don't know what's going on stateside. Be sure to fill your letters with interesting things about you. Have you started work yet, is the car in good shape? I would like to have more pictures of you so I can at least keep myself up to date on my wife. The sweet beautiful girl I married.

Days have been long with not much else to do but remember all the wonderful times I spent with you, yes even you tickling me. I can't say I miss it but honey I sure miss you. To be with you again is all I dream of.

I'll sign off for tonight darling. I love and miss you.

I continued to write although he hadn't received any of the letters that I'd sent. Joe began his letters with a new salutation. "My Darling Wife" or "My Dearest Wife," replaced the usual "Hi Honey," "Beautiful" or "Rusty." I thought this reflected his loneliness and his wanting me to know how he thought of me now that we were married.

My job was going well. The bus ride from home to the office took about twenty minutes. When I got off at Main and Gibbs Street around 8:15 and walked to the office on East Avenue, I was at my counter before we opened at 8:30. Sometimes during lunch break I'd finish a letter to Joe I had started the night before and gave it to the mailman when he delivered the office mail.

19 September 1954

My Darling Wife,

Today is Sunday, and I have a taste of what every Sunday will be like from now on. Not much was done except to ride around and see how the Koreans live, and not too good either. We took a jeep, visited a few points of interest, and took pictures. When I get home, I can really enjoy telling some of the stories behind all of them. Next August 25th I'll be leaving here to come home again. It seems like a long time, but I have nothing but time. I suppose I can't complain; I've just arrived but it sure would be nice to be home again with you. I am lucky to have a wonderful wife like you. As soon as I get home, we'll start on some little ones just like their mother.

I made out the allotment for $200 to the bank; if things go alright, we will have a good sum of money to get started on. I don't plan to stay in the service, so we can settle down, raise a family and live like a happy family is supposed to live. I don't like being separated from you and I am going to do my best to keep us together the rest of our lives. I haven't decided whether I am going back to school or just find a job. Whatever it is, I am going to do something that will keep you with me always. I am sick of moving around. I want to settle down and you're the perfect one to do it with. I am assigned to a good company and I've got a good job to keep me busy until I get home, then I'll have you to keep me busy. I sure miss having you next to me at night when I go to bed. Soon it will be getting cold and you won't be here to snuggle up to. I'll have to start counting the days until I can once again be with you. Maybe I never showed it, but we did have some memorable times when we were together. Remember living in our little place at Devils Elbow and the long trip home? I recall taking a picture of a beautiful sunset one evening too.

Well that's if for tonight honey, write often and soon. I am still waiting for your letters. I miss you.

I framed the picture of the sunset. Each time I looked at it, I was reminded of the happiness during our "honeymoon" at Ft Leonard Wood.

Now that I was home, I had to take the road test for my New York State driver's license. Those few months on the road in Missouri gave me more than enough experience to pass the test.

21 September 1954

My Dearest Wife,
 Hi Honey, here it is Tuesday night around 9:00 and I just took a shower and getting ready for bed so I thought I'd

take the time and drop you a line.

Today was my second day of work and I have to try hard to keep myself busy. This place is very different from stateside. Everyone works hard counting off the number of days left until they go home. Me, well I have too many days to start counting them now. Someday I will and I suppose you'll be doing the same. May God save that day especially for us. We all had hopes back home that I wouldn't be going to Korea, and it didn't turn out the way we wanted it to. No difference though, because in twelve months I'll be heading home to you and our future.

Honey it's times like this I really appreciate all you have done and the love you have for me. I can still remember the time in Wisconsin when I got that mysterious telephone call; inside I knew it was from you but the reason was not clear in my mind. Then, when we talked up on the hill, I realized how much you loved me to come there just to make sure you wanted to marry me. I loved you very much that night honey. I can still remember what you had on. Your blue suit. The one you had for our honeymoon. How tiny you looked as you ran down the sidewalk to meet me. Honey how I wish we could live that day over so I could tell you how I feel now, but it is over and I'll have to wait until we meet once more. I remember that day very well honey.

Well anyway honey, these are the things I dream about each night waiting for my return home. It will be a long wait, I have many dreams to keep me company, and I hope you feel the same. Do you miss me honey? I know it's a silly question to ask. I have faith and trust you, remember that. That is all for tonight sweetheart. Be good. I love you.

His next letter was a happy one because he received four of my letters at one time. He said he was disappointed that he wasn't going to be a dad. I understood how he felt. I wanted a child, too, but I wanted him with me when the baby was born.

I enjoyed my job and the friends I made. Knowing I was a newlywed and Joe was overseas, everyone was interested in what he was doing. My manager, Bob McGraw, watched over me like a mother hen. One afternoon a girl in the office asked me to have lunch with her. When we returned, Bob called me into his office and shut the door. I wondered if I'd done something wrong.

"How was your lunch today?" he asked.
"Fine, Helen and I went to the Maplewood Restaurant."
"With Joe away I feel a responsibility to look out for you."
"What do you mean?"
"Have you ever heard the phrase, *Birds of a feather flock together*"?
"Yes, but what has that got to do with going to lunch with Helen?"
"Let's just say it would be to your benefit not to be seen with her. I'm sure Joe would agree with me on this. If she asks again, just say you have other plans."

The rest of the afternoon, I pondered the reason for him not wanting me to be in her company. No one in the office had said anything derogatory about her to me. I respected my manager, but didn't want to hurt Helen's feelings so I brought my lunch from home. I used the excuse I was saving money not to offend her when she asked me to go to lunch. I can only assume the reason for the discussion.

I liked my job, my co-workers and my manager. It was about this time my manager gave me another responsibility; taking the day's receipts to the bank for deposit. From our office on East Avenue and Gibbs Street to the Marine Midland Bank on Main Street was a fifteen-minute walk. About the same distance walking from Ritz's to home after school. The round trip to the bank, making the deposit and return took about forty-five minutes. At first, I was worried about carrying all the cash and checks, but it became routine. My anxiety disappeared and the walk kept me in shape.

Our letters took at least a week or more to reach each other so we were always a week or two behind knowing what was going on.

10 October 1954

My Dearest Darling,

Hi honey, another day and before you know it the end of the month will be here. In your letter, you said you received the one I apologized for what I had done. Honey, there certainly wasn't any need for you to apologize because I love you, your temper, and all of you so don't try and change. I know you'll be more grown up when I get back and I am sure you know I fell in love with you when you were very young and I will always think of you as a young girl honey.

As for making things easy for me, all you have to do is keep writing often so I'll always hear from you.

I am not worried like you think because you are my wife and we have to forget those things that happened. I know how much you love me; in fact, I've always known. It's easy when you know you have a true love, in fact, that is why I married you because we were meant for each other.

Be good and take extra good care of yourself. Bye for now. Sweet dreams. I love you.

I was lonely and reading Joe's letters made me feel closer to him. I pictured him writing, thinking of the thoughts he wanted to say to me, putting them on paper quickly. Often his thoughts were ahead of his writing and ran into each other as he wrote, but it didn't matter. I understood completely. I shared my memories of making love, how I missed his touch and kisses in my letters to him. My longing for him was felt daily. I was waiting patiently for the day we would be together again

17 October 1954

My Dearest Darling,

Hi honey, another day has gone by and another week. We saw a movie "Genevieve". It was good but it brought back

memories of the days we spent together. It's not good seeing pictures like that with married couples. How they act in the love scenes makes me want you more. When I say, want you I really mean it. All last night I thought about you. Every dream is wonderful honey, even if it is just a dream. One day it will be a real dream, to hold you in my arms, kiss you; make love to you until together, we both share the fulfillment of that love.

So you remember my last cigarette at night. Well I still do it, it's a habit I picked up since we were married. I never used to do that. I'm glad you remembered those little things. You always said, "Little things mean a lot", and I think I've learned you are so right. I'll make every little thing count when we are back together. I'm glad you liked the gift honey; it is just my way of showing my affection for you. I have another here, that is rather expensive, but I think I'll hold on to it a little while and keep you guessing. After all, I can't spoil you all at once.

Again, it is time to say goodnight. I'll keep writing often and please do the same. Your letters are all I have to look forward to darling and they mean so much to me now that I am hundreds of miles away. Be good my darling, I love and miss you very much.

. . . . .

Dad listed the house for sale but told the realtor he didn't want a sign in the yard. He said the less the neighbors knew the better. Mom agreed not to say anything to her friends when they came over for coffee, especially Frances Ange, our neighborhood gossip. She always had something or someone to whisper about when she saw you. Childless, she found fault with every kid in the neighborhood.

24 October 1954

My Dearest Darling,

Hi honey, today is Sunday and it was a beautiful day. The sun was shining and it was really warm. I guess it's what we call Indian summer back home. If I remember right, back home around this time it gets cold and it's time for the Northern Lights. Remember I said for you to check for them around this time and if you look some clear cold night I'm sure you'll see them. I've seen them every year around this time as long as I can remember. Too bad I wasn't home so we could look at them together. It's a perfect time of year for making love and you're the person to do it with. The time when I will feel down in the dumps will be around the Christmas holidays. I've been home for every Christmas. I'm going to spend all my time shopping for my wife. I have to find something extra special for you.

  We took more pictures today, back in the hills where we found some small villages. It's remarkable how they live off the land. They grow and make everything they have, in fact, much to my surprise they grow cotton and spin cloth. Seems like it comes right out of storybooks I used to read. I sent the other pictures out to you so before long you will have a chance to see exactly what I am talking about. By the time I leave here, I should have a fair collection of slides to show you.

  Well that is it for tonight honey; write often because I'm always waiting for your letters. I love and miss you.

  I asked Joe to look for a set of porcelain china when he went to Japan for R & R. I had a set for every-day use but I wanted something special for holidays and special occasions. I trusted his taste. I knew his choice would be something I would like.

             29 October 1954

My Dearest Darling,

  Hi honey, soon it will be the end of another month. Little by little they are going by, it seems slow but they are still going by. Right now, the radio is playing some old familiar tunes that bring back memories; they haven't played "Count Every Star" yet. That song means a lot to us and I hope they play it at least once. I heard "Tenderly" and that really brings back some of *the times, we shared together. Most of all I think about our wedding reception when we asked the band to play it. Do you remember when we left the reception? We knew what we were doing didn't we honey. If I had that day to live over, I wouldn't change a single moment of it. We were so tired from the long day, we said we would talk and not make love until the morning and how serious we were. Then I saw you in your nightgown and, I knew we would not wait until morning. I made love to you for the first time. We were both so unsuspecting weren't we honey? Maybe inside that cute little head of yours you had all the intentions of doing what you did. I guess women are smarter that way aren't they. I know it was difficult for you but you accepted what happened honey, and I was there to help you. For the first time we felt the warmth of our bodies and the passion. How I want that now. I miss you so much honey. I think about you all the time.*

The last letter I received from you was really "no. 1". It showed me the feelings you have for me. I'd say that letter, all five pages was full of love for me. I can't complain about a letter like that. I know my letters don't compare but I'll try and write often to make up for them. Good night for now darling. I love you. Be good and take care of yourself.

I continued to save the money Joe sent home. He told me I could use it if I needed to, but I didn't want to touch it. When he came home, we planned to use it as a down payment on our first house. I used my weekly check for savings and paying our bills. In one of his letters, he referred to our bills as "my debts" and that after Christmas he would send me funds to help. I was offended. They were "our" debts and I was hurt by the tone of his letter. I was doing the best I could, not touching our bank account, and I reminded him I wasn't paying rent so I was able to bank most of what I earned. I paid the car payment, insurance, maintenance, and gas and took a small allowance for personal needs. It was the first time I was upset with him since he left. I told him how I felt about his remarks in my next letter.

Joe always liked my hair long and asked me not to cut it. I said I wouldn't if he would do the same. He reminded me Army regulations required his hair to be a certain length, but there was some leeway with officers if they wanted to keep it a bit longer.

Halloween was around the corner, and I decided to make a clown costume to greet the trick or treaters when they came to the door. I sprayed a blonde wig puce green and purple and teased it to the size of a basketball. The one-piece costume I made was orange and yellow with large purple pompoms for buttons on the front. I took my lipstick and painted large circles on my cheeks and a small circle on the tip of my nose. Donning white gloves and a mask, I was ready to great the unsuspecting kids at the door. Later in the evening when the doorbell stopped ringing at our house, I decided to visit Aunt Mary and Uncle John. I kept on my costume but removed the mask and drove to their house. I parked a safe distance away, so they wouldn't see my car. I put the mask on, walked to the door and rang the bell, wondering what the expression would be on their faces. The door opened.

"Trick or treat."

"Aren't you too old to be trick or treating?" Aunt Mary asked with an inquisitive look.

She offered me a piece of candy from the bowl that she was holding. I took the bowl out of her hand, turned and walked away.

"Come back with my bowl," she yelled.

My uncle came running out the door toward me. I removed the mask and wig.

"Fooled you, didn't I?" I asked.

They said they thought it was late for someone to be coming to the door and I was too tall to be a kid. We went into the house and had coffee with doughnuts, and laughed about them not recognizing me.

I told them I was thinking of taking a Civil Service exam. It could mean a larger paycheck and the benefits were too good to ignore.

2 November 1954

My Dearest Darling,
Hi honey, well it is the start of a new month. Sure is good to see it come around. According to my calculations, I have 297 more days; at least I got rid of the 300 mark. Today I received two of your letters. After I read them, I have nothing until I hear from you again. It's so good to hear from you at least for the moment. So you think about me always. Well our thoughts must be running along the same lines, because I feel the same way. I often dream about you at night honey, they are good dreams and I hope they stay that way. They help to make the days go faster. You said your hair is almost grown out. Good, because I think it really looked nice when it was like that. Yes, I'm letting my hair grow out. I'm keeping my part of the bargain, after all that's the least I can do to make you happy. Don't worry, when I get home my hair will be just the way you expect it to be, so you do the same. I'm going shopping for Christmas and it's going to be a problem getting them all out to the right people. I think I'll use your idea of sending them to you. They will probably get there ahead of time but it's better than too late. Here's what I'll do, as soon as I shop for them I'll send them out and write and let you know what I've sent. They will be mail order so I won't see them and the only way you'll know who they are for is by my letters. Yours I'll save and send air mail to get there by Christmas.
Well that's it for tonight darling. I miss you.

Almost four months of separation were behind us, and each day that passed was one fewer we had to be apart. This separation reinforced the foundation of our love. We spoke of our longing, our loneliness and our hope for the future in every letter we wrote. The support we gained from those letters strengthened our commitment to each other. As a husband, Joe was aware of his responsibility and I was pleased and proud of him for writing about his desire to protect our marriage.

12 November 1954

My Dearest Darling,

    Hi honey, me again with a few lines of love. How is my sweetheart doing these days? Fine I hope. It's days like Sunday that make me feel so blue. Not much to do on weekends around here except go out and take pictures, and that's getting boring now. No matter though, time still goes by whatever we do.

    I wrapped some of your gifts today and will mail them out tomorrow. I'm saving the last one to mail to you by airmail. I don't want it mixed up with the family gifts. I hope you enjoy all of them, including some others you may receive. I got a letter from Mom today and she said she received the allotment check and you were coming to the house to pick it up. I mailed out the money order so you'll have the $200, to deposit in the bank. Next month the check should go right to our bank. I know we talked about using the money for the down payment on our home but I will still have about six months to serve when I get home.

    I keep thinking about that Ford convertible. Sure would be nice to have one next year to go driving across the country with. The top down and you in the front seat with your red hair blowing in the breeze. I dream of those days now with the absolute feeling in my heart they will come true. All we have to do is wait for the months to pass. I'd wait for you for year's honey, as long as we could be together again. I'll probably say that repeatedly before we return to one another's arms.

    On the envelope, I've written something in Korean. I suppose if a Korean read it, he would say that I had poor handwriting, but it still says what I want to say. It says, "I love you very much". I don't intend to learn Korean but it's something different to put on the letter.

    Well honey, that's it for tonight. I love and miss you.

Joe sent a picture of Thanksgiving dinner with his Company Commander, Battalion Commander and others in H/S Co. He wrote that he enjoyed the meal but missed being home with me. I knew exactly how he felt. This was his third Thanksgiving in as many years that he was unable to be home.

Time passed quickly some days while on others, the hands on the clock seemed glued to the same hour, the minute hand barely moving. Those days put me in a slump, but I knew if I stayed there, I would start feeling sorry for myself. Before bed, I began to read Joe's letters again to re-kindle his words of love and assurance that one day our separation would end.

His pictures from Japan were shall we say interesting, especially those of certain establishments catering to an age-old profession that was legal in Japan. I didn't spell out my concerns because he knew what I meant. I assured him that I wasn't doing anything to jeopardize our relationship, and I trusted he would do the same.

29 November 1954

My Darling Wife,

Hi beautiful, me again with a few more lines from your loving husband. Boy, that three-page letter was a nice morale booster. Now honey, what is the matter with my sweet one? You're not letting a couple of pictures get you down. Everything you said about our future is exactly true and don't think that I'd do anything to mess it up. I agree that for me to do anything like that would be hurting you and I wouldn't do it for anything in the world. I want to keep us both free from infection and before I'd ever pass anything onto your clean white body I'd kill myself. When I married you darling, I knew you were mine, now and always will be and for me to deceive you in any manner would ruin everything I love you for. So, no sweat honey, I promise always to be true to you and wouldn't mess up our lives and our children's for a few minutes of excitement. I know I am not the only one deprived. My sweet redheaded wife is also doing the same. I'm proud of you, the way you look and dress, and the ideals you have.

As for those pictures, you can say they are an education to show you some of what life is like on the other side of the world. Actually, Japan is beautiful but they have legalized prostitution, which breeds a high rate of VD, and I want no part of that believe me. In the future if I send pictures that may be misleading, think of them as informative. I just want to show you that America with all its wrongs is still more beautiful and cleaner than the rest of the world.

Glad to hear your mom and dad sold their home. You'll have to send me the new address and phone number. Have to be sure I have no trouble calling you Christmas. Be good darling and write as often as you can. I love you very much honey. God only knows.

When the gifts Joe bought arrived, I wrapped and put them under the Christmas tree. All the family would be at the house to celebrate. It would be the perfect time to give them their gifts. The house would be filled with family and friends, but it wasn't going to be the same without him.

24 December 1954

My Dearest Darling,
Hi Honey, right now it's 11:30 at night and most of the excitement is dying down. For a while, it seemed like Christmas Eve but as usual, most of the guys have no other way to enjoy themselves so they have to drink to forget they are in Korea. The only thing wrong with tonight is I am blue because I have spent my first Christmas away from you. Honestly, honey no matter what we do it doesn't seem like Christmas.
We decorated the tree and club but there is still something missing. In my case, it is you and the idea of being away from home. Honey I never realized until tonight what I was missing at home. Isn't it always the way that when you have what you want you don't appreciate it until you don't have it? Take it from me darling, you should be thankful to be able to be together at home with those you love. Those I love are miles away from me. There is no one here that comes close to family and friends at home. Tonight we gave our Christmas present to "Willie Lump Lump" (we named him that) that works behind the bar at the Officers Club. He is about or a little older than your kid brother Tom but lacks the affection your brother has received.
I am sorry about the phone call but they never could get thru. Maybe later on when the lines aren't so crowded I'll try again. Goodnight for now. I love and miss you.

I spent New Year's Eve at home watching television with my family. At midnight, I kissed Joe in my heart and thoughts and remembered all the past years we waited for the last moment of the old year to pass and welcomed in the new one with hope it would be a blessed year.

January 1955

2 January 1955

My Dearest Darling,

 Hi honey, well it sure is good to be able to put that year on paper. It will even look better when it says August. At least now, I can say I will be going home this year. That's a day I'll be looking forward to and I know my loving wife will be home counting and waiting for the days to pass with me.

 You know what? The 22nd of this month we will be married 8 months, but the only trouble is most of it was spent away from one another.

 It seems most of my letters are written here by the fireplace on a Sunday night right after church. Here it is the New Year and I missed the excitement I missed on Christmas. Yes, we had a big party and all the liquor you could drink but there was something missing and that sweet was you. I don't think there is anything that could compare with the enjoyment one gets from being with your wife on New Year's Eve at 12:00. I remember the long kisses I used to get when midnight rolled around, the dance we danced in the middle of the floor, both of us so in love with one another. Probably the only dance we had all evening because I was so darn thick headed and didn't have the sense that someday I would miss your loving body close to me. How I wish I had you close to me. All I have now honey are the fond dreams and the good times we used to have.

 You mentioned in your letters that we always seem to mention the same lines repeatedly and most of the time we are thinking the same thing. The truth is honey I can't get you out of my mind and I don't ever expect to either. Honey you know what I would want to have from you more than anything while I am away? Please don't get the wrong idea. Here is what I want. I would like you to wear the nightgown and negligee you *wore on our wedding night and take some pictures that are not revealing but appealing as far as I alone would be concerned. Also, include some wearing a sweater, skirt and bathing suit. Just casual shots around the house, in the bedroom, or on the couch where I could remember you as my wife. They don't have to be sexy honey just revealing enough for me to remember what is waiting for me at home. I would really appreciate it. It's a sorry thing when you have a beautiful red headed wife at home and can't enjoy her. Remember they are for me when you take them. I love you.*

I smiled to myself when I read about the pictures he wanted me to send to him. I had more than enough of the everyday pictures he requested but the one he wanted of me in my nightgown was going to be difficult. Who would take the picture?

I thought about asking Mary, my maid of honor, but I didn't want anyone to know Joe wanted that kind of a picture of me. I thought of asking Mom, but then I wondered what she too would think about Joe wanting one like that.

6 January 1955

My Dearest Darling,
Hi honey, me again with more words of love for my wonderful young redheaded wife that I can't even enjoy. When I say enjoy I really mean it too.
I received your letter today and could tell you are lonely for me too. The time is going by honey but never fast enough to please the both of us. I dream of the past and the wonderful times we had. I am glad I won't have to go on dreaming forever because someday we will be back together. Just think honey we are past the first step and now the second step will be to raise a family. I am sure going to enjoy working on the making of one. I would give anything to feel that now. I know I wouldn't want to share it with anyone but you. From the first day I met you I knew you would be the one to be my wife.

Why is it you always seem to know exactly how things are going to turn out? It was fate that brought us together. At times, I would say it was a little more that made us understand what we did mean to each other.

When I think of how I almost lost you, it gives me a funny feeling just to know that possibly we would never have married. Then I think of you the day we met in Wisconsin when I drove to La Crosse to see you. When we took the drive up on the hill and it all seemed like I was watching a love scene in the movie. Yes, my darling you were wonderful and I'll always remember my sweetheart exactly that way.

Those are the dreams that keep me going Rusty and I don't ever want to forget them.

Well beautiful, now we must say goodnight. Write as often as you can. I love to hear every word you have to tell me. Don't forget the favor I asked you for. I love you.

I didn't forget the favor Joe wanted. I hadn't solved the problem of who was going to take the picture. What I didn't know at the time was the camera had a delay timer. I could have set it and taken the picture without anyone's help.

I made the mistake of giving Joe's present of three sterling goblets, which he intended for us, to his mom. She enjoyed receiving them, and I didn't have the heart to tell her of my error. I did tell Joe about it.

Decades later when I told my mother-in-law the mistake I made, she gave them to me. I gave a goblet to each of my three sons on their wedding day. I often think about the coincidence of Joe purchasing only three of them.

17 January 1955

My Dearest Darling,
　　Hi honey, well how is my sweet heart today? Soon spring will be here.

When spring comes the rains will arrive and over here that's a season to be reckoned with. The rumor is it gets so damp you have to air your clothes out daily or they will rot. It won't get me down because the next season after that is summer, and my time will be short and I think I can get by it standing on my head. All I'll be looking forward to then, will be my return to the states to see you honey. That's all I want, to be in your arms again. My sweet redheaded wife, how I miss you. Oh how I wish I were back with you enjoying the wonder and pleasures of being married to you. There isn't much more I can ask for, and each night I ask the Lord to keep us both safe so that someday we can share one another's dream and love again.

Honey, you seemed rather disappointed when you wrote about me not being definite about the time I would be going on R & R. Well to tell the truth I never decided when I would go. The biggest things holding me back is finances. Is it alright if I borrowed a $100.00 from our account? I'll call you on my birthday and you can let me know. Listen to me sounding like a little kid, but I do want to know it's alright with you. I'll be calling you Feb. 6th. Be good darling.

I thought about his request for a $100.00 to take on R&R to Japan. I knew he was hesitant about asking for any amount even though he was sending the major portion of his monthly pay home. In my next letter, I included a money order for $250. Why not? Joe said it was ours to use as needed, and I thought he needed it so he could enjoy a relaxing time in Japan. I knew he wasn't expecting it. I imagined the look on his face when opening the letter and finding it.

22 January 1955

My Dearest Darling,

Hi honey, me again with some more love for you. I received your letter and was glad to hear from you. From the looks of things, you are as lonely for me as I am for you. Why is it our thoughts run along the same line? It seems every letter we write even though we don't see one another seems to say exactly what we both feel and want to say. I am glad we both seem to think that way. It's hard to feel anything when one is so far away. Being this far away is bad enough for two people who have been married for a while. I suppose you could say it isn't fair to us too, so much in love and married for three short months never to have been able to love one another or the chance to really enjoy one another completely. Somehow, I keep telling myself that it is all a bad dream but then I realize I am over here so very far away from you. Don't worry honey, someday we will return to those happy nights again. Honey, I remember those nights when I used to rest my head on your soft body, how could I forget them?

You mentioned in your last letter you thought of my loving you all the way from the top of your head to the tip of your toes and as you said, "and all the places in between". So you think of that too honey, well so do I. Honey I want you so bad and can't have you. When we are together again I'm going to love you so much that you will beg me to stop. You keep all the emotions inside of you honey. Save them until we are together again. Oh, how I wish you were here with me now, then again I wouldn't want you to see this place.

That's it for now honey, be good and write often. I love you.

I was working on the pictures he wanted. I had those from our honeymoon and me at home but I was concerned about the one he wanted of me in my nightgown. I wrote and told him I thought I wouldn't be able to have that particular one.

26 January 1955

My Dearest Darling,

Hi honey. How is my sweetheart today? Fine I hope. I received your letter the other day and was glad to be able to sit down for those few minutes and enjoy being with you. I was rather disappointed though when you said you couldn't do the favor I asked for. Maybe you misunderstood but you wouldn't have to do anything that would be revealing. I am sure you could have a picture taken of you in your nightgown that wouldn't show only what you wanted. Wouldn't have to be sexy. Use your own judgment on it, but remember I don't want you to show off your body, because I can dream of that.

Seems like you're in the same mood I usually get into. Can't say I blame you because very often I feel the same way. I am looking forward to the day when we return to each other's arms. It's too far away honey, it gets me down thinking about it and sometimes I get very discouraged thinking of us together back home. I'll keep my chin up and just pray each night that we both are capable to standing up to the torments of being separated from the one you love. I'll do it honey because I have your picture here that will keep me strong. It's come a long way with me. "She" was with me at school, camp, OCS Missouri, Wisconsin and now here in the Far East. It's a representation of you and I am glad to have you with me. Like I said before, better to have your picture than have you here in such a horrible environment. I'd rather have you stay perfect in mind and body at home than be here in this backward place. I think of you as a soft, tender being and that's the way you'll stay in my heart and mind. The truth is honey I can't get you out of my mind and I don't ever expect to either.

Now for tonight we must close. It's been wonderful being with you these short minutes wife dear. Be good my darling and I love you very much.

Cold and lonely winter days and nights dragged on. One night looking out the front window, I watched large fluffy snowflakes as they fell silently to the ground. I remembered how I looked forward to the cold weather as a child.

A favorite sport of mine during winter was ice-skating on our private rink in the vacant field behind our house. Sonny and his boyfriends' Joe Zizzo, Fred Rossi and Joe Rivaldo, connected our garden hose to the neighbor's to get the length needed to reach the field. The water ran all day and night into the next day to flood the area. Once frozen we skated, avoiding the shallow spots where weeds protruded above the ice. If our blades went over them, they'd stop our momentum and we'd trip or fall. It didn't matter; it was our private rink. If we were cold, we warmed up at home. Mom kept a low flame under a kettle of hot chocolate on the stove.

My first experience on ice skates was disastrous. My skates were double runners that attached to my boots like roller skates; I didn't like them because I couldn't glide on the ice. "I'm not skating, I'm walking," I complained to my mother. Under the Christmas tree, the following year was a pair of white shoe ice skates with a single blade and a white wool sweater with skating figures across the front hand knitted by my mother. Now I could pretend to be my idol, Sonja Henie.

I didn't "glide" at first. Sonny held me up until I could balance myself. It took most of the season and falling on the seat of my pants, but once I mastered the technique, the rest was easy.

Coming in after skating we took off our skates in the basement kitchen mom used for canning and preserving. She turned on the gas stove, opened the oven door to its lowest position and set a folded wool blanket on top of it. We rested our cold feet on the blanket until they warmed. A cup of hot chocolate hastened the warming.

Forty years later, I joined the Genesee Valley Figure Skaters Association. They had an adult class for those interested in learning how to dance on skates My only problem was skating backwards; fear of losing my balance and falling curtailed my advancement in that area.

I had to purchase skates. The Association had a store for me to go to, to be fitted. The surprise was their sizing and fitting. The salesman measured my foot and put on the skates. There was no wiggle room in the toe. He answered my question before I asked. "You don't need room for "growth" as you did as a child. You are not walking you are skating; your skate becomes part of your foot". His last instruction was for me to wet the skates, put them on, lace tightly, cover the blades with guards and walk on them for the day until the leather dried and conformed to the shape of my foot.

29 January 1955

My Dearest Darling,

Hi honey, I received your letter and read it with a smile on my face. It gives me such comfort to read your letters. No matter what I am doing when they come I just drop everything and sit down and read them. I guess I am like most people who look forward to mail call. Right now while I am writing this one there is soft music playing in the background on my roommates' record player. It has me right in the mood to write to you.

I am going to Japan next Sunday the 6th of February. That is if everything turns out right. Here is what I plan on doing. If I can, I will call you from Japan for my birthday. I will have a better chance of getting thru from there. Now I can't say for sure exactly what day it will be. I'll try to arrange it so you'll be home and not asleep. It should be toward the end of the week around the 11th at home. If we do get through, there will be so many things I'll want to say to you. I only hope I can keep my senses long enough to tell you what I want to most of all, and that is that I love you very much and miss you so. All I can say is be looking for my call.

Honey, they are playing "Tenderly" on the record now. If I close my eyes, I can feel you in my arms dancing. Makes me sad because it brings back many memories. Well it's time to say goodnight. Be good my sweet. I love you.

2 February 1955

My Dearest Darling,

Hi Honey, what a surprise I received today when I received your letters. I nearly fell over when I sat down and opened one of them. Honestly honey I never expected anything like that. You could have knocked me over with a feather when

I saw that money order for $250.00. I felt bad asking you for $100.00 and instead my sweet sent me $250.

You said it was my money I had sent and there was no reason why I should feel bad asking for some of it. Well honey, don't feel that way because I send the money home for us don't ever forget that. If you ever need to use any of it for any reason especially yourself, go ahead, you don't have to ask me. After all sweet, now you are handling it and I am sure you know how. I thought tonight when I was writing to you I was going to tell you I had a surprise for you, but you fooled me. Didn't you? Anyway, the other day I airmailed a little something for you for Valentine's Day. I hope you like it because I do. It is just perfect for nights when you and I are at home alone together making love. When it arrives, remember it was bought especially for my darling loveable wife. I received your Valentine card today and it was you when I read it. I can't seem to find one at the PX, but I think the gift will take its place. I don't have a brush cut, it may seem like one but it's just a short haircut. It will be long when I return.

Goodnight for now darling and thanks again.

I paid the small balance owed on the car. I didn't need any new clothes. I had the clothes from my wedding trousseau and if I needed more, I would make them. I didn't want any debts when Joe came home.

5 February 1955

My Dearest Darling,

Hi Honey, well here I am in Japan. It was a miserable plane trip over but we managed to get here in one piece. We weren't worried about having any trouble but Saturday afternoon a bunch of MIG's tried to shoot down a B-45 about 50 miles west of K-55. I guess some of them still want to look for trouble but we sure gave it back to them.

My roommates and I from K-55 are staying at the Tokyo Electric Hotel for officers only. What a difference from Korea. One fellow said when you see Tokyo for the second time after

Korea you would think you are stateside. Honestly, honey, they have beautiful big buildings, flashing neon signs, movies with attractions like, The Egyptian, Rear Window and Cinerama. I never thought Japan could be so nice. They have adopted the American way of living but their taxi drivers are worse than any in New York or Chicago. They say all they need is a fast engine, good brakes, a horn and you qualify as a driver. They are crazy.

We spent most of the day shopping. We went to the Ginza Market, which is like an overgrown five and ten-cent store that has everything and prices that change like the weather. Then we went to a department store. It was beautiful. I've never seen one like it in the States. It was built in December. The clerks behind the counters are so polite. They bow, say hello and give you the greeting of the day.

As for the gifts I bought, I will have to keep them a secret. I don't want to spoil the fun of you receiving them.

Tomorrow morning, we are going to Mt. Fujiyama. I'm told it is beautiful up there and I want to take some pictures. There is a hotel there that is a summer resort for Americans only. I wish you were here to enjoy it with me.

Be good honey, and may the good Lord bless and keep you for me until I return.

.

The Valentine's Day gift Joe sent was an embroidered silk lounge jacket in majestic blue with a pair of black slacks. I modeled them for my mother.

"Mom, do you think Joe would like a picture of me wearing these?"
"Yes, I think he would."
"He also asked for pictures of me in a bathing suit, skirt and sweater." I acted as casually as I could when I mentioned the one in my nightgown and negligée.
"I think it's a good idea for him to have one of you as his pin-up instead of one on a calendar."

Her response caught me off guard.

"I don't think he intends to have it as a "pin up" Mom. When I buy the film will you take the picture?"

"Yes, but you'll have to show me how to use the camera."

I purchased a roll of film, loaded the camera and showed her how to focus and center the picture. The picture of me in lounge pajamas was easy. The next one in my nightgown made me nervous. I walked into the bedroom to change. I put on the nightgown and negligée; I didn't remove my underwear. I sat in the center of the bed, my knees bent, and my hand to one side and she snapped the first picture. Setting the camera on the dresser, she walked to the bed.

"Move more to the side so I can get Joe's photograph behind you in the picture. The negligée over your nightgown hides your legs."

She opened the front of the negligée and let it fall on each side so my legs could be seen through the sheer fabric of the nightgown. My arms showed through the sleeves and the color of my skin through the top. It was what Joe wanted.

"Just enough for him to imagine the rest. Smile."

If they turned out, Joe would have the favor he'd been waiting for, and I was sure he wouldn't believe my mother took the pictures. I didn't believe it either.

14 February 1955

My Dearest Darling,

Hi honey, here I am back in Korea again. My short stay in Japan was wonderful while it lasted but now it is over. One good thing though, I had your letters to read when I got back plus the package you sent. I was wondering what I did with all those books I had. It made me feel good reading "Happy Birthday to My Husband." Didn't have much of a birthday. Right now, it seems like a dream that I even heard your voice from so far away, but it is true. I got a kick out of you asking, "How is the weather there?" I guess you were like me waiting so long for the call and then finding yourself lacking for words. I was thankful that I did talk with you even for those few minutes. I could hope for more to be able to see and hold you but that is asking for a little more than is possible. Oh, honey It sure will be good to be home with you again.

The last letter from you was dated 2 February and a lot of time has passed since then. I hope nothing has happened. When I called from Japan everything seemed fine, please let me know if something is wrong. I know some days will go by when you just don't feel like writing but I look forward to the mail and I know there must be some time when you can take a few minutes out. Then again, there is always the next day when the letter might come and you realize there was a delay in the mail. If mail doesn't come, you don't have much of a spirit to want to write

Wednesday is Ash Wednesday and it means the coming of Easter and spring. Thinking ahead like that only makes me go back to the memories of what I was doing last year at this time. I was at Ft. Wood getting ready to move up to Camp Mc

Coy. All I had in my mind were the number of days until May 22. May seemed like a long way off then but now it seems closer and August seems the furthest. When May does come though I will be a short timer. I will be looking forward to my rotation. I know someday no matter what we have to return to one another. I think of you and all we hope for in the future and it makes me happy that I have a wonderful wife to enjoy it with. That is why I tell myself every day that nothing could make me stay in this Army and be away from you. I could never live this same life again away from you. No matter what I am destined to do honey, I want to do it somewhere where you can be with me. That's all for tonight, please write often. I miss you.

It was depressing to read that he hadn't received my letters. I was writing letters two and three times a week. I couldn't imagine what had happened to them. How could I reassure him there was nothing to worry about? I tried to fill my letters with my love he wanted to read. I could do no more than that. I had to wait until my letters caught up with him.

I wished often that I could pick up the phone and call him to hear his voice. I would listen to the music that we fell in love to and read his letters often. I imagined hearing his voice in my ears saying how much he loved and missed me.

My mother-in-law called and asked if I could help her make some new curtains for her kitchen. I said I could and suggested we could finish them if I stayed for the weekend. She agreed to my suggestion.

When I slept in Joe's bed, the thought of him sleeping there comforted me and I slept soundly.

22 February 1955

My Dearest Darling,
Hi honey, it was good this morning when they brought in the mail and I received two letters from you and one from the folks. It helped to brighten the day.

So you stayed over the folks place. Sounds like you were up to your sentimental tricks again. I only wish I were there to take care of you when you were in that mood. The other night I dreamed about you again. This time you had a baby and honey for that short period of time you don't know how happy I was. I woke up with the feeling it was true. How I wish it were.

I think a small family will be better for both of us. I always wanted a pretty wife and I have one; and that's the way she is going to stay. I was fortunate to get a wife like you that can do all the things you can and still be pretty and that's the way I want to keep it. Some day I'm going to enjoy that beauty and love but for now all I can do is hope for it and let it build up inside and then, just wait and see.

Just got through counting the days and they are starting to look good to me, but even as I count it comes out to 182 days which is six months or the half way mark on my "FIGMO CHART". That is a chart that is a handy way of marking off the weeks or days, whichever the case may be of the time left before leaving. For the time being we are all satisfied with life here, but someday it is bound to change.

There isn't much work now as far as construction is concerned and there is always the rumor we will move out of here. Some say if we move, the Air Force will have to leave first and that isn't probable in a place like Korea.

Well honey, I've talked long enough. Be good sweet. I miss you.

I grew up with four brothers. Joe had a sister. The only way to prevent having a large family was to practice birth control. Being Catholic the rhythm method was the only acceptable way; of course there was abstinence. A problem we would definitely confront in the future.

1 March 1955

My Dearest Darling,
Look at the date at the top of the page. Boy that March date looks good, but it is still not good enough.

Honey, you don't know how I long to be back in your arms again. At times, it is so bad it makes me mad enough to yell out. I've never had the chance to really enjoy you and our love. I want to come back and spend all my time with you. I don't ever want to leave you again. I want you with me all the time. I've always said it isn't fair for us to be separated as we have. Why is it honey, why do we have to be separated? I suppose I shouldn't talk like that because other people have been separated and they have to go through the misery of separation too. I think when I return to you we should take some time off enjoying and being with one another. I guess you could call it a second honeymoon. The one we had wasn't much of one and I feel you deserve a real one. All I think of is returning to you. That is all I want darling. As long as I can be with you, I'll be satisfied.

I've been thinking about what I will do when I'm finished with the service. I have ideas, but I think I'll wait until I come home to discuss them with you. What I want to do first is settle down with my wife in a nice place and raise a family, small that is. I suppose you will disagree on the size but anyway honey I am always thinking of you and what it was like being home with you for the short time we were together. I enjoyed every moment of it and I'm sorry for the times I wasn't as nice as I should have been. Why is it, like you always said, "You miss and feel sorry for the things you disliked when we were together." For example, I'd give anything for you to be in bed with me tickling me. That's the way it is, you appreciate something a lot more when you can't have it.

Well darling, that's it for now. I love you.

I knew Joe's emotions had hit bottom. They were as low as they could probably be. I felt the same way. He needed my love as much as I needed his. Love and passion are difficult emotions to suppress. You feel depressed and often believe tomorrow will never come; but you get up the next morning and work through another day. Difficult as it was, we had to be patient and wait.

One evening after taking a warm shower, I was writing to Joe when I thought about our honeymoon and the first time Joe and I showered together. The shower in our apartment in Devils Elbow Missouri was so small there was hardly room for the two of us to move our arms to lather up. Joe found the perfect solution. We lathered each other; that was stimulating. Joe wrapped a towel around his waist when he got out of the shower and towel dried me when I stepped out. He covered my head with the towel and rubbed my head to dry my hair. He dropped the towel around my shoulders, kissed me and led me to the bedroom.

I put my thoughts into the letter and before I put it in the envelope, I dabbed the pages with a few drops of Tabu perfume. I hoped it would bring back a few of the memorable moments of his loving me.

9 March 1955

My Dearest Darling,
Hi honey, today has been a fine day with letters from you. The letter I received today was dated 26 Feb and the one yesterday 1 Mar. Shows you that it is possible for the mail to be fouled up and why I was short on mail for a while. I know exactly what you mean about not getting mail and what it does to you when it comes. It sure helps a lot doesn't it sweet? Even more reason we should continue to write often.
By the way, you know I have finished two years in the service as of the 25th of last month and now I get a $15.00 raise a month for serving two years. I'm looking forward to the 1st Lieutenants commission for the next raise. Every bit counts over here. The only trouble is they are going to start taking income tax from the troops in Korea so it won't be a noticeable increase. Bad enough being here, now they are taking away our tax exemption.
As far as the Army is concerned, I guess I was in a bad mood. I've straightened things out here. I didn't get along with

my CO and I transferred to "B" Co. of this outfit and like it a lot better. All the officers are young and we get along.

So you will have a bedroom all your own in your parent's new home. Well sweet, you keep it warm for the day I can be with you again. Someday we will be moving into a home of our own. I hope that day doesn't have to be too far in the future.

When I do return I don't know what our first words will be, all I want is for you to be waiting for me when I get there. Just think, no more separations and we can be together for our lifetime. Something we have always been looking forward to. Soon it will be here. I think we deserve a good future after all we have been through.

By the way, honey, have you received your china yet? It should be getting there soon. I am proud of it and I know you will be too. Just something for my sweetheart.

Wait for me honey. I love you.

Getting ready to move again, I thought back to my early childhood when we moved from the apartment in grandma's house into our first house.

January 1941, the month following Pearl Harbor and American entry into WW II, Dad purchased our first home. The two-story house had three bedrooms, one bath, a living and formal dining room, kitchen, full basement, attic and a detached two-car garage.

Located on the northeast side of town bordering the suburb of Irondequoit, it cost $1,700.00 and included the vacant lot next door. City lots were fifty feet wide by one hundred feet deep. The vacant lot gave us a large yard to play in.

When Dad unlocked the front door Sonny, Jimmy and I ran from room to room. Our voices echoed throughout the empty rooms as we opened and closed doors and ran up and down stairways from the first floor to the second, up to the attic and down to the basement.

Mom was upset about leaving her family. She let Dad know about it every week she had to take the bus to the A & P to buy groceries. Nick De Cesare the milkman knew us by our first names. He delivered homogenized milk in glass bottles and put them into the insulated milk box by the side door. When the bill was due, Mom paid it with cash left in the milk box. All bills at that time were paid in cash. There were no credit or debit cards and the only visit to the bank was to make a deposit into the savings account.

Coal was the fuel for the hot air furnace in our house. In the late fall Dad called the coal yard and ordered the first ton of coal to be delivered. Shortly after, a truck pulled into the driveway. The chain on the front of an adjustable chute was released and it pivoted and swung away from the truck and onto the edge of the open window above the coal bin. The driver pulled the lever handle on a door above the chute and coaxed the coal into the chute. Gravity did the rest. I can't describe the loud deafening sound it made as it flew down the chute into the bin. The driver closed the door and put the chute back in position on the truck. Dad closed the window and the first load of coal for the winter season was stored. I had another use for the coal. In the summer, I'd take a piece and use it to mark the sidewalk to play hopscotch.

The furnace took up a major portion of the basement. It was at least four feet in diameter. There were two heavy metal doors on the front. Coal was shoveled into the heating chamber one on top and ashes were removed from the bottom door. Dad shoveled the cold ashes into bushel baskets and put them by the curb to be collected by the city. Ashes, not salt were spread on icy streets to prevent accidents.

I received the porcelain china Joe purchased. Service for twelve arrived, and not one piece was broken. Made exclusively for the military PX by Noritake, it had a number 5491 not a pattern name. A wide Mirage band of beige decorated with a fine raised gold floral pattern surrounded the cream white center. His choice was perfect.

16 March 1955

My Dearest Darling,

    Hi honey, me again to spend a few minutes with you. Well sweet, I received that nice letter from you. I have it next to me right now and the perfume is wonderful. I could tell when the mailman handed it to me it was an extra special one. I sat down to read it and enjoyed every word. I liked some of your expressions, boy they made me feel like rushing home and grabbing you in my arms and kissing you from head to toe. Letters like that one make me long for home. While reading it people kept sighing at the wonderful aroma of the perfume. You know that is a luxury for us over here. We never get the chance to smell anything so pretty. Its "Taboo" isn't it. I like it and you better have some of it on when I meet you. It helps bring back some loving memories.

    You know something sweet; one thing I have really missed is drying you after a shower. I'd like to have the opportunity of doing all those things you mentioned in your letter too. Give me a try when I return will you? The trouble is I think it would turn out to be one of the hottest nights we spend together and not because of the outdoor temperature. Speaking of this how about those pictures, you promised me. I am looking forward to them very much.

    I had a great experience today at a gunnery range. It's located in the back hills about 30 miles. It's an area where jet fighters practice firing on targets. When we got there four jets were practicing and what a sight! They zoomed about 100 yards overhead and fired on targets. From out of nowhere, they would come out of the sky, dive down and fire. The bullets would land about a hundred yards away and you could hear the "crack" of the shells. They were estimated to be flying 180 mph and that is fast.

Well sweet that's it for now sweet. Keep on writing those wonderful letters. I like them. Thanks again. Be good my darling.

I didn't need a special place to spend our honeymoon. I loved being alone with Joe in Jane's Motel in Sparta, Wisconsin, following our wedding and in our basement apartment at Devil's Elbow in Missouri. We were together, sharing and taking care of one another. In his arms, I felt safe, secure, wanted. The freedom we had imagined we would have, we had.

18 March 1955

My Dearest Darling,
Hi honey, received your letter and decided to answer it right away because I have some time tonight. Friday nights are usually free because there is no movie to watch and not much to do unless you like to drink and I don't do much of that. They have been keeping me busy otherwise.

Right now, I have the job of being the Company Commander while the regular CO is on TDY. It's not easy being a company commander. You find out there are a lot of personal problems that come up plus many jobs that keep you busy. By the time the ten days are up, I'll be a nervous wreck. Just last night somebody tried to beat up someone in bed and not only that they say there are some homosexual acts involved also. The other night they found a guy in bed with another GI. They are putting him out of the Army. You would be surprised the amount of men of that mind-set. Drugs are also a problem. There are others who go to the villages and get VD and other diseases such as "Elephantiasis". Sounds horrible doesn't it. Each day there are reports on my desk that state just that. Then there are letters addressed to the CO from mothers who want to know why their son isn't writing and I have to call them in and say, "Your mama is worried about you. Why don't you write home"? There are many situations you have to be prepared to handle.

What's the matter with your foot little one? I hope whatever it is it hurries and gets better. I don't like my sweet to be feeling bad. Maybe it's because of all the walking you do. Anyway, take care of yourself. Remember you have a husband to take care of and that will be a job after a year here.

Don't forget my pictures sweet, I am waiting. Be good my darling and take care. I love you.

23 March 1955

My Dearest Darling,

Hi honey, by the time you receive this letter it probably will be April. The months are starting to sound better but still not good enough. It is spring now and I suppose back home the flowers are starting to come up. There are no signs of flowers around here, and as far as the smell of spring the only thing you can smell are the Korean's putting fertilizer on rice patties.

Spring time, the time for two people in love to fulfill their desires, but here we are miles apart from each other with nothing to love but fond memories of one another. When will it all end? I hope things turn out so we can always share the happiness that we look forward to so much. I don't ever want to leave you again. I miss you so much it wouldn't be fair for us to be separated again. Our love is strong enough but I don't know if I could stand another separation. I want to get back and settle down and carry out our plans that we have hoped for, for so long. I look at your picture on my desk and I see your sweet face and try to realize that it's not a dream, we are married, but it has been so long that it's hard to visualize the happiness we shared. It's there honey; I can remember the wonderful times we shared for so short a period. Honestly honey I want so much to be back with you to hold you and make love to you.

My job as CO is continuing and it will probably be for another ten days. We have a good company. B Company has taken top honors for the monthly inspections for a long time. Makes one feel good to know he is commanding it.

Well sweet, that is all I have for tonight. Be good my darling and take care of yourself.

I knew the feelings he experienced. I had them too. I longed to feel his arms embracing me, his soft lips on mine, and his making love to me. We had our dreams, promises and memories to sustain the long lonely days and months without each other. At night before I fell asleep reading his letters, I'd imagine him being there with me loving me and talking about his plans for our future. His letters were my lifeline to the promises and the commitment we made to one another.

Spring arrived a little sooner than usual. Patches of ice and mounds of snow remained in some areas but for the most part the worst of winter was over. The streets were void of snow and snowplows. Walking to the bank every afternoon for the office was faster without ice and snow on the sidewalk.

What an improvement from growing up in the early 40's when our streets and sidewalks were cleared of deep snow by horse-drawn plows. The leather harnesses of three horses were attached across the front frame of the plow blade. Behind the plow on a wood platform, a man stood holding the reins. The vibration of the horses and plow could be felt from blocks away. A one-horse plow cleared the sidewalks. Horse manure on the street was a problem but not as bad as having to side step what was deposited on the sidewalk.

8 April 1955

My Dearest Darling,
Hi honey, me again, back with a few words of love for my darling wife. It's been so long since I've seen you that it's hard to believe I have a wife. Don't worry sweet I know you're there and I wish I were with you. I guess I am starting to get it bad. I keep thinking what it was like to be with you the short time after we were married. Last year at this time, I was counting the days until I would return home to you to be married. Just about this time it was down to about 37 days, but

now it is 137 before I come close to seeing you. Time has to go by, I keep telling myself but it is still hard. I want so much to be with you and have the feeling that soon our baby will be on the way. I can't wait to come home in order to start. I know I'll have to but the waiting keeps getting me down. Just the other night I had a dream about you that we were together enjoying all the pleasures of being married. I guess I miss you so much my mind tries to put itself at ease by dreaming of you at night. Lately I've been with you quite a bit, but they are only dreams and I don't get the enjoyment out of them as I would if we were actually together. I love you too much to lose you. I want to come home, be a good husband, and enjoy all the pleasures we had and those we had to set aside when I came over here. We missed doing a lot, but when I return I will make it all up to you. I love you sweet, and you're my wife. God alone knows how much I love you, want to hold you in my arms kiss you and make love to you until you have to ask me to stop. I doubt if that will happen.

My darling pray for us. I love you very much.

We had waited so long to love one another intimately, only to have it end abruptly with him having to go to Korea. Whenever I listened to the lyrics of the songs we both enjoyed I'd close my eyes and remember the loving moments and the fulfillment of our passion we shared together. I longed for him so. His plans for us when he returned kept the fire of love burning in my heart. The fantasy of his loving me when we were single was the fantasy of reality.

12 April 1955

My Dearest Darling,

Hi honey, sorry I fell behind on my letter writing. It's just that I've been occupied. Last night I was OD and there is always something to keep you busy when you have that job. Our Easter Sunday was routine. I went to church in the morning and in the afternoon; a friend of mine from OCS came down from up north and spent the day with us. He came with an old friend of his who flies small Army Liaison planes. They had no trouble getting back and forth with a plane for their transportation. Otherwise, Easter Sunday would be like the rest. I worked Saturday night until 8:00 PM finishing a bridge we built. I am proud of it because it the first I have actually constructed. When I went out there today, I found the Koreans had stolen the guardrail for the walkway and also the curbs and a lot of lumber. Those people will do anything to get lumber free. Made me feel terrible because I was proud of it and we worked hard on it.

As to your question honey, just a thought, what would you say if I stayed in the service? Not saying I am but just your opinion. There is a $64.00 a month raise after three years, plus another $40.00 as a First Lieutenant, and I've already received $15.00 for 2 years' service. Let me know your opinion.

Well sweet, it seems I've put nothing but information in this letter. I feel the same way you do about us. I miss you all the time and think about you and your wonderful loving. For now, I'll have to wait.

I wasn't sure how I felt about him staying in the service. I didn't want to think about another separation. I decided to put it out of my mind until he came home so we could make the decision together. My apprehension was the possibility of another hardship tour, separation, and having a baby away from my family.

20 April 1955

My Dearest Darling,

Hi honey, well a big difference in the mail has finally come through. I received four letters in the last two days, three from you and one from mom. From now on sweet, if the mail is late it will be best if we don't worry because with the rainy season it probably causes the delay. I won't be going to Japan in May. They won't let me go until June because they want you to have four months between R & R. I was planning to call you for our anniversary. If I get there, I'll call you in June. After I return from that R & R, I will have a short time to go. I'll bet those last few weeks will simply drag by. I guess I can wait it out. I'll have to; there are no two ways about it.

Let's not worry about the future honey. No matter what I decide here, it will still turn out the way it was meant to be. To be honest I don't even know what I'll do. When I return we can figure it out, right now I am looking forward to just seeing you and those many nights together. I think of you every day my darling. I want so much to be with you. Let's look forward to a life of happiness together because that is what I want most for you.

25 April 1955

My Dearest Darling,

Hi honey, I've just returned from a long trip to Inchon. It took us two days to go up and back. It's not too far but when you're traveling with heavy equipment over dirt roads at 15mph, it's a lot different from stateside. Another reason that makes me want to come home. At least there are fine roads and you can make good time on them.

Well how has my sweet wife been doing? With spring at home, it must be nice. They say springtime is the time for making love. We are missing all that are not we sweet. I am sure we can have more fun next spring and more to come.

I miss those summertime family picnics when everyone gets together. Uncle Tom playing the accordion, the kids playing ball, the hot dogs on the grill. everyone enjoying themselves. Most of all I miss you my darling. I want to hold you in my arms and whisper I love you. It has been so long since I've told you in person. It will be like falling in love with you all over again. This time I am really going to love you with all my heart and soul. It wouldn't be right for me to say now how sorry I am for the way I acted at times. I acted as I shouldn't, but I promise you I shall be different and make things the way you want them. In my letters long ago, I said I wanted to spoil you and I want to do just that. In order to love you as much as I want I'll have to.

Good night my sweet. I love you,

If I was reading correctly between the lines at the end of this letter, remorse for some of his past attitudes while we dated added to his loneliness. There was no need for him to feel that way. Our love for each other weathered the storms.

2 May 1955

My Dearest Darling,

Hi Honey, well here we are in the month of May. It sure does look good to be this far. May brings back memories of last year when I was looking forward to returning home for our wedding. In a couple more weeks we will have been married a whole year. Last year I couldn't wait for the time to go by. I only had a few days left before I would see you. Now I have 114. It is rather discouraging but I am sure it will go by as it has before. When I see you again it will be just like being married all over again. Honestly sweet, I am really looking forward to that wonderful day. It will be worth the wait to be with you once again. We'll make each night more enjoyable than the last one. I didn't have much of a chance to show you a very nice time. This time we will have more of an opportunity to see some of the beauty in our great country. I hope next year at this time we will be looking forward to having a baby. I want so much to have one and I hope the good Lord blesses us with a very fine child, or maybe more.

I guess my last few months here are going to be tiresome ones. The Battalion has started to work 6½ days a week. Saturday and Sunday, I worked all day, and last night I was up until 12:00pm. We had to have a report in by today and as usual had to work a little later than usual. Probably be some time before we have a complete weekend off. I miss sleeping late on Sunday. All we look forward to here is for the time to go by.

Well my sweet the time has come for me to close and say goodnight. I wish I were there in person to say it.

Someday I will be. Until then my darling be good and I love you.

Our first anniversary was three weeks away. I couldn't help remembering last year and the emotional day two weeks before the wedding when I almost postponed it.

I had something more pressing to think about. The car and its damaged rear fender. How was I going to tell Joe about it? It was raining the day I decided to drive the car to work. There was a public parking lot near the office so I parked it there. When I went to pick it up after work, I saw the damaged fender. I went back to the office and called the police. They met me in the parking lot and filed the report. When I got home I called the insurance company. They sent an adjuster to the house the following evening. The damage to the fender was fully covered, but it didn't lessen my anxiety of having to tell Joe about it.

8 May 1955

My Dearest Darling,

Hi Honey, today was a pleasant surprise. We worked today again on Sunday and I was in my office and I received two letters from you. One of them had the pictures of you and your folk new home. The home I must say is beautiful. What I loved the most was seeing you again even if it was just in pictures. Honestly honey I fell in love with you all over again. When I looked at those pictures, it made me feel great I have a wife as beautiful as you are. I've looked at them three times today. Actually, they were the first pictures of you I've seen since I left the states. I kept looking at them repeatedly because each time I would see you I would think you were real and would try to talk to you. My darling would you believe me if I said I fell in love with you again? Keep sending more pictures of yourself. You don't know how much they do for me. I can't wait to see the others of you when they come. I've waited so long for them it will be a wonderful gift just to see you. I miss you so much and those pictures help me visualize you and everything back home. Here you don't see things like that. So keep up with the picture taking. I'd love to have more of them.

The one with your hand on the car door shows you've developed in the right places. You sure have grown up haven't you sweet? I have something to look forward to when I return. The contrast is something I can't explain. I must say if that is the camera I sent you, it sure takes good pictures.

I am glad when you put on paper that you love me very much. It makes me feel that I have a lot to look forward to. Please don't let anything change sweet. Let everything be the same as the time I left you. Our first night together is going to be just like the first time all over again. Are you going to be bashful? I'm not that is for sure. Just keep on waiting honey, work hard and soon it will come. It's something to look forward to. I miss you and love you.

The pictures that Joe wanted and waited so long for were in the mail to him. I had hoped they would arrive on or about our anniversary. They had turned out exactly as he wanted them.

15 May 1955

My Dearest Darling,
Hi Honey, Sunday again and it was a beautiful day. Mail must still be tied up because I haven't received any for a whole week. It is rather disappointing when I look forward to it so much. Maybe you are saying the same thing there, but I have been writing. I am looking forward to those pictures you were going to send me. The others did so much to boost my morale. I could use more of them.

Time is going by and soon I will break the 100-day mark. Here they call it the "sound barrier", but I won't be completely satisfied until I leave for good. These last few months are going to be the hardest for both of us. I hope all goes right so there is no interference in our plans. We have waited so long and been so patient. We have so many things to look forward to my darling.

It is going to be another honeymoon all over again. Just think, the first time I'll be seeing you in a whole year and making love to you that night. It is going to be like the first time. Maybe the first night will be a baby to us. I hope so because I want so much to have children. Our time together was so short we didn't have the chance to start a family. I can wait these last few months and longer if I have to just to be yours again. Until then my sweet be good and I love you.

Joe foresaw the future in this letter. Almost nine months to the day after he returned, James, our first son was born on May 30, 1956. Ten and a half months later Robert was born on April 25, 1957. Six years later Jeffrey was born on April 27, 1963. We didn't have a daughter Joe had hoped for but we had three handsome sons.

In my next letter, I reminded him our first anniversary was a few days away. It was also the three-year anniversary of my junior prom. It didn't it seem possible I had been out of school and already married to my high school sweetheart. There were moments I thought about the first time I noticed him, his smile, and our first kiss. I missed his hands on my face when he kissed me, the sound of his voice saying I love you.

22 May 1955

My Dearest Darling,

  Hi Honey, well the day has come hasn't it. Happy Anniversary honey, but I must say it doesn't seem we have been married all this time. I wish I could have spent this year with you instead of away from you. Anyway, it means now the time will go by and I'll be back in your arms once again.

  After the long wait on your letters, I finally received the one with the pictures I have been waiting for, for so long. Especially the one of you in your nightgown. Honestly honey you are beautiful. I've waited so long for them and it was worth waiting for. I sure would like more pictures of you. I'll be looking forward to them.

  Speaking of the Junior Prom, it reminds me, this will be two years you have graduated from high school and myself four years. Many things have happened to me since we left that school. In a way, I feel proud of myself being what I am. When I left there, I had no idea where I would wind up. I am thankful that I didn't come here when I first left high school. It feels good having only three months left. It doesn't seem very long ago I first arrived here and the feeling of all the time ahead to go. Now I am down to 94 days and with good luck, there is a possibility I'll be in the states when those 94 days are up. Everyone that has left here left 10 to 15 days ahead of time. This sounds good, but not the sort of thing I want to count on. If I make it home in good time, I will be happy, if not I hope to make it there without too much delay.

  There is one thing that bothers me. How I'm going to know when and where to have you meet me. I can't be sure when I'll get there and I can't be sure where I'll land. For you it would be difficult not knowing anything about the West Coast. Maybe it would be better if I got on a plane in San Francisco and flew directly home. It would save a lot of money and confusion.

  Don't worry about the car sweet. I'm glad you weren't in it. I'd never forgive myself if you were hurt. As for sending me something, you could never send me what I want the most *and that is you my sweet-what else. If you can't do that, the next best thing I would like is more pictures of you to bring back those memories of when I made love to you.*

Staying in the Army is a thought, isn't it? I think about it often but don't want to make any definite decisions until we are together again. After all, we are husband and wife and we should think accordingly.

Till then, be good and I love you.

The tone of this letter seemed brighter. With the time growing shorter until his return, it was beginning to reflect in his writing. The light at the end the dark tunnel of separation was almost here.

Joe's mother called and asked me to pick up a gift she had for our anniversary. "Paper is the gift for the first anniversary," she said handing me a square box. The gift was a package of floral edged paper napkins and placemats purchased at Sibley's Department store down town. I thanked her and said I would use them when I set the table when Joe returned.

25 May 1955

My Dearest Darling,

Well three months from today my time will be up. It sure seems good to know I am down to the where I can look forward to seeing you again. There have been other times when I've been away the same length of time and we survived it didn't we sweet. The time is short and I know it will drop off faster than before. Before you know it, I'll be home so get yourself ready for me because I am coming home to give you the best loving of your life. I've given you all your loving before so I'll have to go some to satisfy you. After this long separation, I think I have stored up enough.

It's been another bad week of little mail. I don't know what the matter is because sometimes a whole week goes by and no mail at all, and then when they do come they come all at once. Its gets rather discouraging but as long as I know you are writing I can stand it.

In my spare time, I have learned to play bridge. I thought it was one of the hardest games to play and it sure was. I reached the point where I can play and my partner doesn't hit me over the head when I bid wrong. When I return I will teach you and we can play once a week.

Soon the summer months will be here and the long hot days. Remember last year when it was so hot in Ft Wood? When I get home the cool months will start and the time for love making. I'll be looking forward to them. As long as I can be with you, I'll be satisfied.

That's all my darling. Write often. I miss you so and your letters are all I have to look forward to.

Joe suffered from a variety of allergies but the worst of them occurred in June. Rose fever and June grasses made his life miserable with sneezing, coughing and difficulty breathing. Stubborn about seeing an allergist he finally gave in years later and had the injections to control and almost eliminate his allergies.

9 June 1955

My Dearest Darling,

Hi sweet, me again to spend a few minutes with you. It seems I only have this letter to tell you how I feel. The days are long, the time seems to be dragging and the thought of coming home seems like it will never happen. To have waited all this time and still have to wait gives me a burning sensation that is hard to describe. I want so much to be able to return to you. Will the Lord be kind and let us return us to one another's arms or is there still more in store for us? We deserve to have the happiness we were unfortunate not to share before. I hope and I'll pray until I see you once again and all will be fine. I am sorry to be talking this way but being so far away and in a position such as I am in, things always seem blue. Pray my darling that nothing happens to spoil our happiness. No matter what happens my sweet, remember I am waiting for you and please wait for me.

All I look forward to now is my return and the idea of settling down and raising a family. When we are together again, we will make up for all the lost time I was here. I want to make you happy my darling and not deprive you anymore of the happiness you should have. I've always promised you that, but never actually had the chance to show you. Well my sweet I've gone on too much. I love you and will be home soon.

The tone of this letter seemed a bit depressing. With such a short time to go until he came home, I didn't understand why he felt the way, he did. Maybe his Rose fever allergy was affecting him earlier than usual. Whatever it was, I felt his depression in the last few letters he had written.

I was writing often to him. He sounded stressed out and depressed. I felt helpless that I couldn't respond to his needs more quickly. I sensed his frustration, but I couldn't hurry time. I assured him he hadn't done anything wrong; quite the contrary, I told him his letters sounded a bit blue, even though he was still telling me of his love for me.

19 June 1955

My Dearest Darling,
Hi honey, received your letters and enjoyed reading every one of them. The length of one of them really surprised me. I was comforted reading it because that letter helped remind me of the wonderful wife I left behind. That was a nice letter sweet.
The depression has left me honey and I am out of that slump I was in for a while. I think your wonderful letter had something to do with it. I guess it must have been that time is getting close and the worry of everything turning out well caused it.

It has been hot here with many days without rain. I guess the poor farmers are going to suffer this year because the rainy season is way over due

The days are getting down. I'll have just 9 weeks in a few days. You must have your calculations wrong because my date to leave is August 25. It is just like the time when we were waiting to get married. I am just as anxious this time as I was then. I can't wait to get off the plane and have you run to meet me. I am also anxious for the day to come when we are waiting for our baby to arrive. I think of all the things I ever wanted, is for you and I to have a baby. I hope the Lord hears our prayers.

Yes, I have my rose fever again. I don't let it bother me though. I've had it for too many years to get me down.

I have a feeling some of your letters to me have been lost. You talk of Paul's graduation in your past letters and I never received any. Tell him congratulations and good luck in high school. Has he started chasing girls yet? Won't be long before he will be getting ideas.

When I come home, it will be just you and I the first time we meet. When I get off that plane, the first thing I want to see and hold in my arms is you. Don't worry sweet it will just be the two of us together. It will be just like the time in Wisconsin honey when you ran down the street with open arms. Soon I'll be home making love to you enjoying the happiness only you and I can enjoy.

In this last year, you have become more beautiful and I love you just looking at your pictures honey. You are my darling sweet.

Well that's all for now. I'll be seeing you soon. Pray for us.

I was relieved to read he had received some of my letters. Reading between the lines of his last few letters, told me something was bothering him. I would have to be patient and wait until he was ready to tell me what was wrong.

28 June 1955

My Dearest Darling,
I guess I had better catch up on my letter writing before I let too much time go by. I found out some good news. The Sgt. Major of the Brigade Hdq. used to be the First Sergeant of H/S Co when I was there and I know him very well. He told me where my new assignment was back in the states. I figured it would be SCARWAF but lucky me I am out of it. My new assignment is Fort Belvoir Virginia. It is right outside of Washington, nice housing, many places to go to and see and 400 miles from home. I'm completely satisfied with that and I'm sure you'll like the idea also. Just think honey right outside of Washington and so many places for me to take you to. I am so happy especially for you having to live in Missouri.

With an assignment like that, it makes me think about signing up for another tour with the Army. After all the bad deals, I'm due for some good ones. This is something we can discuss when we get back together. Just 58 more days to go and I'll be home. Less than two months now. That is a good feeling, isn't it? I am so lonesome for you honey. See you soon. Be good my darling and write to me often. I miss you so.

Knowing where he would be spending the balance of his time in service was the prescription Joe needed to boost his moral and get him out of the slump I thought he was in. We would definitely discuss his signing up for another year when he came home.

I didn't mind the time we lived in Missouri. We were alone without interruption from family except for the time Mom and Dad visited us. We went to the movies on Post or to the Officers Club for dinner or stayed home and played cards with new friends. I thought it was a great honeymoon. I drove the car to and from the Post on Route 66 and didn't get a speeding ticket or have an accident.

4 July 1955

My Dearest Darling,

    Here it is the 4*th* of July and I am in Japan. Guess it is better than a letter from Korea. Last year at this time, we went to Merrimac Springs and had a great time. It was the first time in my life I had a chance to celebrate with fireworks. Remember how we couldn't resist buying them? We must have spent $25.00 on them alone. Soon after that, your folks came to see us and we had some fun together for those few days. I imagine everyone at home is packing picnic baskets and heading for Webster Park, you, and the kids going swimming. Boy, I sure miss all that fun. Here it has been very boring with possibly a ball game this afternoon and maybe a fireworks display. I think it might rain and that will spoil the little enjoyment possible. All I care about is that in 52 more days I'll be back home with you.

    I guess now that it is almost over I may as well tell you Remember that letter I wrote that sounded like I was down in the dumps? Well I had good reason to be. We had just received word from our Battalion Commander that all SCARWAF units in Korea would be extended a 3-month period. I'll tell you honey our morale hit an all-time low. Here we are planning to move the unit back in August and then suddenly that hit us. I guess we have Colonel Dugan and Colonel Graham from Brigade and Group Headquarters to thank for it not going through. As it stands, they have opened the pipeline for replacement of all SCARWAF personnel and they should be coming over soon. Looks like I will be home in August after all. When I found out, I just didn't have the heart to tell you. For some reason I kept telling myself it wasn't true and luckily, it was changed. That is why in that letter I sounded so and asked you to pray for my return and still ask until once we meet again. I guess possibly that you can tell by reading between the lines what is in my mind.

    Well sweet, chin up and soon I'll be home. Pray for us. Love ya!

His "love ya" was a sign to me that he was feeling better and his morale was on an uphill climb. I was relived knowing he was finally out of his depressed state. I was anxious too. Even the office noticed my anxiety. Upon returning from the walk to the bank one afternoon Mr. Mc Graw mentioned that I had cut off five minutes of the time it took me to complete the errand. I guess there was an added stride or two in my walk.

24 July 1955

My Dearest Darling Wife,

Happy Birthday! You're one year older. How does it feel to be a young woman? I'll bet you have really grown in more ways than one. I am willing to take all those new charms and try them myself.

Today is the day I have been waiting for honey. After writing all these letters, day after day, week after week, month after month, I finally arrived at the letter where I can sit down and write these words. I received my "port call." You probably have a good idea what it means but I won't keep you in suspense any longer. That is the day I report to Japan to leave for the states. On or about the 17th of August I will leave Japan for the good old U.S.A. How about that? I will be out of here 8 days sooner. In three more weeks, I'll be returning to you and all the happiness I have ever wanted. I am now a short timer among the next batch of officers to leave here. All I have to do now is wait for August 17 to come around and if all goes right, I'll be coming home. By the time you get this letter I'll have about 18 days to go. I am so happy especially for you my darling.

You have waited patiently for so long you deserve all the love you have coming to you. I am just the man and the only one that can show you that love.

I am glad Sonny and Angie decided to wait until I come to christen the baby. Going to make me feel proud being a Godparent. I can honestly say it will be the first experience and I want them to know I appreciate they chose us.

My mind is filled with what it will be like to see you after all this time. You can believe it is filled with nothing but love for you. I am going to be happy with you honey and that is all I want for both of us. Well it is time to say goodnight. See you soon and be good. I love you very much.

I confess that turning twenty was a little emotional for me. No longer in my teens I realized that I had reached the first bench-mark of the decades to follow. At the time, I had no thoughts of how they would come and go so quickly.

The best birthday gift Joe gave me was his "port call" date. He would be home in approximately three weeks. The waiting, longing and loneliness were almost at an end.

When I told my manager I would be leaving the company and going with Joe to Ft Belvoir, Virginia, he told me there was a CIT in Washington, D.C. and Alexandria, Virginia and offered to see if there was a vacancy at either one for me. The following week he said I had a job waiting in Washington if I wanted it. I told him I did.

Joe had asked me not to cut my hair because he wanted it to be long when he came home. In the past year, it had grown to my shoulders; long enough to please him.

31 July 1955

My Dearest Darling,
Hi Honey, well here it is the end of the month. Now we finally start the month I leave here. I never thought my time would finally come. In about 16 days, I expect to be in Japan getting ready to leave this place for the last time. Each day that goes by, I dream of being with you and loving you once again Oh sweet will it ever be possible that I'll be with you once more? I have been hoping and praying for so long I really can't believe we will be together soon. I'll never let you out of my sight once you are with me again. I want to be with you so

much honey. I feel I have been away for so long and missed an important part of our married life. I want to make it all up to you my darling. I'll do everything within my power to make you the happiest wife on this earth. For so long now I have written similar words in my letters to you. I have kept all your letters and I am going to take them with me. Someday in the future I want to sit down and read them to bring back some of the memories of being here.

Tonight I am O.D. and it is raining. I didn't mind walking out there with the rain beating down on me because inside I knew that this is probably the last time I'd have to do this job over here. Feels good to know I'm a "short timer."
This time I am headed in the right direction and I am looking forward to the day, I get off the plane seeing you running toward me with open arms. Then I'll know it's true and I'll believe it.

Well sweet, it's time to say goodnight. Be good my darling. I love you very much.

Providence had me keep all of the letters Joe wrote to me the year he was in college, basic training, OCS and Korea. My letters to him in Korea were stolen when he left so he never had the opportunity to read them again after he returned home as he had planned.

I was hardly able to contain my joy or concentrate on anything at work. Almost every waking moment I was thinking about Joe coming home. The girls I worked with said I would blush whenever someone mentioned Joe would be home soon. Of course I did. I knew that they knew why I was blushing.

5 August 1955

My Dearest Darling,

Another day has gone by and soon I'll be leaving here. Today my orders were cut. A week from tomorrow, which is Saturday, I hope to leave for Japan. It doesn't seem real to me that the time is so close before I will hold you in my arms once more. I don't even believe so much time has gone by since I've held you.

Sunday I am going to receive Communion being it's my last day here. I pray the Lord gives me a safe trip home and we can be together as planned.

When you receive this letter, you may as well stop writing because I won't receive them before I leave. I'll continue to write and before long, I'll be there in person. Be good my darling.

. . . . .

Thursday, August 18

I put my coffee cup in the sink and was about to get dressed and go to work when the phone rang. I picked it up.

"Hello." A pause.
"Good morning, honey."
My heart pounded, my eyes filled with tears and I couldn't say anything when I heard Joes voice. Then all my thoughts came out at once.

"Joe, where are you? Are you in the states? Are you at the airport? When will I see you?"
"Honey, slow down. You're talking so fast and asking so many questions I can't get a word in. First, you don't know how good it is to hear your voice. Second, I can't wait to get home to take and feel you in my arms, kiss you and make love to you."
"I can't wait either honey. Where are you?"
"I'm in San Francisco. I just got off the plane and have to get my luggage and check on my flight home. I think I should be home around 3:00 this afternoon. I'll call you back when I have my time of arrival and we'll talk"

"OK."

"I love you. I'll be home soon."

Waiting for the plane to taxi to the terminal, I wondered what those first moments were going to be like. What would I say to him? What would he to say to me? The airport attendant wheeled and locked the portable stairway against the plane. The door opened; passengers exited one by one. Finally, Joe stood in the doorway. He looked around, saw me running toward the plane and walked quickly down the steps.

His feet had barely touched the ground when I felt his arms around me and our longed for kiss. I could hardly breath from his crushing embrace. I looked into his eyes and silently thanked the Lord for his safe return.

I called my office and told Mr. Mc Graw that Joe was home and I wouldn't be in. He said to take a few days off and let him know our schedule so he could notify the Washington office of my rival.

Joe decided to purchase the new car he wanted.

"A white Ford Convertible with turquoise interior to go with your red hair," Joe said as we drove to Ken Ralph Ford, a dealer in Fairport.

We walked into the showroom and Joe told the salesman what he wanted. "Follow me," the salesman said with a smile. We left the showroom and went to the lot at the rear of the building. The salesman pointed to a white convertible that still had its white top protected with a clear plastic covering.

"This just came off the trailer this morning. The interior is turquoise. Is this your car?" Joe smiled and looked at me.

"Yes, it is."

Shortly after, we left for Ft. Belvoir, Virginia where Joe would be stationed for six months until discharged in January 1956.

We rented a furnished apartment at Huntington Towers located near Washington with a view of the Potomac River. I alternated driving the car and riding the bus to work in Washington on the days that Joe carpooled to Fort. Belvoir.

The future that we had looked forward to and dreamed about for so many years had finally begun.

Epilogue

In the stillness of an early morning or clear star filled night, I have been shaken by the realization that my youth is gone and I never saw it leave. Older and I hope wiser, I look back where I started from and reflect on my past. Is it possible a life time has gone by? My future was an open road stretching far in front of me. I had no preconceived notions of how the twists and hairpin turns to come were going to test the values I was taught in childhood. Unforeseen circumstances reshaped the person I was then and who I am now. My mind perceived a future without roadblocks. My dream and desire were to marry the man I loved, have a home, raise our children and grow old together. However, I was young and naive; I trusted the man I loved to be at my side forever as my protector, my knight in shining armor.

I believed in the fairy tale ending of happily ever after. Snow White, Cinderella and Sleeping Beauty all had a prince rescue them from a wicked stepmother, but I didn't have a wicked stepmother. I had an overly protective, strict Catholic mother who was afraid to let go of her parental authority. I wanted to go places with my friends and be trusted to make decisions right or wrong, but I wasn't allowed to. I envied my brothers' freedom to come and go without accountability and resented the double standard, but I obeyed the rules dictated to me by my mother even though I didn't like some of them. Rules followed me from my father's house to my husband's house, social, religious, and those unspoken. I no longer had parents telling me what I could or couldn't do, but now I had a husband who had his own set of rules I was expected to follow.

      Trudging down the gravel road of paying bills, raising children, doing laundry and preparing meals, I found little time for pampering. I strove daily to fulfill the role of loving wife and nurturing mother. In the process, I discovered no harm came to me when I shed old traditions and established new ones. What did it matter if I left dishes in the sink while I took the children for a walk on a sunny day? I'd wash them when I got back. If I decided to let the dusting go and Joe wrote "dusty" on the table, I answered "not a priority". My world didn't revolve around keeping a spotless house. It would be standing long after I left this earth, and how tragic if my headstone were to read - She always had an immaculate home. I have reached an age when I can accept the past and know I will never be too old to change my mind or welcome change if I step outside my comfort zone to explore the world beyond it.

      I lived 52 years with the husband I loved and trusted. The only man with whom I was intimate all my life. Writing our love story, reading his letters, remembering the love he felt for me, his last tender "I love you; I've loved you all my life," I go on.

True love never dies.
It lives forever in the heart, mind, and memories of those who have
received and given love unconditionally.
(Mary Ann Marasco)

Made in the USA
Middletown, DE
22 September 2023